DIARIES TO AN ENGLISH PROFESSOR

DIARIES TO

AN ENGLISH

PROFESSOR

Pain and Growth in the Classroom / *Jeffrey Berman*

The University of Massachusetts Press / Amherst

Copyright © 1994 by

The University of Massachusetts Press

Afterword copyright © 1994 by Maryanne Hannan

Printed in the United States of America

LC 94-10564

ISBN 0-87023-927-9 (cloth); 928-7 (pbk.)

Designed by Mary Mendell

Set in Berkeley Medium by Keystone Typesetting, Inc.

Printed and bound by Thomson-Shore, Inc.

Library of Congress Cataloging in Publication Data

Berman, Jeffrey, 1945–

Diaries to an English professor : pain and growth in the classroom

/ Jeffrey Berman.

p. cm.

Includes bibliographical references (p.   )

ISBN 0-87023-927-9 (alk. paper). — ISBN 0-87023-928-7 (pbk. :

alk. paper)

1. English language—Rhetoric—Study and teaching—Psychological

aspects. 2. Literature—Study and teaching (Higher)—Psychological

aspects. 3. Diaries—Authorship—Psychological aspects. 4. Books

and reading—Psychological aspects. 5. Psychoanalysis and

literature. I. Title.

PE1404.B464   1994

920.0973—dc20   94-10564 CIP

[B]

British Library Cataloguing in Publication data are available.

To Jerome Eckstein, professor
of Judaic Studies, University
at Albany, and Sophie Freud,
professor emerita, Simmons College
School of Social Work, for their
wisdom and abiding friendship,
And to my Literature-and-
Psychoanalysis students, the
real authors of this book.

/ Contents

/ Acknowledgments

It is a pleasure to acknowledge my gratitude to the many people who helped me write this book. My University at Albany colleagues Britta Maché of the German Department and Randall Craig, Eugene Garber, Mark Nepo, and Steve North of the English Department read one or more chapters of the manuscript and made valuable suggestions. I am grateful to the many kindnesses extended to me by my department chair, Warren Ginsberg. Thanks also to past department chairs—John Gerber, Eugene Garber, and William Dumbleton—for allowing me to teach courses in literature and psychoanalysis. Marshall W. Alcorn, Jr., of George Washington University, encouraged me to explore some of the theoretical implications of diary writing. Andrew Berry, Linda Cunning, Mary Martin, Stephanie Meyer, Julie Nark, Anna Rosen, and Tim Walter also provided encouragement, as did my former editor, Jason Renker.

A University at Albany Faculty Research Grant-in-Aid offered timely financial assistance; and the university administration, particularly Jeanne Gullahorn, vice president for research and graduate studies, provided me with the necessary computer equipment to complete the project.

I am grateful to the staff at the University of Massachusetts Press, especially Clark Dougan, senior editor, for his enthusiasm and expertise. I also wish to thank the two anonymous readers of the manuscript for their constructive criticisms. Thanks also to Craig Noll for his careful copyediting.

An abridged version of Chapter 5, entitled "'The Grief That Does Not Speak': Suicide, Mourning, and Psychoanalytic Teaching," first appeared in *Self-Analysis in Literary Study*, edited by Daniel Rancour-Laferriere and published by New York University Press.

To Maryanne Hannan, I owe a special thanks. Reading her Afterword, I had the sense that she had captured unerringly not only my comments on student diaries and my teaching style but also aspects of my character. Without Maryanne's contribution, this book would have been incomplete. To my wife, Barbara, and my daughters, Arielle and Jillian, I can only say, once again, "Thank you for your love, faith, and support." Finally, in dedicating this book to my students, who entrusted their diaries to me, I regret that I cannot thank them individually by name.

1 / Introduction

Diaries to an English Professor owes its existence to the many undergraduate students who have taken my literature-and-psychoanalysis courses at the University at Albany, State University of New York. I began teaching psychoanalytic literary criticism in 1976, three years after arriving at the university. Long interested in psychological approaches to literature, I was curious to see whether students could use a weekly "Freudian" diary to apply psychoanalytic theory to their own lives.[1] In outlining the course, I told my students that, just as we would use our class discussions to analyze fictional characters' dreams, fantasies, desires, and defenses, so would the students be encouraged to turn their attention inward and, with the help of insights acquired from readings and class discussions, examine their own lives. The diaries, then, would be the "laboratory" part of the course, allowing students to pursue the Delphic oracle's injunction, Know thyself.

Safeguards

I knew from the beginning that introspective classroom diary writing was fraught with potential dangers. For the experiment to succeed, numerous safeguards had to be built into the course. My overriding concern was that no student be harmed by the process. The following precautions were therefore essential. First, students had to be assured that their diaries would remain confidential. I alone would read the diaries when the students turned them in every Tuesday, and I would keep the diaries locked in my office until Thursday, when I would return them to the students. No one else would read the diaries or know the diarists' identities. Second, since diaries are highly subjective, recording a person's most private feelings and thoughts, it would be inappropriate to grade them. Free from the pressure of grades, students would be willing, I hoped, to write honestly and openly about themselves. Third, for those students reluctant to engage in self-analysis and self-disclosure, other options had to be available, such as using their diaries to work out ideas for their formal, graded essays. Students could thus choose for themselves how self-analytical they wished to be—and at any point in the semester they could decide not to reveal anything further about themselves. Fourth, I assured my students that I would not "psychoanalyze" their writings. Not only am I unqualified to make such interpretations—I am an English professor, not a psychoanalyst—but interpretations outside a clinical context would surely be experienced by students as threatening and intrusive. Instead, I told my students that I would limit my responses to supportive statements. To be sure, I knew that it would be difficult if not impossible to be entirely neutral, since every time I remarked that a student's diary was "interesting" or "important," I would be making a value judgment. Nor is asking questions itself a neutral activity. Nevertheless, I promised my students that I would be as noninterpretative and nonjudgmental as possible. Finally, I told them that I would strive to maintain proper boundaries, avoiding both overinvolvement and underinvolvement and respecting their privacy.

Hearing the Diaries

With these safeguards in place, I felt reasonably certain that students would feel secure enough to write about themselves without fear of exposure, coercion, or criticism. I could foresee, however, one problem with the experiment. The privacy of diary writing precluded any public sharing of knowledge. In writing about themselves, diarists would not know what their classmates were writing about; there would be no sharing of insights, no dialogue among the students, no sense of interconnectedness in the classroom. I had used diaries before in nonpsychoanalytic courses, and while students found them helpful in clarifying and developing their ideas, the classroom remained an impersonal setting. Would it be possible, I wondered, to read a few diaries aloud each week without disclosing the diarists' names? In this way, students could share experiences with their classmates without revealing identities. As an additional safeguard, I told the students that if they did not want me to read their diaries aloud, all they had to do was state their request at the end of each entry.

To make sure that we did not spend the entire class period on the diaries, I decided to read only five entries aloud each Thursday and then immediately hand all of them back to the students, with no class discussion of the diaries afterward. Thus, only about 20 minutes of one class per week, out of a total of 160 minutes per week, would be occupied with the diaries. There were two other advantages to having no class discussion of the diaries: first, each student would have to reach his or her own conclusion about the diaries read aloud, without being influenced by anyone else's remarks; and second, none of the five diarists would be inadvertently hurt or angered by a thoughtless comment expressed by a classmate.

And so I tried the experiment, with astonishing results. Students wrote powerful and moving diaries on far-ranging subjects, including love, sex, family, interpersonal relationships, education, and religion. The diaries were, for the most part, conflict-oriented, with both men and women writing about personal problems they wished to solve. Many students wrote far more than the one- to two-page diary entries I recommended. Nearly all the students gave me permission to read their diaries aloud, and when I did so, the other students sat as if riveted to their seats, listening with intense concentration. The anonymity of the diaries allowed students to feel empathically connected to their classmates without violating anyone's privacy. Many students reported at the end of the semester that, as a result of writing weekly diaries and hearing other students' diaries read aloud in class, they reached important breakthroughs in their lives. Although writing about personal problems was sometimes painful, the students felt better afterward and were convinced that writing was therapeutic. Those who revealed traumatic events said that writing the unspeakable was a turning point in their lives.

Since 1976, I have taught the same introductory literature-and-psychoanalysis class nearly every semester, including many summers, generally in classes ranging between 25 and 35 students. To date, over 1,000 men and women have taken the course. Students in a related course, Narcissism and the Novel, also write weekly diaries. In the mid-1980s, when the idea of writing this book first came to me, I began asking students in both courses for permission to photocopy their diaries for possible later use. In the following chapters I will present some of these diaries to you, in the students' own words. *I have received written permission from all the students whose diaries appear in this book.*[2] I have changed their names and created other disguises to maintain their anonymity. Apart from light editing, primarily to correct errors in spelling or punctuation, I have reproduced the students' exact words. Paradoxically, their ungraded diary entries are often much better written than their graded essays—suggesting that, when students write about what is important to them, they write very well.

What Students Write About

Chapter 2 begins with a selection of diaries from a summer school class. These diaries demonstrate many of the themes that students write about and raise crucial issues regarding the rewards and risks of introspective classroom diary writing. I also investigate pedagogical problems that sometimes arise and how they may be handled. The other chapters examine some of the subjects that students write about every semester, subjects which I could not have predicted before I began receiving diaries. Chapter 3, "Sins of the Fathers," discusses the wrenching problems often experienced by children of divorced parents. Chapter 4, "Hunger Artists," is devoted to the alarming number of college women suffering from eating disorders. Chapter 5, "Suicide Survivors," examines how students cope with the devastating loss of relatives and friends who have taken their own lives. Chapter 6, "Sexual Disclosures," focuses on what men and women reveal—and conceal—about this important subject. All of these chapters reveal dissolving authority: students' loss of control over their families, bodies, and lives. Chapter 7, "Teaching Empathically," explores how diary writing intensifies the student-teacher relationship and stimulates personal growth and discovery in the classroom. The Afterword, written by Maryanne Hannan, a former graduate student of mine and presently an adjunct instructor in the Department of Classics, offers a lively and detailed examination of the kinds of comments I write on student diaries.

Self-Analysis in Literary Study

Except in a few cases, I have not tried to reproduce the class discussions of literature that may have served as a background to a particular diary. It is difficult to know precisely what triggers a diary entry: sometimes it is a story that the student has read the night before, or another student's diary read aloud in class the previous week; other times it is an event in the student's life that may have had little to do with class readings or discussions. Nor have I presented here a systematic discussion of psychoanalytic theory or its application to literary criticism. I encourage but do not require students to use diary writing to integrate their developing understanding of literature with their growing self-understanding. By giving students the freedom to write about whatever they wish in their diaries, I give them the freedom *not* to write about literature. The main focus of the diaries—and this book—is on how students write about themselves: what they both reveal and conceal about their lives, what resistances they experience to self-analysis and self-disclosure, what they discover about themselves as a result of writing, and what they can teach and learn from other students (and teachers).

In presenting these diaries to you, I should emphasize that they constitute only one component of my literature-and-psychoanalysis courses. As the course syllabus in the Appendix indicates, students fulfill all the requirements that are traditionally part of college literature courses: they have daily readings; write formal, graded essays; and take midterm and final examinations. They *also* write weekly diaries.

I realize that some readers of this book will question the appropriateness of self-analytical diary writing in a literature-and-psychoanalysis course. My response is that, *precisely because* the course takes a psychoanalytic approach to literature, it offers a valuable and appropriate context for students to explore the affective as well as cognitive implications of self-discovery. There is a widespread tendency among teachers and literary critics to avoid talking or writing about anything that is "personal." And yet, not only is the classroom an ideal setting for personal self-analysis, growth, and development, but literature itself, particularly twentieth-century literature, is highly personal. Literature is filled with a cast of memorable characters who, in their attempt to analyze themselves and heal their inner tensions, compel our identification and serve as models for personal self-discovery. I don't claim that the self-discovery occurring in the classroom is as intense or sustained as in psychoanalysis, but students consistently tell me that they have been impressed by the insights acquired through introspective diary writing.

Thoreau's observation that most people lead lives of quiet desperation is evident in many diaries. Late adolescence is a turbulent period in the life cycle, and it is easy for teachers to underestimate the extent to which students are preoccupied with personal problems. For a variety of reasons—economic uncertainty, the breakup of the nuclear family, escalating social and political problems, drug- and alcohol-addiction, AIDS—students today seem to be more troubled than those in the past.[3] Although my sample constitutes a nonclinical population, a surprising number of students are, judging from their diaries, at risk. Readers who think that college students are enjoying the best years of their lives will be startled, as I was, to discover the conflicts and insecurities bedeviling so many of them, including those considered "the best and brightest." These students, I should add, generally come from middle-class families, are not members of disadvantaged minorities, have done very well in high school, and are succeeding in their academic studies at a selective public university.

Representative Students

In selecting diaries for inclusion in this book, I have not necessarily chosen the most dramatic, poignant, or best-written ones. Rather, I have selected diaries that reflect both the content and form of student writings. Friends and colleagues to whom I have shown early drafts of the manuscript inevitably ask, "Are these students truly representative?" "Do you draw students who are especially troubled or who perceive you as a therapist?" My answer is inevitably the same: I have no reason to believe that my students are significantly different from those who study at other excellent public universities. Each semester the number of students who write about the same subjects is relatively constant—and the way they write about these subjects is also relatively constant. In a typical fall or spring class, for example, about 25 percent of the students write about problems associated with being children of divorced parents, 17 percent write about experiencing an eating disorder, 35 percent write about another person's suicide or suicide attempt or their own battle against self-destruction, and 30 percent disclose sexual experiences or feelings which they identify as problematic, such as sexual abuse (including incest, stranger rape, and acquaintance rape), promiscuity, and homophobia. About 60 percent of the students in every class write on at least one of these subjects. These figures may seem high, but when I began researching national statistics, I discovered that divorce, eating disorders, suicide, and sexual abuse are far more widespread than people realize. If anything, the percentage of my students who write on these subjects is *lower* than national statistics would indicate.

Whenever appropriate, I try to situate my students' diaries in the larger social context of the late 1980s and 1990s. My purpose in doing this is not because I view myself as a culture critic or as a therapist but because, in presenting student diaries, I want to show how they reflect significant problems in contemporary American society. Rather than limiting myself to a discussion of textual issues, I have tried to indicate how the private topics on which students write mirror the public discourse about divorce, eating disorders, teenage suicide, and sexuality. Although I do not analyze or interpret my students' diaries when I receive them each week, I have not been able to avoid some analysis and interpretation of the diaries when writing this book. I hope that neither past students nor readers find this offensive. I have sought a balance between allowing the diaries to speak for themselves and providing enough commentary to show how they reveal central themes and patterns in students' lives.

The diaries have opened my eyes to problems confronting students, and this new understanding has had a profound impact upon my teaching. It is a revelation to see, for example, how many students suffer from low self-esteem and are constantly battling depression, or how many other students feel humiliated over an experience which they have never disclosed to anyone. There are few students who do not write about an event which they assume no one else has experienced or is capable of understanding. Although some of the diaries that I receive are depressing or disturbing, they also reveal the inner resources upon which students are able to draw. Their stories have affected me deeply, as I think they will affect you.

Summer school compresses a normal fourteen-week semester into six weeks; hence, students write five diaries instead of twelve. There were twenty-six students in the following class, ranging from freshmen to seniors. They were generally in their late teens or early twenties, but four of them were in their thirties. Most were full-time students during the academic year and were taking a summer course because they wanted to graduate early or needed to make up credits. The class met two evenings a week, from 6:00 to 9:30. The students' majors ranged from English to business, and many had full-time jobs. Some were taking the course because of an interest in literature and psychoanalysis, but most were there because they needed three credits of English. Had the course been reading prose fiction or the contemporary novel, the class population would have been largely the same.

The course was as rigorous as an undergraduate summer course can reasonably be. We began by reading Freud's *Introductory Lectures on Psycho-Analysis* and spent two three-hour classes discussing the strengths and limitations of psychoanalytic theory.[1] We then turned to classic nineteenth- and twentieth-century short stories, including Nathaniel Hawthorne's "Young Goodman Brown," Edgar Allan Poe's "Fall of the House of Usher," Herman Melville's "Bartleby the Scrivener," F. Scott Fitzgerald's "Babylon Revisited," D. H. Lawrence's "Rocking-Horse Winner," and Shirley Jackson's "Lottery." We read two novellas—Franz Kafka's *Metamorphosis* and Saul Bellow's *Seize the Day*—along with two novels: Sylvia Plath's *Bell Jar* and J. D. Salinger's *Catcher in the Rye*. The students also read my own book, *The Talking Cure*,[2] to see how writers have portrayed psychoanalysis in novels and plays. There was a midterm, a final examination, and a five-page essay.[3]

In order to suggest the range of students' concerns, I want to focus on several men and women in this class and how they responded to diary writing. Wherever possible, I provide the context of their diaries. The degree to which the students engage in self-analysis varies considerably, as does the degree of self-disclosure. The dialogic nature of classroom diary writing will soon become evident. Following these diaries is a discussion of the theoretical and pedagogical issues arising from introspective writing and how I respond to the problems that sometimes develop.

Establishing Trust

In the beginning, students were understandably skeptical about the diaries, viewing them as burdensome. "What exactly do you want?" one person asked. When I told him that he could write on whatever interested him, he seemed uneasy at the thought of so much freedom. There was also the problem of trust. Despite my assurances that I had built many safeguards into the course and that students in previous classes had found diary writing valuable, some students remained wary. Many opening diaries are quite tentative and guarded, and it takes some students longer than others to share their feelings with the class. Trust does not develop easily in a university that is perceived to be large and impersonal. And yet trust can be established by following the safeguards I have outlined: guaranteeing complete confidentiality, not grading personal writing, respecting students' decisions not to engage in self-disclosure, remaining empathic and nonjudgmental when commenting on diaries, and maintaining teacher-student boundaries.

AMY
"I Saw a Fire in His Eyes"

There was remarkably little hesitancy in Amy's first diary entry, which conveyed a desperation that was immediately apparent to me. "My mother makes me nervous, my father makes me scared. I have to get away, I have to leave this place and go far, far away. I don't want to be hurt anymore, I don't want to be scared." The context of Amy's comments remained obscure, but she elaborated on her feelings in her second entry:

> I was always very close to my family. I found it quite difficult growing up being only three years younger than my brother. He was always the

perfect one, and I was always considered the "black sheep" of the family. Sure, I was not perfect, but I honestly felt that I was no worse than any other teenage girl. From day one, my father thought differently. I could always tell that my father held something against me, which scared me more as I got older. We were growing further apart, and he started to drink a lot. I could feel that something terrible was going to happen.

After I graduated from high school, something happened which will have a great impact on me for the rest of my life. My father started to hit me—well, he really didn't hit me, but he beat me, until I lay in the corner and couldn't move. Every time it happened, it was when my mother and my brother were out of the house, and after he had a few drinks in him. It was, needless to say, the worst experience in my life. I still have dreams of him slamming my head against the wall and floor, and telling me that he wants to kill me. These dreams that I have now were once a harsh reality, something that I prayed every day I would make it through.

You probably are saying to yourself, "Why didn't you tell someone or leave?" My father told me that if I left, I would be disowned by my family and never allowed to come back. I had no money. So I lived every day like it was a new nightmare, and endlessly wished that I would wake up. The biggest reason why I stayed was for my mother. I knew that it would break her heart if I left.

This summer is the first time I've lived at home in a few years, and I will never do it again. Even though my father does not hit me anymore, I can see a fire in his eyes every time he looks at me, which is waiting to explode. I am still scared and live each and every day in fear. If I could help myself, I would, but I don't know what to do.

Amy's diary raises several questions which I encouraged her to explore further. Why was she considered the black sheep of the family? What did her father have against her? Why did he beat her until she couldn't move? (And why did she make a distinction between being hit and being beaten?) Why couldn't she confide in her mother? The most haunting image in the diary is the fire in her father's eyes, an image repeated in the next entry:

Last night I was sitting in the kitchen studying. In came my father for the purpose of making his first martini of the evening. As I watched him, I noticed the intense feeling that he put into making his drink. I don't know exactly why I was so involved in observing him, but once I started, I could not stop myself. The familiar sound of cracking ice now filled my ears. He was holding the ice cube in his left hand and smashing it with great force with a knife handle in his right hand. He seemed so absorbed in his actions that he did not look away once, even when my mother called to him.

It was extremely scary for me to watch my father, but I still could not look away. The smashing of the ice lasted for what seemed to be hours but in reality was only a few minutes. While he was smashing away, I saw a fire in his eyes which I have seen many times before. This really bothered me, but I didn't dare say a word. I knew exactly what he was doing, which was taking his aggressions out on the ice cubes. I wished that I knew what he was doing, but then again the truth would have frightened him [sic] me. I think that might have been a Freudian slip because I typed the word "him" instead of "me." Maybe he is also afraid of his thoughts. Anyway, my father left the room, and I went on with my studying.

Last night I heard the same sound of ice smashing in my dream. I was in a field and the sound was getting louder and louder, but I didn't know where it was coming from. I walked over the hill in the direction of the sound. As I reached the peak, I looked down to see a single person pounding a cross into the ground. Someone had just been buried, and it was my father. The sound of the hammer hitting the cross into the grave was a duplicate of my father smashing his martini ice cubes. I think I know what this dream represented, but I am afraid to admit it.

Amy's diaries are written with power and compression. Concerned primarily with narration rather than analysis, she remains detached and controlled, avoiding self-pity and sentimentality. She contrasts the fire in her father's eye with the chilling way in which he vents his aggression on the ice cubes; she is terrified of her father but cannot stop gazing at him. The smashing ice invades her dreams, along with a fearful secret that is never explained in any of her diaries.

MARIA
"My Father Also Physically Abused Me"

Amy allowed me to read her entries to the class, and they inspired three other women to relate similar experiences in their diaries. Each of the three identified with a different issue raised in Amy's writings. Maria was the first to respond, acknowledging that she too had been physically abused by her father:

> I really don't know where to start. This is very hard. My father also physically abused me all of my grade school years (I am female), and being raised in an extremely Italian, extremely Catholic, strict household, there was no hiding or haven with my mother. Her excuse was the old faithful reply: "He's your father." One night, when I was about fifteen, I came home five minutes late; my father beat my head against a wall until I bled from the ears. I was never hospitalized, and I have no idea what kind of damage it did.
>
> For years I was haunted with nightmares, and I still can't escape this fear of my father, but the one thing you have to realize is that if your father did such a terrible thing, there must be something wrong with him. Not to say that your father is some lunatic, just that there must be some anger or hate in him that manifested itself through you. Get it? Nothing that he did to you was your fault, and the answer to stopping these dreams is understanding. Not necessarily forgiveness, but an understanding that no matter what you may have been as a child, pain in the ass or not, the anger in him wasn't caused by you, and your job is to understand that the man has problems. Just try to understand, and you'll feel better.

JANE
"My Mother Is an Alcoholic"

Jane was the second woman to respond to Amy's diaries, identifying with the plight of children of alcoholics:

> I really understand what the woman who wrote about her alcoholic father was saying. It is very difficult to live with a parent who has this disease. It took me years to acknowledge that my mother is an alcoholic, and still more years to say it to others. I even feel guilty writing about it here in this diary. But that is a leftover response from when I was younger and used to feel horrid if I even dealt with my mother's illness in anything but the most sympathetic terms. Actually, there is nothing wrong with acknowledgment and dealing truthfully with this

disease. There is nothing wrong with feeling anger, either. It took the longest time to realize that my anger was healthy. I think that, at this point in my life, I have a more balanced approach to this than ever before. At least I can see objectively the reasons and causes for my mother's alcoholism.

We still do have our problems, though. I think it's because she would never get treatment for her illness. We still have a lot of arguments, especially concerning my sisters and brothers. I think my mother tries to milk her problems and lean on me, which is OK, except that in many instances she uses her problems in such a way that I get angry. I don't like to let my mother get away with things she thinks she can get away with because of her position. As much as I hate to say this, it is a lot like dealing with a naughty child or, more accurately, a manipulative child. But it never fails that when we do have an argument, like this weekend, I have bad dreams at night. In all of them, I perceive my mother as hopelessly lost in her alcoholism, never to return to the way she used to be. The most frightening thing, though, is my fear that one of my sisters or brothers will inherit this disease, and this fear always comes out in my dreams.

My mother would be shocked if she knew I wrote about this. But I think it is better to deal with this on a regular basis than to shut it off. Also, I am happy to share, with the young woman who wrote of her father, experiences of a similar nature. It is a really traumatic thing to go through, and I think it's important for people with alcoholic parents to know that there are a lot of us out there trying to cope with it.

LINDA

"I Can Never Forgive What Was Done to Me"

Linda, the third woman who responded to Amy's diaries, submitted an entry entitled "After such knowledge, what forgiveness?"—a line from T. S. Eliot's poem "Gerontion," from which I quoted at the beginning of the course.[4] Linda was an assertive speaker and gave the impression in class of being optimistic and self-confident, yet her diaries reflected the pessimism and spiritual paralysis of Eliot's early speakers. She was particularly gloomy about the value of self-knowledge, believing that "we delve deeper and deeper until we find what we think we are looking for, only to have our hopes dashed on the hidden reefs and drowned at sea." She elaborated on this fear in a later diary, revealing that, like Amy, she was filled with anger and fear as a result of her father's abusive treatment of her:

It helped me greatly to learn that not everyone had the perfect happy home life that made me envy most of my friends while I was growing up. My father, too, abused me, though it was sexual abuse and not what some might consider traditional physical abuse. To a large extent I was mentally abused as well, again by my father. I think that hearing the other woman's problems made mine seem smaller and perhaps easier to cope with, though of course I realize that child abuse in any form is not a problem which is small or insignificant in any way.

The diary that bothered me the most was the one that expressed the belief that in cases similar to these, one ought to forgive through understanding. I strongly disagree. I can never forgive what was done to me, and I probably never will understand why any single person should be able to so completely strip someone of their self-esteem. Or why any eleven-year-old child should have her childhood stolen from her. Or why a twelve-year-old should be made to feel like a prostitute. Or why a thirteen-year-old should be so harshly manipulated in every possible way. Or why a twenty-year-old, who can intellectually recognize where the true blame lies, should be so emotionally torn and feel so terribly, terribly guilty. Or why anyone should be allowed to hurt someone else so very much that the hurt never seems like it's going to end.

Dammit. I thought I could do this without crying. Jesus, I hope my housemates don't walk in while I'm writing this. I don't actually know why I'm even writing this. It's not exactly a cry for help. I know I should probably seek professional help concerning this whole thing, but I'm not sure I ever will. Sometimes pretending like it never really happened is so much easier. At least that's what he does. My father, I mean.

I think that's probably part of why I always wanted to be a set designer. I've been disguising myself my whole life, and doing it so well that no one even notices. So well that I ought to have a closet full of Oscars. So well that everyone, including my mom, whom I love dearly, thinks that it's all in jest when I say that I hate my father and that he's a sonofabitch and that he did a shitty job as a dad while I was growing up. Yeah, people think that I'm "Daddy's little girl," and nobody seems to notice how I cringe when people use that term to speak about something as unrelated as "Babylon Revisited."

When I first began receiving diaries on physical and sexual abuse, I was shocked, for they were written by confident-looking young women who did not appear outwardly abused. I did not realize then that most abused women carry scars that are not easily visible. Nor did I realize that, since 1940, major studies indicate that between 20 and 35 percent of women report a childhood sexual encounter with a male family member.[5] Also disturbing is the number of students who in every course write about the problem of alcohol abuse, which, judging from the diaries, is far more prevalent than drug abuse. Ironically, students are so casual about alcohol abuse that they rarely call attention it; alcoholism remains more of a subtext in student diaries than a dominant theme.

WENDY
"She Forgot to Look Both Ways"

Wendy began her first diary by saying that she was having difficulty understanding Freud's theory of dream interpretation and felt uneasy about having her diaries read in front of class. In her second entry, however, she reported that her attitude toward the class was changing and that she was beginning to remember her dreams. In her third diary she wrote about interpreting for the first time a recurrent dream based upon an event she had witnessed several years earlier:

When I was only thirteen years old, I was just a freshman in high school. I used to walk to school with my older sister. We always took the same route to school. We had to cross the main road without a traffic light. There was a grade school only a few blocks away from my school. The little kids had to cross the same busy road as we did. For many years, the residents tried to get a traffic light put up but were unsuccessful. I never realized that I would witness the life ebbing out of a little girl on the pavement.

One day, I was walking to school as usual. We were running late, so we had to walk fast. We approached the intersection where we had to cross the street. Just as we finished crossing, we saw a little girl waving to a friend of hers on the other side of the street. She was so happy to see her friend that she forgot to look both ways before crossing. As she stepped off the curb, a car drove by. She dashed out in front of the car before the startled driver had time to react. Her small body made contact with a thump, and her white sneakers lay on the ground in the pool of her own blood. The driver of the car sobbed, saying that she hadn't seen her until it was too late. She was right. It seemed like the whole incident occurred in slow motion, then sped up suddenly at the end. My sister and I were horrified at what we had just seen.

It took me a long time to get over what I had seen. I guess I never did though. I had nightmares about that little girl's still body. These dreams continued until recently. I never made the connection between the accident and what I was dreaming. I realized that I had to face myself and bring it all back into the open again. Although it was painful remembering what happened almost eight years ago, it helped me a lot to do it. I found that in my subconscious I blamed myself. "If only I had looked more carefully—if only I had yelled a warning." I always felt that her death was senseless. She was so young and had so much left to do.

I don't think that I will ever forget what I saw, I know I won't. At least now that I've dealt with my emotions, I won't be so afraid of them anymore.

MARK
"I Blame a Lot of My Shortcomings and Little Setbacks in Life on Him"

Mark, like Wendy, was troubled by bad dreams. He began his first diary by expressing skepticism over the assumption that the present is an outgrowth of the past. "If we believe that our attitudes and feelings are 'predestined,' so to speak, what would be the incentive for an individual who had a real crappy childhood and only had himself to blame for his own shortcomings to try to improve his life?" He opened his second diary with an analysis of a recurrent dream, revealing midway through the entry why he was so troubled by the idea that the child is father to the man:

When I turned six, my father died. He left for England on a business trip on September 12, and I vividly remember, I think, the whole exit because this was the morning of my sixth birthday. I have dreamed this incident time and again, and it's the same way each time. My mother and I are standing at the front door of a house watching my father bring his luggage out to a car waiting for him. He then comes back and wishes me a happy birthday again, kisses me, then kisses my mother and says she'll be all right alone, and then leaves. And during this whole incident, I know that my father is going to die, but I don't say anything. It's as if, while dreaming, I have the knowledge to stop him from leaving, and thus stop him from dying, but I can't make myself speak.

Now this is obviously a very traumatic experience for anyone, especially a six-year-old boy. I would agree that the last contact that someone has made with another person who dies is a contact that sticks out in the mind. But I just don't know. My mother has spoken to me about those last few moments many times, and I'm afraid that all I am doing is replaying the incident that she tells through my mouth. Now I'm going to try and figure out why I think, or feel, like I do. As you said in class, we understand things—death, for example—on the intellectual plane but not on the emotional plane. I was very young when my father died, and I was vehemently jealous of my older brothers and sisters for knowing my father and being able to spend time with him, while I was usually left behind when they went golfing or swimming, or whatever, because of my age. Emotionally I felt cheated.

Could it be that I retell this story and have this recurring dream as part of living up to the distinction of being the last son to see him alive—a sort of morbid sense of pride? I hope not, but this is what I am inclined to believe. I blame a lot of my shortcomings and little setbacks in life on him, because it's convenient, I guess. I don't know why I wrote about this; I can't put much of what I'm learning in your class into this dream/reality. I guess I just wanted to get it off my chest to see what someone else thought.

Mark continued to explore in later diaries his ambivalence toward father figures. In one dream he was a fireman caught in the middle of a blaze, smothered to death when the roof on which he was standing collapsed. The dream, he noted, arose in response to a local news item in which several firemen were burned to death by a falling roof. Analyzing the dream, Mark observed that he had always disliked firemen and policemen and that he was sometimes in trouble with the latter. Ironically, the father of one of his former girlfriends was a fireman, and Mark did not like him. He interpreted the dream as self-punishment for harboring hostile feelings toward male authority figures. In his own words, "My dislike or disrespect for firemen was punished, and I felt guilty that I thought this way when I saw that they were indeed good for something and that they had mothers, just like my own, who grieved over the death of a loved one."

Like Esther Greenwood in *The Bell Jar*, Mark felt anger toward his father for dying early. "He really hurt me by doing that, and I just recently fully realized my pain." Growing up without a father created severe financial problems, and he resented people his own age whose parents financially supported them. Identifying not only with Esther but also with Saul Bellow's tragic-comic protagonist Tommy Wilhelm in *Seize the Day*, Mark added that he was always broke and, more ominously, had frequently sabotaged his chances for success, especially in high school, when he played the role of the "dumb jock." After giving several examples of unwise actions, Mark vowed to live up to his potential:

> I'm not some ignorant drunk who wants to sit on his ass and collect welfare off the rest of society. Rather, I am someone who knows that he can do great things but is afraid of not getting the chance because of lack of money and stupid moves. I pray to God that I laugh out loud when you read this journal; I pray that my anxiety for the future makes me push all that much harder to make myself into someone I can be proud of.

GEORGE
"The Other Day I Realized I Was Chasing a Ghost"

George began his second diary by relating a fantasy in which he was an idealistic political leader with the ability to change the world through heroic devotion to peace and equality. The fantasy ended with his assassination by a fascist extremist, though not before the dying hero delivered a noble monologue inspiring millions of people for centuries to come. "My dying words remind everyone that peace and love are the most important things in life, and then I die a martyr, a legend, a Christ figure." George's next diary contained another fantasy of martyrdom which he traced to his insecurities as a child:

> Growing up I was always very skinny and frail, not just physically but mentally as well. Whenever I played football with my friends, I was

always one of the worst, and it made me cry often. I would desperately try to hold back that flood of tears until I thought I was going to choke, then I'd break down and weep. Of course all my neighborhood playmates would tell me I was a baby and to cut the shit, but honestly I couldn't help it.

Then one day as I was crying, realizing how ashamed of myself I was, I stopped. I promised myself, with the deepest resolve, that I would never cry again, and I haven't since I was fourteen. Now I am twenty. The price I have paid for a controlled behavior is a distance from whatever I do. I don't let people come too close, and I don't like that in myself.

I also had problems with girls. I was too skinny and not so attractive, and at thirteen, kids can be extremely cruel. I felt I was ugly, and nobody would ever consider me that good-looking, popular guy that everybody loved.

Now in the present, through my fantasies of martyrdom, I like to refer to myself as the ugly duckling that grew into a swan. I know that sounds like I'm full of myself, but that's impossible. I will forever carry around that weak, unattractive self-image.

Now I am older, and dates aren't a problem at all. In fact, I split up with my girlfriend because I wanted to date tons of girls. I did. This summer I've spent literally hundreds and hundreds of dollars on girls, dinner, etc.

The other day I realized I was chasing a ghost, a thirteen-year-old fantasy to be the epitome of male studness as on television or in the movies. But I was forgetting one thing. The girl at home right now in Brooklyn who loves me. The person who takes my bad points as well as good points. The person who after leaving her and chasing a fantasy could only say, through tears, "Of course," when I asked her to take me back.

Some people might say, "How could she take him back after he broke up with her for other girls?" But all I can say is, thank God she did. She is truly my best friend. Now we are taking it slow, but things are progressing back to the way they were. I'm convinced that things are going to be even better because I have gotten this monkey off my back. One last note, on the phone with her the other night, I cried too. Not much, but it's a start, and for the first time ever, it felt good.

SAM

"I Am a Person of Extremes"

Sam, a lawyer in his late thirties, newly remarried and intent upon reviving an old interest in literature, began his first diary by commenting on the folly of getting married when statistics indicate a 50-percent divorce rate. He was equally critical of the marriages that apparently succeed, believing they are based upon deception. In a later diary Sam returned to the theme of marital disillusionment, speaking personally for the first time:

> I recall clearly a year or so after my divorce how very bored and tired I became with the single life. Or rather, the "Night People's Mating/ Dating Game," as I called it. I wanted out, and yet I feared being trapped in another miserable relationship. I was terribly cold-blooded, and I methodically went shopping for the ideal wife. It took about a year of hunting and dating, complete with checklist, and when I finally found her, I allowed myself to be caught. We had a good friendship, and a lot in common. It was not the head-over-heels, stars-in-the-eyes love rela-tionship that I had the first time, which ended in disaster. I am too cynical to let that happen again. Now I'm content, I suppose, secure, well fed, taken care of, satisfied, and bored.
>
> Ironically, I find myself yearning again for singledom. Oddly enough, now I find my memories are of wild, irresponsible fun. I want the total freedom to do, say, and be totally me. Now I'm feeling tied by bonds of laughter, companionship, and money. I don't want to be lonely again, though; I don't want my life to career out of control. Maybe I can't stay in a middle ground. I am a person of extremes.
>
> I keep wondering if this is the best I can do. Would I ever be happy, even if I did get free and found someone else later in life? Maybe the same vicious cycle would start all over again. I'm not sure I can ever be satisfied; my standards are so high that no one measures up for very long. The flaws become glaringly irritating after a while, and I'm afraid I'll always be searching for . . . well, I'm not sure what. It may be someone, or something, or perhaps a way of life.
>
> I know I have a "good" marriage now, it's working, but it isn't satisfy-ing, not really—I feel unfulfilled and somewhat hollow inside. At times she makes me feel like I'm being squashed, and my true complete per-sonality is under tight rein around her. I'm never free to be 100 percent

me; she doesn't like the 100 percent me. So I show her the sides of me that she knows and loves, and she is happy, but I'm stifled. I think she would become a charter member of the Man Haters Club if I took off. But I won't, at least I don't think I will; I'll just go on while I stay troubled and wondering. I wish I could see a way to handle this without anyone getting hurt. I suppose it's just a matter of risk and priorities.

Sam's last diary was written when we were discussing *The Bell Jar*, and the novel affected him greatly:

The curious mist which enshrouded the motivation behind my self-destructive tendencies cleared a little. It was hard for me to believe that we were discussing Esther and/or Sylvia Plath. It could have been me, or rather the me which was the dominating personality between the ages of seventeen and twenty-nine. I don't buy the sex stuff, at least not as it pertains to me, but the rest of it was right on the money. A low self-esteem with corresponding masochistic tendencies.

I was one of those people who thought that if a little was good, then a lot would be great. Definitely a man of extremes: extreme use of drugs that went way beyond the conventional recreational use limits, extreme use of alcohol, and extreme use of sex. I never went through a formal analysis with a professional, although I would probably benefit greatly, since even now I have a great deal of anger and guilt, though I'm not sure why.

I'm working through it myself, however, as I have always done. The drugs and booze were to keep me numb and release the inhibitions so I could feel free to do the things I was driven to. I suppose I was taking revenge, like Esther, on several individuals around me, as well as on myself. I, too, had an idealized father whose impossibly high standards I strove to live up to. I have since relegated him to the category of normal human, friend as well as father. The sex was simply an exercise in distance; I used women emotionally and physically, always under the haven of "friendship" so that none of them saw me for the person that I was. I really could be brutal . . . and I enjoyed it greatly. Don't get me wrong, I was very selective and stayed with only one woman at a time. The relationship would end when it threatened to become permanent. Once the "I love you's" were said, the death of the affair followed shortly.

Maybe it helped to make me feel better, since the rest of my life was so out of control. Life was pretty tough for awhile, and like Tommy Wilhelm, I made some dumb decisions which contributed greatly to my sufferings. I worked through both the drug and alcohol problems slowly. Needless to say, now I have it controlled to where I abstain from narcotics and drink socially and sparingly.

Yet I guess I still have the martyr complex to an extent. It is hard for me to place my dissatisfaction with things on my own doorstep; I tend to place the blame with another, but at least I am aware of this. Like Esther, I have an awful problem of feeling superior. This tends to make it difficult to be around people, males and females, since too often the flaws and imperfections in their personalities or intellects become irritating to the point where socializing is impossible. Actually what it does is make your social circle very select and small in numbers. Acquaintances are many, but friends are few. They have to be people to whom I feel equal or even perhaps somewhat inferior to. I can't believe I'm saying this. I've only admitted this to one other person, and she too is narcissistic and "superior." We laughed and were relieved that we weren't the only ones who felt like this. Oddly enough, when we first became friends, we were intimidated by each other, but once we admitted this to each other, equality moved in.

DONNA
"They Were Running Away from Me"

During the first week of the term Donna revealed that she had been tormented by nightmares, resulting in a recent breakdown and institutionalization. Because the disclosure came in a class comment, I didn't know whether she would write about this experience in her diaries, since, if she did so, everyone would know her identity. Donna evidently did not mind the loss of anonymity and returned frequently to the hospitalization, each week supplying additional background information. In the second diary she wrote that, although she could not remember any of the disturbing dreams she had in the hospital, she wanted to be able to make sense of them. In the third diary she stated that, as a result of the course, she was beginning to remember one of these recurrent dreams:

It was always the same dream. My parents and I would be on the main street of my home town, and I would be waiting for them at a local department store once they had completed their banking. Unfortunately, my parents never come to me, and when I leave the store in search of them, the entire city is deserted. I become panic-stricken because I can't bear the thought of losing my parents. I walk all over in search of my parents, unable to locate them anywhere. I decide my only alternative is to walk to my grandparents' house and convey to them my dilemma, but as I approach the house, I see my parents running down the steps as if something terrible has just happened, or as if they are trying to get away from something. Usually, after awaking from this dream, I would give considerable thought to the reason my parents never came to meet me, and why they could possibly have been running away from me, and I always came up with the same reasoning: they were running away from me!

Why do I think my parents are trying to desert me? I don't know. I guess it's really hard for me to accept the fact that people actually love me. I've just recently come to terms with myself, and although my self-esteem remains at an all-time low at the present time, I feel that, with the proper changes in my lifestyle, I can become more self-gratifying, more self-loving, and begin to place my own needs before the needs of others.

In the next two diaries Donna expanded on the consequences of her low self-esteem, intimating that the terrifying dreams for which she had been hospitalized were symptomatic of deeper conflicts. In her fourth diary, written during our discussion of *The Bell Jar*, she confronted the subject of suicide:

A very intelligent man once told me that he felt "no sympathy for people who contemplated suicide." My response to that statement was one of silence because I am sympathetic to suicidal people, since I myself have given thought to suicide in the past. It's frightening to talk about, and people more often than not view those who admittedly associate themselves with suicide as "crazy." Suicide isn't "crazy" as many think; rather, it's a frightening thought. I thought about it once, and someone dear to me told me that "suicide is a cop-out." I guess I never really wanted to die; I wanted to be loved and understood. I needed to feel important to someone. I paid for my harsh words of suicide with a stay at a local hospital, where I lived with people very similar to those discussed in *The Bell Jar*.

Once you're in it, it's very hard to get out. Everyone tries to be nice, but their kindness goes unrewarded because what you want is not sympathy but a way out. I don't mean death, but a way out to make a new place in society. But once you do get out, you realize that there are still people in these places who will never be allowed a second chance because they are not like everyone else. They know true suffering, they know the true meaning of life because you either learn to live again or you die—perhaps not physical death, but mental death, the inability to think for oneself, that's true death.

After reading *The Bell Jar* I was able to understand better some of the mood swings and depressed states I had been having. Sylvia Plath's problems seemed a little deeper than my own, though. Whereas she truly wanted to die, I, on the other hand, did not, I wanted affection. It may sound odd to you that a person would seek affection through death, and now it seems odd, even "crazy," if such a word exists. I never wanted to die. I just wanted the attention that often accompanies suicide "victims," attention which doesn't stem from affection but from pity and fear.

People who have never contemplated suicide are afraid of those who have because if you have those thoughts, there is obviously something wrong with you. But there really isn't anything wrong with you, it's just that those who have similar thoughts are dead or too afraid to talk. I've had these thoughts and I've learned that it's not so wrong, but it is wrong to see these thoughts through.

BILL
"I Withdraw All Previous Diary Entries"

Two students found introspective diary writing objectionable, and their reactions illustrate the problems that sometimes arise. Bill's early entries were little different from those of his classmates. In his first diary he agreed with a statement I made in class that psychological health depends upon the ability to tolerate ambiguity in life, though he felt that Freud brooked no dissent from his readers in the *Introductory Lectures*. "Why does He find it necessary to lead me by my hand? What is He trying to prove? His theory? or His ability to devise such a theory?" By capitalizing the pronouns, Bill made it clear that he thought Freud regarded himself as a deity. The second diary was an elaborate martyrdom fantasy not unlike Holden Caulfield's messianic wish to save children from falling into the abyss of adulthood. Attempting to lead a throng of screaming children away from the brink of a cataclysmic waterfall, Bill found himself trampled to death.

Bill's third diary was about witnessing a boy attempt suicide at a school for emotionally disturbed children. Bill admitted that our interpretation of *The Bell Jar* had changed his mind about self-inflicted death. Whereas he used to believe that people who wanted to die were burdens to society, better off dead, now he interpreted suicide as a cry for help, deserving compassion and understanding.

Bill's "Declaration of Boycott" in his last diary caught me by surprise. "I withdraw all previous diary entries and refuse to submit any further entries. Reason for this being that I see no advantage in listening to or adding to the collection of trivial teenage confessions which seem to be the vogue this summer." The reason for Bill's sudden hostility was not clear to me at the time; he did solid B work throughout the course and did not seem dissatisfied either with his performance as a student or with mine as a teacher. In retrospect, I can see Bill's opposition from the first diary. He may have believed that, like Freud, I was attempting to lead him by the hand. He came to regard the diaries as a waste of time, and his last words were unambiguously defiant in content and spelling: "Since I really hate havinfg [*sic*] to write this shit, I wont [*sic*]."

ERIKA
"I Would Prefer Not To"

Erika also disliked diary writing, and she was the only student who did not give me permission to photocopy her writings at the end of the semester. I was disappointed because her entries were witty and trenchant, evoking the corrosive satire of Karl Kraus. She would have agreed with Kraus's sardonic characterization of psychoanalysis as the disease of which it purports to be the cure. Her diaries abounded with mocking references both to Freud and me; she believed that we were both manipulative and sexist. No matter how hard I tried to distance myself from Freud's antifeminism, Erika saw me as hostile to women. Nor was she sympathetic to my claim that psychoanalysis and feminism were potential allies in their aim of empowerment.

Erika never changed her dim view of psychoanalysis, nor did she overcome her mistrust of diary writing. Since she did not restrict me from reading her entries aloud, I shared two of them with the class, hoping they would spark a useful debate on the merits and demerits of psychoanalytic literary criticism. My efforts backfired, however, and she came to feel increasingly isolated. Her antipathy to Freud alienated the other students, further strengthening her determination not to compromise her dissenting point of view. In the belief that she was being walled up by an oppressive patriarchal ideology, Erika reminded me of Bartleby the scrivener: she quietly but adamantly asserted to everyone that she "would prefer not to" be like everyone else. She was thus telling me that, although she had no choice about being in my class and fulfilling my requirements, she did not have to copy my version of reality.

I don't think I felt "unmanned" by Erika's defiance, as the lawyer does in his confrontations with Bartleby, but I did feel frustrated by my failure to earn her trust. I inferred from some of her writings that she had been wounded by her father, and I did not want to become another persecuting authority figure. Nor did I wish to become vindictive, as Freud was in his only major case study of a woman, *Fragment of an Analysis of a Case of Hysteria*. Annoyed that Dora had broken off treatment unexpectedly, Freud writes condescendingly about her in the postscript to the story. "I do not know what kind of help she wanted from me, but I promised to forgive her for having deprived me of the satisfaction of affording her a far more radical cure for her troubles."[6]

Yet even as I write the above paragraph, I realize my failure to remain empathic toward Erika. Comparing her to Bartleby and Dora reveals the wish to see her as a troublemaker, rebel, or patient. On a conscious level, I criticized Freud's patronizing attitude toward Dora; on an unconscious level, I identified with his feelings of rejection. Although I doubt that the majority of the students regarded me as manipulative, Bill and Erika did, perhaps with justification. Because teachers give off contradictory signals about encouraging students to disagree with them, Bill and Erika may have detected my uneasiness over their sharp criticisms of Freud and of my psychoanalytic approach to literature. Fortunately, Erika did not curl up and die in a fetal position at the end of the semester, as Bartleby does at the end of Melville's story. Rather, she earned an A in the course and proceeded with her education.

Honesty and Truth in Diary Writing

Before discussing how the students finally evaluated diary writing, I want to address important theoretical and pedagogical issues arising from any form of personal writing in the classroom, including honesty and truth, voyeurism and prurience, transference and countertransference, teacher-student boundaries, teachers' self-disclosures, and the rewards and risks of introspective writing. These issues will be of particular importance to teachers who encourage their own students to write self-disclosing diaries.

Honesty and truth are, strictly speaking, two separate issues: one can write honestly but not truthfully (one may believe sincerely in a delusion, for example) and truthfully but not honestly (in telling a lie, a person may unintentionally express the truth). To address the first question, do students write honestly in their diaries? Are they sincere in what they say? In every class students express doubts about the honesty of their classmates' diaries. It is not enough for me to say that, to the best of my knowledge, all the diaries appearing in this book are honest; I believe this, but I cannot be certain.

Although I do not grade their diaries, it is easy to see why students might wish to deceive me. They might fabricate stories to tell me what they assume I wish to hear or to impress me with their unique lives or colorful prose. They might sensationalize a diary so that I read it in class or include it in my book; or they might believe that, notwithstanding my statements to the contrary, their diaries will contribute to my final evaluation of their class performance. Students might wish to portray themselves as victims in order to receive special attention or validation. People sometimes lie to make themselves appear better—or worse—than they actually are. For those who enjoy admitting crimes they have not committed, confession becomes an art form in itself. Some people may fabricate simply for the pleasure of invention; there is little doubt that deception is as much part of human nature as truth telling is.

To determine how honest they are in their diaries, I ask students to fill out anonymous questionnaires at the end of the semester in which they answer, among several questions, two in particular: (1) Were you honest in your diaries (that is, did you tell the truth as you saw it and not invent the experiences and feelings you were writing about)? and (2) Do you think the other students in the class were honest in their diaries? Student responses to the questionnaire are instructive. Close to 100 percent of the polled students have reported they were honest in their *own* diaries; no student has reported that he or she was not honest, and none or one or two students in each class have reported they were "not sure" whether they were honest.[7] By contrast, between 60 to 70 percent of the polled students believed *classmates* were honest in their diaries; the remaining students were "not sure" about their classmates' honesty. How do we explain the discrepancy between these answers?

I suspect that the reason so many students doubt their classmates' honesty is because they cannot imagine the harrowing experiences contained in these diaries. It may be that students who have enjoyed a protected upbringing are the ones who are the most skeptical of their classmates' credibility with respect to eating disorders, suicidal thinking, and sexual abuse. If students were able to read all their classmates' diaries, however, I suspect that they would find the diaries more believable. Reading a single diary entry may provoke readers to question a diarist's credibility; reading an entire semester's diaries allows readers to see the continuities of a writer's self-representation from week to week, thus strengthening readers' trust in the diarist's credibility.

Student diaries may be honest, but are they true? Diaries are perhaps the most subjective and solipsistic of all genres. Students may believe they are telling the truth in their personal writings, but they would no doubt see a very different picture of the truth if they heard the viewpoints of relatives and friends. Even when people believe they are scrupulously telling the truth, they are still selectively remembering and forgetting experiences, editing biography and history to make them conform to their own self-perceptions. Some historians and philosophers claim that all interpretations are misinterpretations; postmodernists, in particular, assert the fictionality of all self-representation. Elements of both self-discovery and self-creation inhere in probably all autobiographical writing.[8] Even Freud, who remained supremely confident that psychoanalysis could help patients dredge up long-repressed memories, sometimes feared that memories of the distant past are either irretrievably lost or hopelessly distorted. Freud was also fond of quoting one of Nietzsche's aphorisms from *Beyond Good and Evil*: " 'I did that,' says my memory. 'I could not have done that,' says my pride, and remains inexorable. Eventually—the memory yields."[9] All truth claims, even when sincerely made, are subject to qualification and challenge. At best we convey, to quote the apt title of one recent book on the subject, the "varnished truth."[10]

Voyeurism

In overhearing intimate aspects of students' lives, we may sometimes feel that we are voyeurs, gazing at private material that we have no right to witness. Students occasionally express uneasiness upon hearing their classmates' intimate revelations, and readers may feel similarly uncomfortable about portions of this book. Do self-disclosing diaries render us into Peeping Toms?

I don't think so, largely because, as I discuss in more detail in later chapters, nearly all students who comment upon their classmates' diaries do so sensitively and compassionately. An empathic reader is not a voyeuristic reader. Rarely will a student make a caustic or callous comment about another student's revelations. I have no reason to believe that students who do not comment on their classmates' diaries remain unmoved by them. Students do not exploit their classmates' vulnerability or derive pleasure from others' misfortune. The anonymity of the diaries prevents students from unmasking classmates' identities. Some students may surreptitiously gaze around the room during the reading of the diaries in an effort to locate a diarist's identity, but this is seldom a problem. Students are not rubbernecks, and diarists do not cater to prurient interests.

Transference and Countertransference

Diary writing intensifies the student-teacher relationship. All students project feelings for their parents onto teachers and authority figures, but diary writing heightens this phenomenon. Transference, as it is called in psychoanalysis, pervades the classroom. Freud's most complete definition of transference appears in *An Autobiographical Study*:

> In every analytic treatment there arises, without the physician's agency, an intense emotional relationship between the patient and the analyst which is not to be accounted for by the actual situation. It can be of a positive or of a negative character and can vary between the extremes of a passionate, completely sensual love and the unbridled expression of an embittered defiance and hatred. This *transference*—to give it its short name—soon replaces in the patient's mind the desire to be cured, and, so long as it is affectionate and moderate, becomes the agent of the physician's influence and neither more nor less than the mainspring of

the joint work of analysis. Later on, when it has become passionate or has been converted into hostility, it becomes the principal tool of the resistance. It may then happen that it will paralyse the patient's powers of associating and endanger the success of the treatment. Yet it would be senseless to try to evade it; for an analysis without transference is an impossibility.[11]

Transference and countertransference (the analyst's unconscious projective tendencies) are similarly impossible to avoid in the classroom, manifesting themselves in every aspect of the student-teacher relationship. Grades, for example, are fraught with symbolism for students and teachers alike, conveying an evaluation that extends far beyond mastery of a subject. Grades touch upon issues of identity, self-worth, power, and motivation and ultimately re-create aspects of the parent-child relationship. Teaching is itself a form of parenting, and classroom diary writing awakens powerful unconscious forces within students and teachers alike.

For decades analysts have debated the role of transference and countertransference in psychotherapy, but only in the last few years has there been discussion of how these phenomena manifest themselves in the classroom. In a 1989 issue of the *AWP Chronicle*, Robert Langs, a psychoanalyst who has written extensively on unconscious communication in psychotherapy, calls into question Freud's definition of transference as a constellation of *inappropriate* perceptions of and reactions to the analyst. Langs maintains, on the contrary, that the concept of transference is misleading because the patient's perceptions of the analyst are generally accurate. Langs would avoid the term "transference" altogether and replace it with the role of "*non-transference*, or *valid unconscious perceptions* in the teaching relationship."[12]

Langs rightly points out that it is self-serving to invoke concepts such as resistance and transference to explain a patient's (or student's) failings when it may be the analyst's (or teacher's) actions that are responsible for professional failure. He is also right to call attention to the subtle unconscious communication existing in the classroom. Many of his suggestions for maintaining the proper student-teacher relationship are important, such as a clear sense of ground rules in attendance, grades, tests, and reports.

Some of Langs's other comments about teaching strike me as rigid, however. He insists that both the patient-analyst and student-teacher relationships depend upon strict detachment; consequently, any departure from what he calls the "ideal frame," such as a student and teacher meeting for lunch, having a casual conversation outside of class, or sharing any personal material with each other, may be disastrous. He also holds that there should be total privacy for the class, with no observers, and that the teacher should maintain anonymity and make no personal disclosures. In warning against teachers' overinvolvement with their students, Langs creates a paradigm of underinvolvement which is, ironically, reminiscent of Freud's discredited theory of analytic neutrality, where the psychoanalyst is urged to model himself "on the surgeon, who puts aside all his feelings, even his human sympathy, and concentrates his mental forces on the single aim of performing the operation as skilfully as possible."[13]

Teachers' Self-Disclosures

My own teaching experience leads me to believe that total privacy is not necessary in the classroom and that, far from compromising the student-teacher relationship, the sharing of personal material can heighten the learning experience. There are occasions when teachers are justified in dropping the mask of anonymity and revealing personal experiences, as Langs himself does effectively in his article. Teachers can talk about themselves in the classroom in ways that open up dialogues with their students. A teacher's pertinent self-disclosure can embolden students to make connections to literature that might otherwise remain obscure. As discussed in chapter 5, when I explore with my students how a fictional character's suicide affects other characters in a story, or how an author's suicide affects our response to his or her writings, I usually reveal the devastation I experienced when my best friend committed suicide. Talking about this in class encourages students to write diaries about similar losses in their lives. Students appreciate teachers who strive to be honest and open about themselves, who are not afraid to be self-critical, and who can be both authority figures and fellow beings.

Minimizing the Risks of Diary Writing

Self-analytical classroom diary writing yields great benefits but also poses considerable risks. Only in a safe and secure setting can one deal with the potentially volatile emotions generated by introspective writing. Freud's cautionary note in "Observations on Transference-Love" applies to the teacher no less than to the analyst: "The psycho-analyst knows that he is working with highly explosive forces and that he needs to proceed with as much caution and conscientiousness as a chemist."[14] Without proper safeguards, the potent chemistry of psychoanalytic diaries can become toxic.

And yet transference and countertransference dynamics need not always be fraught with explosive energy, as some scholars have stated. Ann Murphy asserts that in "encouraging our students to unlock and express their ideas, feelings, and beliefs more effectively, we are, like psychoanalysts, insisting that they confront lost or denied elements of themselves," a project she regards with deep suspicion.[15] Her fear is that, in unleashing these powerful forces, we might not be able to put the genie back in the lamp. "When we ask students to keep journals, for example, or assign to them writing tasks which push them inward to explore their own lives and selves, we may very well elicit material we are utterly unqualified to handle."[16] Murphy's conclusion is that as "pseudoanalysts," we are untrained to probe our students' psyches. More recently, three academics writing in the *Chronicle of Higher Education* have warned against the dangers of compelling students to write about themselves in journals, compositions, and other writing assignments. Stressing the potential harm done to students by requiring them to engage in inappropriate self-disclosure, they suggest that personal writing may heighten the vulnerability of those students who, victimized in the past, may find themselves victimized again by their writing instructors.[17]

Although introspective diary writing does intensify the teacher-student relationship, thus heightening the possibility that students may become inadvertently harmed in the process, teachers can avoid this situation by resisting the urge to be pseudoanalysts. It is not the teacher who probes his or her students' psyches but the students themselves. They analyze only what they want to analyze, when they want to analyze it, and they can stop whenever they wish. The students control how much of the genie they want to release at a time. While some students may be disappointed that I do not interpret their diaries, they are also relieved that they alone are challenged to discover or create meaning for themselves. By refusing to play the role of analyst, omniscient professor, or savior, I maintain my professional distance from them without becoming remote.

Maintaining professional distance also implies the strict avoidance of any sexual contact between teachers and students, a policy that several colleges are now trying to adopt. But there have been challenges to this position, most recently, by William Kerrigan, a well-known psychoanalytic literary critic. In a roundtable discussion in *Harper's Magazine* in which four academics attacked campuswide bans on sexual relationships between faculty members and students, Kerrigan asserted that "there is a particular kind of student I've come across in my career who was working through something that only a professor could help her with. I'm talking about a female student who, for one reason or another, has unnaturally prolonged her virginity."[18] Kerrigan's statement touched off a furor at the state university where he teaches, and far beyond, and he later issued a clarification stating that he agreed with the adoption of regulations banning teachers' sexual involvement with students who are in their classes.

How can we assure our students that we will not betray their trust, exploit their vulnerability, or project onto them inappropriate feelings? It takes time to establish trust, without which introspective diary writing cannot work, and that trust can be shattered quickly through a sarcastic comment on a diary or an essay, a missed office hour, insensitivity to a student's disappointment over a grade, or inappropriate conduct.

Trust is important in teaching but crucial in diary writing. Teachers must be keenly sensitive to the ethical issues arising over personal diaries. Students must not be pressured into analyzing and disclosing more than they want to, and they must be free to determine their own topics and set their own pace. They must have the freedom to avoid self-analysis and self-disclosure entirely, if they wish. The belief that we deceive ourselves so that we do not perish of the truth highlights the dangers of self-discovery. Students need to be assured, moreover, that their diaries are not being judged in any way or used to influence their grade. And they must never be put on the defensive as a result of disclosing material in their diaries.

In determining which diaries to read aloud each week, I am careful to avoid any entry that might cause embarrassment or discomfort to another member of the class. Diaries on racism—an explosive problem on college campuses—must be handled with special sensitivity. Students write increasingly about ugly racial incidents which they have been involved in or have witnessed. Because relatively few minority students take my literature-and-psychoanalysis courses, it is obvious that when they write about being victimized by a racial attack, I cannot read the diary to the class because their identities would be exposed. Even if an African American, Hispanic, or Asian American gave me permission to read one of these diaries aloud, I would not do so because it might distress another member of his or her racial group. Nor would I read aloud a diary written by a white student about being attacked by a member of a minority group.

I usually read aloud diaries that are critical of me. Students are surprised when they hear these diaries read aloud and feel validated that their criticisms are taken seriously. By contrast, I do not read aloud a diary that is critical of another classmate. If a diary is particularly personal, I sometimes contact the student before class to make doubly sure that he or she will not feel uncomfortable about having the other students hear it. I read the diaries in a calm voice, avoiding emotionality.

The Teacher's Double Role

I often play a double role to my students. I am their English professor—a balding, bespectacled, middle-aged man who assigns essays and exams, compels their class attendance, enforces deadlines, grades their work, and wishes them success in their future studies. I am also, for many of them, a confidant and friend, a person to whom they entrust their thoughts and feelings and with whom they remain in touch after the semester ends. By setting rigorous standards while grading their essays and striving for empathy while reading their diaries, I try to fulfill both roles. Significantly, students seldom confuse these two sides of me or make unreasonable demands on me. When they visit me during office hours, we discuss the usual academic issues: papers, exams, advisement, and so forth. We rarely discuss the diaries. Indeed, there is a tacit agreement that the diaries are part of our private relationship. Contrary to what one might expect, assigning final grades to students who write introspective diaries is only slightly more difficult than grading other students' work. Nearly all diary students indicate, in the anonymous evaluations they turn in at the end of the semester, that they believe I have graded fairly their written work.

Evaluating Diary Writing

How did the summer school students finally evaluate diary writing? With the exception of Bill and Erika, all the students concluded in their final diaries that writing weekly entries heightened their self-understanding and self-esteem. They felt bonded to their classmates and discovered that they were not alone in being confused or hurt or angry or conflicted. Observed one student: "It makes me feel so much better to know that I am not the only one who gets jealous and feels sorry for myself at times. The diaries made me feel as if I were almost normal and not the terrible person my parents keep telling me I am."

The three students who were abused by their fathers—Amy, Maria, and Linda—welcomed the opportunity to share their experiences with the class. Amy was particularly touched by her classmates' kind words in their subsequent diary entries, which I read aloud. "It really helped me to realize that other people have gone through the same situations. It also took a load off my chest by sharing it with people who seem to care. I have learned that people do care what happens to others and are willing to take the time to try to help. Somehow, this makes me feel a lot better about things."

Maria identified so intensely with Amy's diaries that she began dreaming again of being physically assaulted. "When I heard that diary about the young woman's father who beat her, I almost broke out in tears. Not just because I was also beaten by my father but because of her bad dreams. I've always had these dreams of a man coming to my room and trying to kill me. The dreams stopped about a year ago, but when I heard the fear in that diary, I felt it myself. That was the diary which made the strongest impression on me." Maria added that, as painful as it was to relive these old memories, writing made them less terrifying:

> I found that writing the diaries for class was extremely meaningful for me because I had to face things about myself. Not just in my mind, but actually down on paper. There's a big difference between the two. When you think something about yourself, you can deny that you ever thought it, you can forget it, but when you write it, there's no escaping the reality. You scream at yourself, HEY! YOU! YEAH, YOU FEEL THIS WAY! There is no escape from a typewriter or a pen.

Linda reached a similar conclusion, commenting on what I called the "distanced intimacy" achieved by reading anonymous diaries to the class:

> I think the diaries have been a tremendous help. It's funny, but the stuff that I revealed about my father's sexual abuse of me is something that I've only told three people in the world, only one of whom is a very close friend—and that was over the phone. I guess this distanced intimacy is a

terribly important thing. And I plan on sending this diary to my best friend, who graduated and now lives at home. I'm not sure what kind of response I'll get, but as I get older, I find that I'm getting more and more bogged down by my deep, dark secret. I guess it's time to tell people. Or some people, at least. And now, if this gets read in class, I will have told a roomful of people, the majority of whom are total strangers. God, what an odd thing to do. Distanced intimacy really is amazing.

Writing enabled other students to mourn deceased parents. "I am a very private person and am not prone to 'wearing my heart out on my sleeve,'" Mark wrote in his final diary. "But I think that my most important diary is the one wherein I expressed my deep anger and maybe a little animosity toward my father for dying on me at an early age. He really hurt me by doing that, and I just recently fully realized my pain. Probably the most important lesson I learned in your class is that it is all right and natural to be mad at someone for what may appear irrational reasons."

Hearing these diaries proved valuable to the students who had not suffered any of the traumatic experiences described by their classmates. The following comment is representative:

One thing that I realized when listening to the diaries is that so many of them could have been written by me. It is amazing to realize that so many people's lives are like your own. I am also grateful that some of the diaries related to my life in no way whatsoever. My heart really goes out to the people who experience so much grief in their life. The diary that affected me the most was the one about the girl whose father abused her. It makes me think how lucky I have been in life. I come from a very honest and open family. They would never do anything to hurt me, and they have stood behind me in everything I have done.

If diary writing teaches us anything, it is, in the words of another student, that "things are not what they seem on the surface." Few students would have predicted at the beginning of the summer that they would write about such wrenching personal conflicts, many of which were acknowledged for the first time. In a class of representative college students, the notion of "normalcy" was dramatically called into question. No less than the fictional characters who are baffled and buffeted by experience or driven to desperate measures by a seemingly indifferent society, several of the students viewed themselves as martyred and misunderstood. Like Esther Greenwood and Holden Caulfield, they had gone through turbulent identity crises, were physically or sexually abused, experienced suicidal fantasies, and endured crushing guilt. The diaries offer irrefutable proof that the college years are among the most confusing, lonely, and dangerous periods of the life cycle.

"Painful Experiences Hidden from View"

The diaries also demonstrate that suffering usually remains concealed from public view, neither seen nor heard by most people. If, at the beginning of the semester, those students fortunate enough to have been raised by loving parents in a protected environment found it difficult to relate to the experiences of their less fortunate classmates, by the end of the semester they were sensitized to a darker world which many of them thought existed only in fiction. It was not "just literature" that I was reading to them for twenty minutes a week but real-life stories written by their classmates. As a student from another class remarked at the end of the semester:

> The journals make me realize that as I sit in a class and go about normal academic affairs with people with unremarkable exteriors, I am unaware of painful experiences hidden from view. Hearing the journals about suicide, sexual abuse, and mental cruelty, written by people who conduct academic business with smiles, makes me realize how important it is to be sensitive to the pains they don't display.

To this extent, introspective classroom diary writing has the effect of removing some of the wadding in our ears and reminding us, with a knock on the door, of the unhappiness of so many people in our midst—images borrowed from George Eliot's great novel *Middlemarch* and Anton Chekhov's haunting short story "Gooseberries," respectively, both of which suggest that literature heightens our sensitivity to suffering:

> If we had a keen vision and feeling of all ordinary human life, it would be like hearing the grass grow and the squirrel's heart beat, and we should die of that roar which lies on the other side of silence. As it is, the quickest of us walks about well wadded with stupidity.[19]

> Behind the door of every contented, happy man there ought to be someone standing with a little hammer and continually reminding him

with a knock that there are unhappy people, that however happy he may be, life will sooner or later show him its claws, and trouble will come to him—illness, poverty, losses, and then no one will see or hear him, just as now he neither sees nor hears others.[20]

The Writing Cure

Introspective classroom diary writing reveals students' capacity for growth and development, the resiliency of the human spirit. It is here that the talking cure and the writing cure, psychoanalysis and literature, coincide. "Strictly speaking," Marlow says in Joseph Conrad's *Lord Jim*, "the question is not how to get cured, but how to live"[21]—by which he means living with the "legitimate terrors of life." Similarly, a biographer notes that for Kafka, "writing was not so much an alternative to living as a terminal cure for it."[22] The writing cure that literature affirms bespeaks not only an awareness of the undeniable anxieties and terrors of life but also the power of art to restore us to health.[23] Introspective classroom diary writing is therapeutic, not because it causes our problems to disappear magically, never to return, but because it heightens our understanding of those problems and helps us find ways to live with them.

I believe that Freudian theory can help us achieve self-empowerment, and that is why I teach courses in literature and psychoanalysis. Freud gave us a process by which to approach the truth, not the truth itself, as Heinz Kohut remarked shortly before his death. "Freud's writings are not a kind of Bible but great works belonging to a particular moment in the history of science— great not because of their unchanging relevance but, on the contrary, because they contain the seeds of endless possibilities for further growth."[24]

And yet I also believe, paradoxically, that students will discover the self-healing power of diary writing no matter what explanatory system they use to understand the self. As Seymour Fisher and Roger Greenberg observe, "Research evidence has consistently indicated that a patient's belief in interpretations and his consequent anxiety reduction do not depend on the accuracy of the interpretations."[25] Judd Marmor makes a similar point. "Inasmuch as the types of interpretation given by analysts of different schools of thought vary significantly, it is obvious that the *specific form* and *content* of the interpretation cannot be as crucial a therapeutic factor as each school seems to believe. In other words, the specific content of the insight is not in itself critical for the change process, as long as that content represents a plausible and internally logical explanation for the patient's difficulties."[26]

Talking or writing can be therapeutic, then, regardless of the explanatory system that is used and regardless of whether anyone hears or reads the words. This has been demonstrated convincingly by the experimental psychologist James Pennebaker in his book *Opening Up: The Healing Power of Confiding to Others* (1990). Pennebaker conducted several experiments in which he asked college students to write for fifteen or twenty minutes a day. Students in the first group were requested to write about only emotions surrounding traumas in their life; students in the second group were requested to write about only superficial topics. Students in the first group, the high self-disclosers, consistently experienced greater emotional relief and reported fewer illnesses than did students in the second group, the low self-disclosers.

Excited by the results and eager to determine whether writing about traumas actually improved physical health, Pennebaker conducted another experiment in which students in high and low self-disclosing groups consented to have their blood drawn the day before writing, after the last writing session, and again six weeks later. He discovered that while students who wrote about traumas reported feeling sadder and more upset than those who wrote about superficial topics, the blood samples of the high self-disclosing students revealed a heightened immune function—specifically, a greater number of white blood cells, or lymphocytes, that ward off disease. Not only did other blood and cardiovascular changes take place, but brain-wave tests indicated that when people wrote about traumas, there was a much greater congruence between the left and right sides of the brain than when people wrote about trivial concerns. Pennebaker's resounding conclusion is that while writing about traumatic experiences is often distressing and produces resistance, writing leads almost always to short-term and long-term improvements in physical and psychological health.[27]

Whereas Pennebaker's students wrote only for themselves, I encourage my students to share their experiences with the class, and in doing so, they derive even greater benefits from writing. Hearing other peoples' stories brings clarity to their own, and they develop the ability to interpret experience from multiple points of view. The class as a whole becomes an empathic audience, with students commenting in their diaries on their classmates' experiences. The resulting dialogic relationship is especially valuable at a time when so many students find themselves lost in a large, impersonal educational system where they have little contact with other students or professors.[28]

Rejecting the Role of Victim

Students also discover that, although they may be in some ways victims, they can take charge of their lives and reject any self-defining perspective that becomes confining or unhealthy. "One of the possibly harmful psychological advantages of being a 'victim,'" Margaret Atwood writes, "is that you can substitute moral righteousness for responsibility; that is, you can view yourself as innocent and your oppressor as totally evil, and because you define yourself as powerless, you can avoid doing anything about your situation. 'Winning' is not always 'good,' obviously; but neither is losing."[29]

According to Harvard psychologist Jerome Bruner, we "*become* the auto-biographical narratives by which we 'tell about' our lives."[30] From a constructivist perspective, we do not discover reality so much as create it; by changing our stories of ourselves, we change our lives. Viewed in this way, therapy is the act of creating a healthier story of our life.[31] Diary writing encourages students to tell their stories, compare them with those they hear in class, identify the dangerous elements in these stories, and construct new ones in which they gain self-mastery.

As the summer drew to a close, many of us had the sense that something extraordinary was ending. One student wrote in his last diary, "I know I'll never understand everything about myself, or about other people, but in writing the diaries I have begun to dig a little deeper into my unconscious self. And hearing the most personal, often frightening writings of the other members of the class made me realize that we are all thinking together. I doubt I will ever forget a single face of any of the people in the class because of the diaries we shared with each other."

I don't know if any students experienced the mourning that patients feel upon terminating analysis, but I felt the sadness that inevitably accompanies the end of a good class. As usual, there was not enough time to say good-bye. A few students have remained in contact with me, like Linda and Jane, who send me greeting cards periodically and keep me up-to-date on their lives. I often find myself thinking about the students who have not kept in touch. I don't know if Amy has managed to extinguish the fire in her father's eye or if

Maria's dreams of an assaultive man coming into her room have ended. I hope that Mark is pursuing his dreams of greatness and that Sam has resolved his marital problems. In the last diary he wrote: "I just had a quick narcissistic fantasy of you publishing parts of my diaries in your book, and me publishing the same material in one of my novels, and a future scholar making the connection. Déjà vu?" I hope that Bill and Erika have forgiven me for leading them by the hand and intruding into their lives. In thinking back upon all the students in the class, I am reminded of Holden's final words in *The Catcher in the Rye*: "Don't ever tell anybody anything. If you do, you start missing everybody."[32]

3 / Sins of the Fathers

Unfeeling, heartless creator! you had endowed me with perceptions and passions, and then cast me abroad an object for the scorn and horror of mankind. But on you only had I any claim for pity and redress, and from you I determined to seek that justice which I vainly attempted to gain from any other being that wore the human form.—Mary Shelley, *Frankenstein*

Divorce is so common nowadays that it is easy to underestimate the devastation arising from the breakup of the family. Numerous studies indicate that divorce is the most stressful event children are likely to experience while growing up. Children are often more overwhelmed by their parents' divorce than by a parent's death—and more confused. They cannot understand why a divorced parent no longer lives or speaks with them, and they fear that the custodial parent may not be there to protect them in the future. Whereas children can begin mourning a parent's death immediately, receiving the support of relatives, friends, and teachers, it is more difficult for them to mourn a parent's departure from the family, if only because of the uncertainty over whether the parent will ever return. Unlike death, parental separation and divorce are not always final, and children cling to the fantasy that one day their parents will be together again, a fantasy that in most cases does not come true.

Children also find themselves implicated in their parents' arguments, burdened with guilt, anger, and sorrow, wondering what they did to cause the divorce. Contrary to the benign image of divorce portrayed in *Kramer vs. Kramer* and other films, children often find themselves caught in the deadly cross fire of their parents' battles. Children often blame one parent in particular for the divorce—either the parent who no longer lives with them, or the one who remains. It is common for sons and daughters to believe that one of their parents is divorcing them.

Children of Divorce

Judith Wallerstein's groundbreaking research has deepened our understanding of the impact of divorce on parents and children. Her two studies *Surviving the Breakup* (1980) and *Second Chances* (1989),[1] based on years of interviews with divorced families, reveal that while only a few children believed that their parents had been happily married, the overwhelming majority preferred the unhappy marriage to the divorce:

> The family rupture evoked an acute sense of shock, intense fears, and grieving which the children found overwhelming. Over one half of the entire group were distraught, with a sense that their lives had been completely disrupted. Less than 10 percent of the children were relieved by their parents' decision to divorce despite the high incidence of exposure to physical violence during the marriage.[2]

Wallerstein found that five years after the divorce, more than one-third of the children were struggling; they were clinically depressed and doing poorly both in school and in their interpersonal relationships. For many of them, anger continued to be the predominant emotion in their lives. Fifteen years after the divorce, 40 percent of the young adults in Wallerstein's study had been in therapy to work through issues associated with the breakup of their families.

Wallerstein's findings have been confirmed by a federally sponsored survey of more than 17,000 American children. The study indicates that one in five children under the age of eighteen has a learning, emotional, behavior, or developmental problem that can be traced to the breakup of the two-parent family.[3] The survey suggests that the most important factor contributing to the increase in childhood psychological disorders is the family dynamics arising from conflicted or shattered marriages. For children who grow up in single-parent homes, emotional and behavioral problems are two to three times higher than for children who grow up in traditional double-parent families.

These figures become more disturbing in light of the continued high incidence of divorce in the United States. The divorce rate doubled from the late 1950s to the late 1970s, declined slightly in the 1980s, but still remains high. Recent statistics indicate that the divorce rate per thousand population was 5.3 in 1981 and 4.7 in 1990. Over two million people were divorced in 1989, prompting one researcher to observe: "If one takes into consideration the children and the parents of divorcing persons, it is reasonable to assume that over six million persons were directly affected by divorce during that single year."[4] According to a *Newsweek* article, demographers predict that "by the beginning of the next decade the majority of youngsters under 18 will spend part of their childhood in single-parent families, many of them created by divorce."[5]

Writing about Parental Divorce

When I first began receiving diaries about parental divorce, I was startled by both the number of students who wrote about this experience and the frequency with which they returned to it in diary after diary. Although few of the stories we read in class involved divorce, many students chose to write about this subject in their diaries. For these students, divorce was the central event in their lives, around which they defined their identity. They described divorce as frightening, filled with sadness and yearning, and they felt overwhelmed by conflicting emotions—anger, hurt, anxiety, and guilt, feelings which persisted long after the divorce. Some students whose parents were divorced ten or fifteen years ago reported that they still had not come to terms with the experience.

Divorced children, Wallerstein remarks, experience two profound losses: the ending of the intact family, and the absence of a parent, generally the father. I, too, have found that most students writing about divorce feel abandoned by their fathers, many of whom mysteriously depart from their children's lives. As we shall see, the "sins of the fathers" is a major theme in these diaries. Some students closely identify with the plight of the Frankenstein Creature in Mary Shelley's novel. Like the Creature, they believe that their fathers are unfeeling, heartless creators, endowing their children with life only to desert them.

Diary writing is especially valuable for children of divorce because it enables them to express ambivalent feelings arising from the family's breakup. By actively confronting the trauma of divorce, they voice previously unverbalized feelings and arrive at meaningful interpretations of the event. Insofar as many students still feel anger and resentment, diary writing becomes a safety valve, allowing them to vent explosive feelings and get on with their lives. Although writing about parental divorce and other traumas is painful in the short run, almost all students conclude at the end of the semester that diary writing is therapeutic.[6] Writing about parental divorce encourages sons, in particular, to seek out their fathers and reestablish a relationship. For these students, writing may be a reparative act.

I want to focus on seven undergraduate students in this chapter and explore how they wrote about parental divorce. Six were juniors or seniors ranging in age from twenty to twenty-two years old. The youngest was two and the oldest was seventeen when the divorce occurred. In each case, the divorce resulted in the son or daughter living with the mother and feeling rejected by the father, who gradually broke off contact with the family. All six students were still angry at their fathers and protective of their mothers. To use Wallerstein's term, the students were "aligned" with their mothers. On a more subtle level, antagonism toward the mother appears in a few of these diaries, but it is evidently difficult for students to acknowledge this. I also include the diaries of a seventh student, a woman in her forties, who wrote about the intergenerational implications of divorce.

All seven students viewed themselves as generally healthy survivors of the breakup of the two-parent family, but they all wrote about significant conflicts which they traced to their parents' divorce. These conflicts involved fear of rejection, lingering anger, and mistrust of intimate relationships. I don't claim that the seven are a representative sampling of divorced children, but they are typical of the students in my classes who write multiple diaries on this subject.

Surprisingly, men and women write very differently about parental divorce, and one can usually tell whether a male or female is writing a particular diary, even if one does not know the diarist's name. These gender differences manifest themselves in terms of identity, self-other boundaries, parental identification and counteridentification, and interpersonal relationships. All seven experienced their parents' divorces as traumatic, but they were traumatic in distinctly different ways for men and women. Intrigued by these differences, I began investigating the growing research in gender theory and discovered, as Deborah Tannen demonstrates in her best-selling book *You Just Don't Understand*, that "gender is a category that will not go away."[7] As I present the following diaries to you, I should point out that none of my interpretive comments appeared on the diaries themselves. Nor did the issues of gender or divorce arise in our class discussions.

MARA:
*"Every Relationship I've Ever Had Has Been with
Someone Who Has Qualities of My Nonexistent Father"*

Mara, a junior, wrote five diaries about her feelings toward her parents, who divorced when she was two years old. Growing up without a father was painful and confusing to her, resulting in low self-esteem, mistrust of men, and an unusually close relationship with her mother. Mara notes that the desire for her mother's exclusive love and attention was so intense during childhood and adolescence that it may have prevented her mother from having a life of her own. This realization, bringing much grief and guilt, compels Mara to pay her mother back for the years of sacrifice:

> I grew up with only my mom and find myself looking for someone who resembles my father. I really hope that I don't find someone like him, considering that he left my mother and me when I was two. This seems like such an unfeeling thing for him to do. How can someone father children and then leave them only to contact them, at the most, ten times in their life? I guess this answers my question about why I have such cynical views of relationships. I hope that through my writing I can overcome this fear of rejection that I suffer from. If not, I will seek outside help.
>
> I would never want to go through what my mom did after my father left us. She put herself through graduate school and sent me to the best schools. I truly appreciate *everything* she has done for me, and I know that I can only repay her through respect and love. I guess I probably have an Oedipal complex toward my mom, since she was like a father to me. I definitely resent any male telling me what to do, and I protect my mom from being taken advantage of by other people. I feel like I had to grow up too soon and wish that I could relive my childhood so that I could look with a more open mind at what my mom had to do.
>
> Now that I am twenty, I am more mature and realize that my mom did

everything for my own good and that she still does everything for me. This upsets me, since I don't want her not to do something she wants simply because it might bother me. Most people don't understand the relationship my mother and I have. I can speak to her on any subject, and she will truly listen to me. She may be the only real friend I have to confide in.

I do have very good friends, which is something I will always be grateful for. Most of my friends know that I don't see my father or even know where he is, yet there are many who ask stupid questions when they find out that my parents are divorced, like "Do you see your dad?" which I of course answer "no" to. Then the really annoying questions come out such as "Why?" Don't you think if I knew why, I would see him? Obviously I don't see him because he did not love me. There, I said it. Are you happy? Does it make you feel better than me? Anyway, I guess it is good that my mom is a family therapist and that she can help me with the problems I've had to face in my life. Well, I've said all I have to say, and I hope you don't think it was too depressing. I feel a lot better now that I've said all that I want to.

I may be insignificant to some people, but I hope I make a difference in some people's lives. It's not like I don't have friends, because I have some very good ones. Sometimes I just feel like another faceless person in a sea of humans. I make myself feel like this, however, because I alienate myself before someone else has the chance to. That way it doesn't hurt as much if they don't like me. Rejection is my biggest fear, which stems from the first rejection I ever felt—when my father deserted me. I never did put it like that before. But that is what the prick did. Well, I couldn't stop myself from typing that last line. The truth hurts, but somebody's got to say it.

I guess the main idea of this journal is how pissed I am that my father fucked up my life so much. What a selfish person! May he rot in hell. That made me feel a lot better, even though it was harsh to say. But that's how I really feel. I think that if he walked into my room right now, I probably wouldn't recognize him first of all, but then I'd spit on him.

Well, I've decided to take your advice and analyze how my nonexistent relationship with my father has affected my relationships with other men. Whenever I meet someone I am interested in, I get very nervous and lose all sense of composure. I don't like to let my true feelings show, and I'd rather admire them from afar. I think the reason for this is the fact that I can't deal with rejection from another man. I am truly a pessimist in this area, and if I sense the slightest reciprocity in feelings, I wonder why someone would want to get closer to me. This shows my lack of self-worth. Obviously I am not the antichrist or anything close to that, but I do feel very lacking in the overall self-esteem aspect of my life. I find it very hard to open up to people, especially guys, and I do feel guilty for not being able to open up to people.

Every relationship I've ever had has been with someone who has qualities of my nonexistent father. Either looks or the whole irresponsibleness of his character. I find it very hard to tell someone how I feel about them unless they tell me their feelings first. This is, of course, a defense mechanism—I need to be reassured of my place in people's lives. If I feel that a person doesn't like me for some reason, I always get very angry at myself for getting hurt. This is rather ridiculous, of course, yet this is an integral part of my personality.

I may seem to be very self-confident, and in some respects I am, but I am just an emotional wreck inside. I do put on a front, I suppose, when I interact with people. However, my true friends know my shortcomings and still love me. I also put newly met people through a test which they will pass with flying colors or fail miserably.

The test goes like this. I feel that people should have to prove that they are worthy of my affection. After typing this sentence, I realize it must sound pretty fucked up and arrogant for me to say this. However, I've always had to prove my worth to other people, and I feel I deserve the same respect. Now that I think about it, I realize that the only person I have to prove myself to is myself. Anyway, I don't really know what kind of test I put people through—I guess it's psychological. I process all the feedback I get and assess its value. As I grew older, I realized that I used to be very obnoxious in order to hide my insecurities, but now I realize that I can't go through life being mean to people so they won't or can't get close to me.

This self-realization is a big step for me. I don't really remember when I stopped being mean, but a lot of my longtime friends notice the change, and they commend me on my efforts. I try to have a more open mind to things now, but the insecurities are there, and I guess they will always be a part of my life.

This past weekend I met a guy. He seemed really nice, so I gave him my phone number, and we spoke for a while. Then he called me every night until Tuesday. This I think is rather weird. Guys never call right away, especially when they say they will. So we went to the movies last night. It turns out that he is too normal for me, and I find myself in a position that I never have been in. I am the one breaking the heart now. Or at least I think I am because from the feedback I got from him, he really likes me, and I feel guilty that I don't return the affection.

I wonder if other people who don't like someone feel guilty, or if they don't care as long as they aren't getting hurt themselves. Well, I figure that I am guilty because when I see that someone doesn't like me, I am hurt and wonder what's wrong with me. But now I see that it is the fault of the person who doesn't return the affection. So now I have to let this guy down gently, and I don't know how to do it. Anyway, I know what it feels like to be let down but certainly not gently. I will try my best, but the advice I got from male friends tells me to just not take his phone calls and "he'll get the hint." I feel really guilty and I don't know what to do, but as my mom would say, "It's just a fine point." I would really like to know why I feel guilty. I couldn't sleep last night because of it. I hope I can understand why I feel guilty—maybe it's because I've been hurt before and wouldn't want to be the cause of someone else's pain.

As the holidays approach, I always get very nervous. Why? you may wonder. Well, it is really hard on my family during the holidays because there is always someone who is missing. My father. Since he left when I was two I've never spent a holiday with him, although I don't mean that everyone else in my family didn't try their best to make it fun. The absence will always be felt by me. I'm sure my mom notices it herself. Having no one to give "Merry Christmas, Darling" cards to must be very hard to deal with. Even though she has had boyfriends, she has never remarried, and I think that was my fault.

The last sentence I just typed brought me to tears. I feel so incredibly guilty for my mom's being alone. She never said anything to that effect, but I can sense her loneliness. As a child, whenever my mom went out with a guy, I always threw a fit. I'm sure this was because I didn't want my father to be replaced, based on the never-ending hope that he may return. This I realize now is a lost hope.

I wish I wasn't such a selfish bitch when I was a child because then my mom would be happy. I wanted my mom all to myself. No one else was allowed to hug her as much or to love her as much as I did. Now that I'm older, I realize that I stopped my mother from being truly happy, and now I try to make up for it by telling her how much I love her and will do anything she asks because I know it will make her happy. I love her so much and will lay down my life for hers if I had to. But I realize that even that can't make up for all the grief I caused her as a child. Now I find myself unable to find happiness because I don't deserve it as much as she does.

I don't think that anyone can understand the depth of emotion I am feeling right now. It is hard for me to type these words, but I will try. I just wish that I could change all the terrible things I did to hurt her as a child into loving ones. But there's no way for me to do that. The only thing I can do is keep trying to make up for my past mistakes. I remember all the times at Christmas or Easter that I was such a bitch to everyone and didn't give a shit about their feelings—only my own mattered. Now I will try to change this. All I want to do is make my mom happy. But she doesn't understand that this is the hardest thing of all.

Mara's story about her parents' divorce involves an abandoning father, a self-sacrificing mother, and a guilt-ridden daughter who feels she does not deserve to be happy in her own life. What is striking about the story is the idealized portrait of the mother, who is mythologized into a larger-than-life figure—wise, selfless, compassionate, and devoted entirely to the needs of her child. Mara refuses to criticize her mother, insisting that *everything* she did was for her daughter's own good. The description of the mother is not unlike the idealized portrait of the kindhearted De Lacey in *Frankenstein*, the parent surrogate who initially befriends the Creature, only to disappoint him later.

And yet as Dorothy Dinnerstein has remarked, "There is of course no such thing as a wholly benevolent mother, with no antagonism whatsoever to the child as an autonomous being. But even if there were, she would be experienced by the child, in its struggle to become such a being, both as an interfering influence and as a lure back into non-being."[8] Nancy Chodorow and

Susan Contratto make a similar observation about the fantasy of the perfect mother: "Belief in the all-powerful mother spawns a recurrent tendency to blame the mother on the one hand, and a fantasy of maternal perfectibility on the other."[9] The belief that one has a wholly benevolent mother requires one to be a perfect child, thus increasing the burden of guilt when one inevitably falls short of perfection.

RACHEL
"It Took Me a Long Time to Realize
That He Left My Mother, Not Me"

Rachel, a senior, wrote five diary entries about her parents, who separated when she was ten. Like Mara, Rachel still feels anger and bitterness toward her father, and the rage spills over into a recurrent dream in which she imagines his violent death. Rachel's relationship with her mother is very close—too close, in the daughter's judgment:

This has been a tough week. The schoolwork is beginning to mount up, and the pressure of an eighteen-credit course load is settling in. My concentration level was incredibly low this week. It's funny how my mind always wanders away from schoolwork and never to it. But anyway, it all started last week when I had a terrible fight with my father. My father and I have had nothing to do with each other for the past nine years. We do not get along. Although there is a lot more to it than that, for now this will have to suffice. He telephoned me the other night, and we had the worst fight in recorded history. For some reason, I told him that when he died, I would not go to his funeral. I don't even know why I said this. That night and for the next few nights I dreamed of his funeral. I could not tell whether I was actually there or just looking in from the outside. This dream kept waking me up over and over again. The saddest part was that I was not really troubled by it, just confused. Was I guilty? Or did a part of me really want him to die?

Ever since that night, I have noticed that I have been very nasty to my male friends. I have been very impatient with them and even cruel. I guess in my mind I am taking out the negative feelings I have for my father on my male friends. It is like I push them so hard to try and see how much they will take from me. Those who put up with the most must love me the most. I realize this is a problem, but I am coming to terms with it. I did not realize how serious this entry would turn out until I started.

The other night I had the strangest dream, which I have been trying to analyze ever since. My parents and I were driving to the Middle East. This is odd for more than the obvious bizarreness of why the Middle East. It is even odder that I was with both my parents. They have been divorced for ten years, and needless to say, they make the *War of the Roses* look like child's play. Why were we all together, and why were we getting along?

As we drove through the Middle East, there were men all around us with turbans on their heads. They were almost all soiled with blood. There were terrorists everywhere, and guns were being shot at random. My parents, though, were incredibly calm. They were just staring at each other, as if they were in love. They were laughing and getting along famously. I remembered thinking how ironic it was that they could get along only when there was a war going on. Bombs were exploding in the streets, but my parents were oblivious to it all. My mother was even sitting on my father's lap. I was so furious with them. I started screaming, "What the hell is wrong with both of you? You both hate each other. Don't you see that there's a war going on? How can you be so absorbed only with yourselves?"

It was at that moment that I saw my father falling down a hill. He wasn't shot, just falling. The only sense I can make of this dream is this part. I think his falling may have symbolized his falling off the pedestal I had once put him on.

This week was not a psychoanalytic one. It was a week of tests and papers. It was also a week of resume writing and thinking about the future. I find it hard to think of the future without first thinking of the past. Some memories are so vivid—the senior prom, high school graduation, getting my driver's license, my first love and sexual experience, and entering college. College has been the fastest four years in my life. I remember my feelings the first time I drove to Albany. I remember becoming all choked up at the prospect of leaving my home and the friends I had since kindergarten. I walked out of my nice safe home in suburbia into a cramped dorm room where I would have to share for the first time in my life. When I left my house I kept thinking of that line, "You can't go home again." I realized that my home would never be the same again. I remember crying bitterly. Even more than coming to the realization of my home never being the same again, I also thought of how my relationships would change in my family. After all, it's a lot different not being under the same roof. Maybe this is the basis of today's journal.

When I was in high school, my mom and I got along great. I had a lot of freedom to come and go as I pleased. Since college, though, things have changed. My mother and I are still very close, but when I go home for the holidays, she expects me to spend all my time with her. This makes it hard for me to see my old friends. They don't understand why she feels this way, and then I defend her. I say that she's lonely, and since my dad doesn't live with us, it's understandable. But sometimes I don't understand. Although she never comes out and says anything like, "Don't see your friends tonight," I can sense her disappointment when I say that I'm going out. This puts such tremendous guilt on me.

The thing is, I do spend a lot of time with her, and I enjoy that time immensely. She is my biggest supporter and my best friend. I just feel so suffocated every time I go home. As close as we are, and maybe it's because we are so close, I've never been able to discuss my feelings with her. I feel such guilt even writing this because I realize how lucky I am to have a mother as great as mine. Needless to say, though, I'm scared. I'm scared about moving back home after graduation. I'm afraid that I won't have control over my life, and that I will lose the independence it has taken me so long to gain.

Although I really enjoy this class, it has made me think about my father more often than I'd like. When I was younger, my father and I were very close. I loved him more than anything in the world. I didn't really care for my mother. Maybe it was the Oedipal conflict. Looking back on it, now that I have taken this course, I suppose it was. All I know is that I wanted him all to myself and didn't want to share him with my mother. He was a god in my eyes. Everyone even said that I looked just like him. This made me extremely happy. He was everything to me.

When I found out that my parents were getting divorced because of his infidelity, I was devastated. I went into a serious depression, where I wouldn't leave my home for the entire summer. I remember one time that I asked my father who he loved the most in the world. He said me, and I really believed him. I asked him who he loved second, and he wouldn't answer. I always wondered why he wouldn't tell me. I guess it's because it wasn't my mother. I felt so much guilt inside me that I had known something for so long, and that it eventually destroyed my parents' marriage. I really hated him.

In time, I grew close to my mother and refused to have any relationship with my father. He has tried many times to build a relationship with me, but I have refused. It took me a long time to realize that he left my mother, not me. Even with this realization, though, recent events have made me stick to my decision to keep him out of my life. It was and is the hardest decision I have ever had to make. The few times I have spoken to my father in the past few years, I have always mentioned my boyfriends. My last boyfriend and I went away a lot together, and I made sure to tell my father about that. I guess I wanted him to be jealous, or to give him a coronary. I wanted him to pay for not being around and maybe even let him think that I was promiscuous. I missed not having a father around. I resent him so much for this.

Sometimes I wonder who will give me away at my wedding. I'm not even engaged yet. Why should little things like this even enter my mind? Well, now I'm graduating. My father has written to ask me if he can attend the ceremony. I have not yet responded. I have my own life now, and I don't see how he could fit in. I don't even think I want him to. He doesn't know me anymore. When he left, I was a little girl of twelve. Now I'm almost twenty-two. I have never idolized anyone again. I have trouble trusting people, especially men. I also tend to push people so hard just to see if they will stay. I wonder all the time if I will have a happy marriage. I would hate to put my children through what I went and am still going through.

When I went home for spring break, I decided, all of a sudden, that I hated the wallpaper in my bedroom. This wallpaper, which had been perfectly fine for the past ten years, had suddenly become repulsive to me. I started ripping it off piece by piece. My mother came in to see what I was doing and was rather surprised to see me violently ripping off the wallpaper. It took hours to get it all off, but I wouldn't quit until I was finished. It was as if I was in some kind of trance. My mother was nice about it and said that if I didn't like the wallpaper, all I had to do was say so. She said that I had probably outgrown it and that we should paint the walls. Although I agreed, I couldn't choose a color. My mother brought me hundreds of samples to look at, but I kept putting it off.

It was almost as if I unconsciously didn't want to paint the room. I didn't care that the walls were chipped and pale. They were so ugly, but I didn't care. In fact, I sort of liked it. I don't know why. Maybe I feel that I don't want to improve my room at home because then I will feel like I'm moving back in permanently. If it looks too nice, maybe I'll put off getting out on my own.

When I read this journal over, I can't help thinking it's ridiculous. Do you think that there is any significance to any of this? Why was it so important for me to rip off that wallpaper, and why did I rip it so violently? Also, why not choose a color? I am not usually so indecisive.

Rachel's story of her parents' divorce resembles Mara's in several key ways. Once again there is an absent father from whom the daughter feels bitterly estranged, a devoted mother, now single, who has assumed all the caretaking responsibilities in the family, and a conflicted daughter caught in the dilemma between loyalty to mother and commitment to self. When she left high school for college, Rachel had the feeling, echoing Thomas Wolfe, that "you can't go home again." She talks about forsaking a comfortable suburban home for a tiny dorm room, but she has enjoyed the freedom of her college years. Her independence now seems threatened by the regressive return home. Rachel's feeling of suffocation can be seen in her fifth diary, describing a recent visit home when she began pulling off the old wallpaper in her room. The incident uncannily recalls Charlotte Perkins Gilman's haunting short story "The Yellow Wallpaper," in which a young woman newly married feverishly rips off the wallpaper in her room in a desperate effort to escape from the enslaving domesticity of a patriarchal society.[10]

TRACEY
"It Seemed Like I Possessed an Alarm System That
Was Sensitive Only to My Mother's Fears and Pains"

Tracey, a senior who was taking my Narcissism and the Novel course, wrote four diaries about her parents' divorce. She identified closely with the theme of paternal neglect and child abuse that we were discussing in *Frankenstein*, *Wuthering Heights*, *Great Expectations*, and *Sons and Lovers*. She was particularly interested in the distinction between conditional and unconditional love. Although her parents did not separate until she was nearly seventeen, Tracey's feelings toward her father began to change when she was still a young girl and witnessed his violence toward the family:

> You asked us to focus on the question "Is the love from your parents conditional or unconditional?" Reflecting back on my childhood and looking at the present, I would have to say that it was different for each of them. On the one side my mother's love was unconditional, and on the other side my father's was conditional love.
>
> My parents have been separated and divorced for a few years now. They had a mother-child relationship, not one of equality or adult partnership. My father is an overgrown child who has never been able to face his responsibilities to his family. Ever since I can remember, his friends were his first priority and his family was second. He has never gained any respect from me because he has never earned it. And yet he expects it from both his kids. How can a father who says "promises are made to be broken" teach his children honesty? What about a father who speaks to his mistress on the phone while his children are sitting in the same room? What kind of father would try to kiss his daughter's best friend?
>
> I have an older sister who, like me, has a terrible relationship with my father. She is not the subservient, obedient little daughter that my father wanted. Instead, my sister was quite rebellious. At first she wanted to gain his love more than anything in the world, but after she saw through my father's facade, she wanted only to rebel from him. I remember the day when my father found a letter that my sister was going to send to her boyfriend. It contained information confessing her bad feelings toward my father and her belief that he had a mistress. My father dug it out of the trash and posted it on the refrigerator door so that everyone would see it. I felt bad for my sister, and I feared the silence between my sister and him. I did not want to lose my father's love, a love which I now know was not true but instead false.
>
> After my father realized that he could no longer love my sister, he began to focus his attention on me. I was not rebellious like my sister. I

loved both my parents and thought they were wonderful. I learned to play ice hockey, a sport which my father lived for. He gave me so much attention that my sister became jealous.

As I grew older, I began to realize that my father wasn't so great. He hurt me the most when I saw him treat my mother like "shit." Ever since I was a little girl I've always been close to my mother. She told me that when I was a little girl and I saw her cry, I would sit on her lap and give her a big hug. I would always reassure her that "everything will be better next year. Don't worry, Mommy." But every year it got worse, and my mother worked even harder to keep the family together.

She has gained the respect from me that my father thinks he so deserved. She has kept the family financially and spiritually together. I have seen her cry and have felt her pain and grief. I have seen her smile and have felt the sunshine in my heart. I have seen her come home after twenty-four hours, her energy drained from working, and have felt fatigued and weak myself. My mother is fifty-eight years old, and it horrifies me to think that someday soon she may not be around. It really frightens me to think that my mother, who has been my source of strength and guidance, may one day not be here.

My attitude toward my father changed as I grew older. The strengths of my mother revealed the weaknesses of my father. My love and admiration for him vanished, and my actions revealed it. My father has only proven to me that he is a selfish child. I cannot love my father the way he wants me to. I can only remember the pain he caused my mother and the damage he did to my family.

We have discussed in *Frankenstein*, *Wuthering Heights*, and *Great Expectations* the recurrent theme of crimes against the child. It seems like authors show how the child often becomes a plaything to be toyed with by their parents or other adults. I wish we could touch this subject more in depth, but there are so many other themes that the books contain. I have a lot of questions and feelings that arise when I think about this theme.

The strongest feeling I have is anger and hatred. I find it impossible to understand how anyone, especially a parent, can harm a child both physically and mentally. If a child is an extension of their parents, then aren't abusive parents hurting themselves? I don't understand why a child should be a victim of another person's ignorance or stupidity. A child is not born to be a scapegoat but so that a parent can love and cherish it. A parent is responsible for their child's development into adulthood. A child learns from their parents and will often pass this learning onto their own children. What does a child learn when a parent hits their child and leaves bruises on their body? What does a child learn when a parent doesn't care if their child attends school? What does a child learn when a parent tells them that they hate school? If a parent cannot teach their own child to love and care for others, and show empathy toward others, then how do they expect them to learn these important characteristics?

My mother has always taught me the importance of a good relationship with your children. I know that the love, concern, and understanding I received from my mother will be shared with my children.

Although I've read only 150 pages of *Sons and Lovers*, the character of Paul reminds me very much of myself, especially his relationship with his mother. I've always felt a unique bond with my mother, not a simple mother-daughter relationship, but much deeper than that. When she is happy I feel myself glow inside, and when she is hurt or sad I feel the pain in my heart, and it weighs me down.

Ever since I can remember, I've always felt closer to my mother than my father. I recall one incident when a girlfriend and I went to a party and stayed out all night. I knew I should have called my parents, but I didn't because I feared that I would look like a baby in front of my friends if I asked for permission to sleep over at a boy's house. When I came home the next morning, I came up with the story of how my friend's car had broken down and that we ended up sleeping in it because we couldn't find any help. What a dumb alibi, but at the time it sounded feasible.

As expected, both my parents were worried about my well-being. My father yelled and screamed furiously at me and continually asked me where I was. I told him, and he found it ridiculous to believe that no cop car stopped to check a seemingly abandoned vehicle. He was so upset that he had to leave the house to avoid becoming violent with me. My mother, on the contrary, was just relieved that I was alive. Apparently my friend's mom called my mom asking about her daughter, and each one thought the other was sleeping over at the opposite's house.

Well, panic crept in and both families contacted everyone, friends and the cops. I explained the car story to my mother and insisted I was telling the truth. My mother believed me and did not question me any further. Her understanding and forgiveness made me feel very guilty, though. When she went back to bed, I could not stand the guilt anymore, so I went to her bedroom. I climbed beneath the blanket and snuggled next to my warm Mommy. Quietly I whispered to her that I had lied and told her what really happened. I could not hold back my tears as I revealed the truth to my mother. She continued to hold me in her arms and asked me why I was crying so much. I responded, "I don't know. I guess I was just scared." My mother just wiped away my tears and told me she loved me and was glad that I told her the truth. At that moment, I felt like a baby in the womb of her mother, secure and safe from the world, a world that a sixteen-year-old girl was just learning about.

The relationship between Gertrude Morel and Walter Morel in D. H. Lawrence's *Sons and Lovers* reminds me very much of my parents' relationship. There is a definite love-hate relationship between husband and wife. But it is the hate which I sadly remember the most with my parents.

When I was in grade school, I remember waking up several evenings to the sounds of my parents yelling and screaming at each other. I could recall my strong desire to jump out of bed and stop the two from arguing. I wanted so much to tell them how much it was hurting me inside and that I hated them for causing me pain. I could hear my mother's footsteps running away from my father and her fearful demands to "Stop it! Stop it!" The picture in my mind of my mother being struck by my father made me scared and frightened. I would begin to cry for myself but especially for my mother. How could they have loved each other to produce two children? My hands would tighten around my pillow, dampened by my tears, and would cling to it as if it were my security blanket. I felt very alone in the middle of the night.

It seemed like I possessed an alarm system that was sensitive only to my mother's fears and pains. I wanted to wake up my sister and tell her to stop my father. But I could not move from underneath my blankets. I was torn between my desire to help my mother and my fear of being hurt myself. I hated my father so much for the pains he had caused my mother, both physically and emotionally. I wanted so much to hear my mother yell back at my father and tell him to go away. But I knew that my mother could not demand such a thing because she had two children to worry about, and she needed him to support us. I felt guilty for the burdens and restrictions my sister and I placed on our mother. For some reason, though, I knew that my mother had to have loved my father also.

For years, my mother believed that my father would change. She hoped he would spend more time with the children, would be more responsible for financial matters, and would refocus his priorities on his family. But every year things got only worse. My father grew apart from us, and we found it very difficult to talk to him. My mother is the stronger figure in my memories, and my father is only a blur. Divorce was a difficult remedy to my mother's situation, but it was the only way that she could eliminate the pain and gain back some happiness in the years she had left.

Even after the divorce, my mother constantly reminds us to write our father or call him. "After all, he is still your father," she says. But in my eyes he is not. He never was there to see me play hockey or to hear about my achievements in school. The only person who was there throughout my childhood experiences was my mother. She is both my mother and my father, and without her I would not have turned out as caring, loving, and empathic.

There are a few differences between Tracey's story of her parents' divorce and that narrated by Mara and Rachel. Tracey apparently does not mistrust men, dream of her father's death, fear rejection from others, or test her friends' loyalty. The tone of her writing is neither self-lacerating nor fraught with anxiety. There is anger in her voice when she describes her father, but it is measured and does not carry over into other areas. She does not seem burdened by low self-esteem or self-recrimination.

And yet despite these differences, Tracey's story affirms the special sensitivity to her mother's feelings that we see in Mara's and Rachel's writings. She recalls a wonderful moment when, climbing into her mother's bed and confessing the truth about where she was the previous night, she receives her mother's blessing and love. Tracey uses the vivid metaphor of an alarm system sensitizing her to her mother's moods. The mother's smile is sunshine to her daughter's heart; the mother's sadness is darkness to her soul. Loss of mother, in short, threatens the daughter's own existence. The mother-daughter interdependence in these female diaries is striking. Significantly, Tracey describes no such attunement to her father's feelings and moods; he remains a distant other, remote and detached.

For Mara, Rachel, and Tracey, reconciliation with their fathers seems out of the question. They do not identify with their fathers, express curiosity over their lives, or forgive them for hurting their families. Nor do the three female students reflect upon their paternal legacy. It is as if, following their parents' divorces, the daughters have written their fathers out of their lives. Their diaries reflect patrophobia, the fear of becoming like their fathers. By contrast, although the following three male students also feel anger toward their fathers and have broken off contact with them, they are not ready to banish their fathers permanently from their lives.

RON
"You're Just Like Your Father!"

Ron, a senior, wrote two diaries about his parents, who divorced when he was twelve. He begins the first entry by describing himself as a "very responsible person" but then recalls an experience when he was uncharacteristically irresponsible—"forgetting" to make motel reservations for his parents, who were planning separately to attend his college graduation. As a result of reading Freud's *Introductory Lectures on Psycho-Analysis*, Ron arrives at an intriguing interpretation of his memory lapse:

> I am characteristically a very responsible person. Or at least that has been the consensus of most people whom I have dealt with in the past. This is why the following situation has posed such a curious problem for me.
>
> As a senior, I expect to graduate in May. Most of my requirements are completed, and those which are not do not pose much of a threat of failure. Knowing that Albany will be a madhouse on graduation weekend and that hotel reservations will be necessary for each of my parents during that weekend, I decided last June to make arrangements far in advance. This, I thought, was excellent foresight because many seniors would wait until the start of the fall term to make their reservations.
>
> On June 3, I wrote a note to myself saying, "Call motels." I left this

note on my bedroom door and passed it countless times over the next week. Each time I read the note I thought, "Oh, right! I'll do that today." On June 10, I left Albany. When I did, the one thing I left in my old apartment was that note on my bedroom door. I had failed to carry out my intention.

Upon arrival back in Albany during August, I gave no thought to motel reservations until one of my friends brought up the subject. He had just come back from saving a room at the Ramada Inn. "Damn!" I thought, "I knew I had forgotten something." I swore to myself that I would take care of the necessary arrangements that weekend. Needless to say, I didn't.

My forgetfulness in this matter continued until December. When a friend of mine told me that he had looked all over town and couldn't find a reservation anywhere, I finally did call various motels, asking them about graduation weekend. Of course, I met with negative responses at all points. Satisfied that I had at least tried, I called both of my parents in turn and informed them of the bad news. They were each disappointed and tried to come up with alternate solutions to finding rooms. However, they could find none.

Apparently, my parents were upset enough about the bad news to get in touch with each other for the first time in over a year. They discussed how they might work together to find accommodations for the weekend of my graduation and eventually got to smoothing out some of the differences that had led to their most recent (though one-year) argument. True, this was only a small reconciliation, since their divorce ran much deeper than such trivial items, but at least they agreed to work together on this.

Also, my mother agreed after this discussion that she would be civil to my father if she saw him at the graduation. The last time the two had met was at my sister's graduation six years before. The behavior of my parents and the grief they caused my sister and me made the graduation the most stressful day of her life. I remembered this well and always felt bad for my sister because they made what should have been a happy day for her into a nightmare.

Looking back, I see that perhaps, as Freud would have suggested, there was a "sense" to my forgetfulness. It seems reasonable to me that maybe the reason I kept "forgetting" to make reservations for my parents was because I honestly didn't want them to come to my graduation. I had often joked with my sister about this, saying that I wasn't going to tell Mom and Dad when the graduation was to be. That way they couldn't ruin it. Seemingly, this train of thought was not merely a joke, but instead it emerged into my actions as a sort of blockade. Sure, I told them when the graduation was to be. I had no choice. But if there was no place for them to stay, they couldn't come from their homes in Washington and Chicago for just the ceremony.

An interesting parenthesis is that less than a week after hearing that my parents were speaking to each other and were both agreeable to civility on the occasion of a meeting, I found a solution to the dilemma. I realized just after New Year's that I had made some fairly good contacts last year while researching Albany motels for a business marketing class. I contacted two motel managers whom I had interviewed last year, and within two hours they had arranged two rooms each. With the unpleasant prospects for my graduation day seemingly put in check, a solution to my reservation problem lost its element of perplexity. The answer was obvious. Now how does this get classified—selective forgetfulness or just coincidence? I'm not so sure!

My father is a very reasonable, rational, contemplative man. He rarely gets angry. I have never seen him cry. I don't think he has ever been afraid. In essence, I often wonder if my father is able to express emotion at all.

I have always marveled at the manner in which my father is able to maintain composure in even the most provoking of circumstances. He has always had all the answers at just the right moments. Everything he says, no matter how wrong it may seem at first, invariably stands up to the most stringent of analyses. The logic behind even his most infuriating and insensitive arguments is impeccable.

While I am awed by the degree to which my father can be completely unaffected by his emotions, and appalled by the way in which he can be seemingly impervious to the dictates of conscience, I can't help but respect and admire these self-same qualities. I often find myself struggling with a problem and not being able to derive a feasible solution to it. In these cases I wonder how my father would approach the situation. I detach my feelings from my intellect and am immediately faced with at least one solution from the viewpoint of each extreme. The viewpoints often conflict, thus leaving me with a choice to make. When I was younger, I invariably chose the one that "felt" right. But now, more and more, I find myself choosing the one that "sounds" right. I am becoming more like my father all the time.

When my father left my mother, it was a very difficult time for her and for me. My sister was in college, which left me to watch my mother's pain by myself. I had to deal with her violent mood swings without anyone's help. Here I was, a twelve-year-old faced with the responsibility of watching over a mother who had already tried suicide in the previous few months. It was a very hard time for me through middle school and high school. I began to lose my sensitivity to anyone's emotions other than my own. I had been exposed to too many emotions too quickly—all coming from my own mother.

I tried to speak to my father about his reasons for leaving. Nineteen years of marriage is a long time to throw away. Anything that I felt, I told him. His simple answer was this: "I'm not happy with your mother. I need to do what's right for me."

I hated him for that response for awhile. What about what was right for the rest of us? What the hell made his wishes more important than mine, or Mom's, or my sister's? Eventually, the reason in his response sunk in. If he wasn't happy, how could he make the rest of us happy? There is a sobering validity to this line of thought. It hurts to think that my father broke up the simplicity, the love, the safety of my family. But I admire the strength, the courage, and the wisdom behind his actions. I have never seen my father as happy and as successful as he is today. He rebuilt his life around his old one, keeping only those parts of it that made him happy.

Ruthless, unfeeling, insensitive, uncaring. All words I've used in the past to describe the way my father can seem. And yet, I'm growing to be more and more like him. Often, when my mother wants to hurt me, or when she is angry with something that I have done, she will tell me with a tone of disgust, "You're just like your father!" Just knowing how she feels about him, how much she hates him now, has the desired effect on me. I am able to relate her feelings to a phrase that most people would be proud of and, in turn, be insulted. But I'm becoming just like my father. I see it happening. Where I used to aspire to love and marriage, now I aspire to success. Where I once put others ahead of myself, now I put myself first. Where I used to help people because they needed my help, now I help them because it makes *me* feel good to do it. In short, I have become selfish if it benefits me to be so. I have become insensitive if sensitivity makes me unhappy. I have become logical!

I am a reasonable, rational, contemplative man. I rarely get angry. Nobody ever sees me cry. I can't remember ever being afraid. In essence, I often wonder if I am able to express emotion at all . . . because if I could, I think I would hate myself.

Ron's cast of characters resembles those we have seen in the other narratives. There is the estranged father, who walked out on the family; the hard-pressed mother, who cared for the children; and the bewildered child, unable to accept the parents' divorce and forced to grow up too quickly. The experience left Ron feeling numb and self-preoccupied, resentful of the hardships imposed upon him by the divorce.

It is here that Ron's diaries depart significantly from the women's. There is no mention of suffering from low self-esteem, going into a depression, or remaining at home to care for his mother. The close attunement we saw in the three mother-daughter relationships is conspicuously lacking in the mother-son relationship. Ron does not reveal the same degree of bondedness and indebtedness to his mother, the same wish to have her all for himself, the same blurred boundaries between self and (m)other. When describing his mother's violent mood swings and suicide attempt, he remains psychologically detached. Mara's wish to sacrifice her own life for her mother's happiness, Rachel's fear of being suffocated by her mother's desire for closeness, and Tracey's belief that she possessed an inner alarm system alerting her to her mother's moods are all missing from Ron's diaries. In short, whereas the three daughters express allegiance to their mothers and to the world of emotion, family, and self-sacrifice, the son expresses allegiance to his father and to the world of reason, work, and self-development.

Ron's growing identification with his father and counteridentification with his mother are also revealing. The description of his father—"ruthless, unfeeling, insensitive, uncaring"—has suddenly become a self-description. He finds himself inscribed in a series of binary oppositions suggestive of his maternal and paternal legacy, respectively: intuition and reason, family and work, intimacy and autonomy. By choosing his father's values, Ron fears that one day he may find himself divorced from his better self.

It would be wrong, however, to view Ron as harshly as he views himself. Anyone who writes sensitively about the fear of becoming insensitive is still sensitive. His commitment to reason, intellect, and justice never wavers. It is not that he has lost the capacity to feel; rather, his dilemma lies in resolving the split between his maternal and paternal selves.

MICHAEL
"My Father Had Cheated on the Most Wonderful Human I Knew"

Michael, a senior, wrote three diaries bearing upon his parents' divorce, which occurred when he was in second grade. The opening diary records the moment in high school when he first learned about his father's infidelity. The second diary, written in the form of a short story, tells of a magical ring he received from his grandmother on his sixteenth birthday. The third diary, a poem, reveals the son's kinship to his father, the absent figure in his life.

> I guess it's about time to get around to the father issue. I'm going to have to write about it sooner or later. My parents are divorced. They've been divorced for quite some time, must be around fourteen years now, as I was in the second grade when they told us. It actually went pretty smoothly at first. I didn't think it was going to be that bad. Stupid me. Shit started happening, custody problems, alimony problems, problem problems. My father, of whom my only remaining good memory is watching him shave when I was five or six, became the scariest, cruelest monster I had ever known. I don't really know what happened. There was a period of what must have been about three years that I didn't see him.
>
> During all this time my remaining household split in two. My sister developed a bond with my mother and me that remains today, some twelve years later. We have a love that is boundless. My brother, on the other hand, went absolutely nuts. He was ripped in two. Spouted hatred and violence at all of us and then ran off to be with his father. A father who would tell him how awful we all were but who still refused to support him or send any money to his mother for support. So we were

left to try and survive his rage and to support ourselves in a very upper-middle-income neighborhood on food stamps and welfare.

But time goes by, and things do change. They don't get entirely perfect, but they do get better. Now, many years later, I do have a relationship with my father, though not without its share of anger and resentment. More important to me, I have found a love and brotherhood with my brother who had scared me so as a child.

The one hardest thing I ever had to deal with was a shocking realization that came to light one Sunday evening, driving back to our house with my mother and sister. It was not many years ago, maybe five or six. I always thought that I pretty much understood what had gone on with the divorce. Well, we were discussing various things about years gone by when we worked our way back to a camping trip I had taken with my brother and sister about a week after my father moved out, before the divorce was settled. I saw something I had never seen before: my sister, a woman whom I nearly worshiped, was practically in tears. I had no idea what was going on. And then I started listening a little closer. She was saying, "How could Dad have taken them with us so soon? How could he have been so stupid?" "They" were a woman and her daughter from my dad's office who came with us. I'd really never ever thought much about it. I stopped her and asked what the hell she was talking about. And then I realized all that she had been saying for the last half hour.

My father had cheated on the most wonderful human I knew. He'd screwed around on my mother. I don't say this lightly. My mother is a saint. She raised three children on practically nothing, kept our house, kept the three of us together without killing each other, and to this day dissuades me from speaking as coldly as I do about my father. The idea of divorce had never really bothered me. I mean, if two people aren't getting along, that's their option. But this was a different story altogether. This was unforgivable. But time goes on, as I said, and things do get better. We've discussed it, and I still harbor great resentment, but that I can live with.

But a scary thing happened last month. We were talking together, my father and me, discussing love and relationships because I was involved with someone and trying to work through some difficulties. After explaining to him the situation and telling him my views and opinions, he told me that I think quite the same way that he does. "We want similar things in life, we have similar goals." I smiled, choked back my thoughts in the name of civility, and swore to myself that I would never, ever, ever think like him or want anything remotely similar to what he does. He'll never know, but that was one of the cruelest, most infuriating things he could have ever said to me. How dare he equate himself to me, after what he's done!

I have a magic ring. It's a band of gold, with my initials raised on its face, and a small diamond chip between the letters. I wear it on the smallest finger of my right hand, with its face on the inside, so all that appears is a thin band of gold. And this ring is indeed magic. You might imagine that this ring never leaves my finger, valuing it as I do. But precisely because it is magic, I allow it complete freedom to be where it wishes to be. And it has been to places I have never seen, reappearing when I most need it, never informing me of its travels. I do miss it when it is gone, but I know there is always a reason. And it has always come back.

Six months before my sixteenth birthday, my father came to visit me one morning and informed me that we were going into Manhattan to visit a jeweler. My turn had come. I thought of the beautiful rings and necklaces that adorned the hands and necks of my brother and sister and cousins. Now I was also to wear a sign of my grandmother's love and pride. That was how I had considered this ritual gift, and as one of the youngest in my extended family, it had seemed so very long in coming. But as we drove into the city, all I could think was, yes, now it is my turn. The jeweler showed us a tray of rings, all suitable for initials, all very beautiful, all very small. At that time, gold went for an extraordinarily inflated price, and my grandmother couldn't be with us to help me choose, as I had always imagined. She had suffered a heart attack and lay quite helpless in a hospital bed.

So there I stood, with the jeweler, my father, and a tray of gold, feeling very confused and lonely. I felt guilt, and I felt shame, and I felt anger, and I felt a world of emotions which had nothing whatsoever to do with the situation before me. For no reason I could understand, I was scared. And before me I beheld a tray of gold, from which to choose a sign of love, a circle, an endless touch, which I'd long equated with only myself, my hand, rather than the gift it offered.

The ring I chose was not the largest, nor was it the smallest. It was relatively conservative, and all who saw it approved, saying it was a beautiful ring. What they didn't know was that it was magic. That was why I'd chosen this ring, or rather it chose me. So the jeweler took it and prepared it for me, and on my sixteenth birthday my father presented it to me with a letter. I still have that letter. I kept it because it infuriated me. It told of pride in me and belief in my future. It was signed by my father. Or rather my father had signed my grandmother's name, as though I'd believe it came from her. I knew it hadn't. She died just months later. Long before she died—in fact, long before the ring's presentation—she'd already forgotten who I was. She could not have written the card or even conceived it. That was not from her, and that was why I was mad at my father for pretending. He never did understand. She had already given me her gift, and the card was meaningless. She had already given me, in those moments that I sat confused and scared in the jeweler's store, the magic that flowed in the ring, and the magic that flowed inside of me.

So the years went by, and many of the emotions I'd felt were long forgotten, lying dormant deep within my memory. And over the years I forgot that the ring was magic. This did not, however, stop it from being so. It always had a life of its own, disappearing for days, weeks, sometimes months and years, always reappearing to spend countless days never leaving my touch. It lived in other houses, on other hands, in other lands, bringing back always its mass, but more important its consciousness. I loved that ring and attempted to show others its beauty and love by giving it away. But it always returned. And for all the hope and faith I had sent my ring away with, I was always strangely relieved to see it once again in my hands. And so, chaotic emotions and conflicting impulses danced and thrashed their way through my last years of high school. Till one day, I found myself sitting across from a woman.

I thought back on the years that had passed since I'd first held this ring. I thought back on how many girls had asked me about it and why I wore it backward. I thought about how I explained that I wore it so that it always faced my heart, for my grandmother had died soon after giving it to me. And I thought about how many girls I had offered it to after that "deep" and touching explanation. And I laughed at myself knowing that just weeks before, it had graced the hand of one who could never know its power.

But before me now was a woman. One I had just begun to know. And

I removed the ring from my finger and looked at it. Then I explained it not at her request, maybe not even for her benefit, but because I needed to understand what I'd discovered so long ago and forgotten. And I said, "This ring is magic." A word presented itself to me from so very long ago: magic. I had so long lived on the one side of its endless being that I had forgotten about the other side. And that day began some beautiful things for me. I hope I never live so long on the far side of anything that I forget there is another side. And she believed me. Magic can be very real. Your mind creates it always.

Of course my mind must have always known where it had left or abandoned the ring. Sure, I kept track of it, knowing a time would always come when I could learn something from it. The ring taught me the value of materials and the value of nonmaterials. It taught me what people want to hear and what is actually the truth, and where the two do and don't meet. It taught me that it's all right to love and to hate and simply not always to know. But always, my unconscious mind knew where to find the ring. There were no supernatural forces here. I'll probably wear the ring to class on Thursday when these diaries are read, just in case mine should be chosen. I look down at my hand and know that magic does exist. What could be more beautiful? What could be more wonderful than a mind that can learn and uncover such things, such wonders, from a little band of gold, from a little magic ring.

Old man, I am indeed yours,
I have your chin,
Though never as deep as yours
Is my cleft.
Inches away, all these years,
I can taste your breath.
I can taste your breath.

When I was so small,
Hardly a mouthful,
I could feel your sticky lips
Around my ear, nibbling, chewing,
Tasting. You wanted to be sure.
And together we sang about the

Kittens, and the little boy blue.
If you only knew how blue.

Old man, how your power grew,
Grew like a thorn,
Armed against those who crowded
'Round your heart.
You scarred us all,
We tasted your blood,
The babes cried for blood.

Then I also grew,
Stretching wide your jaws,
Your lips cracked and bled.
One with whom I'd shared my plate,
Warned me of the decree, saying
That you, and also we, were only
Human, and I know that, he knows it too.
Which is he? He's the one that is you.

Michael narrates the same male story as Ron does, affirming autonomy, freedom, and self-development. We learn surprisingly little about his mother, apart from the fact that she was a "saint" for having kept the family together after the divorce. Unlike Mara, Rachel, and Tracey, Michael does not see himself primarily as an extension of his mother or responsible for her welfare. There appears to be both a gain and a loss in his more detached relationship from his mother. Positively, he is neither entrapped by family responsibilities nor smothered by an overclose mother-son relationship. Negatively, there is no suggestion of the son's playing the role of caretaker or nurturer in the family.

Michael's freedom to explore new relationships is strikingly evident in his diary about a magical ring. Although rings traditionally symbolize perfection and mystical unity, Michael's ring evokes the free-spiritedness associated with curiosity and adventure. Allowing the ring the "complete freedom to be where it wishes to be," he endows it with the autonomy and independence he has achieved in his own life. His confidence in the ring's eventual return reflects unbounded faith in his own powers. The ring becomes an extension of self, a sign of his emergence into the world. The ring travels to other places, spreads its magic to others, and returns home triumphantly.

Whereas Mara, Rachel, and Tracey counteridentify with their fathers, evincing no interest in their lives, Michael, like Ron, comes to recognize that he is his father's son. He opens his poem with the bold assertion, "Old man, I am indeed yours," and he proceeds to develop their kinship. Oral images abound—tasting, nibbling, chewing. Though the father's power "grew like a thorn," scarring everyone with whom it came into contact, the son has now incorporated it into his own being, much as he inherited the magical ring in the preceding diary. The poem ends ambiguously with the son's gaining ascendancy over the father but being warned that they are both "only human."

PAUL
*"The Worst Mistake a Man Could Make Is to
Deny a Relationship with His Children"*

Paul, a senior, wrote five diaries about his parents' divorce. The first two diaries describe his abiding anger toward his father and the emotional damage caused by the family's breakup. The third entry involves a terrifying dream which brings back past memories of life with father. The final two diaries contain a letter Paul was preparing to write to his father in an effort toward reconciliation.

> When I was two years old, my parents decided to divorce. Today I realize that my father was and is a bright man; he was just not a very good father. I wasn't beaten or physically tortured, though he did have a tendency to use his hands a lot on my mom. Over the years, though, I've found that I was hurt much more on a mental level. For a long time, I found myself not able to become close with other guys—only girls; this is fine if you're nineteen or twenty, but it is not so good when you are fifteen or sixteen. I was afraid of close relationships with other guys and tended to take the back seat when it came to hanging out with groups. I also had a tendency not to trust others in a relationship. I felt that everyone "cheats," just as I was cheated out of a father.

> According to Freudian theory, during the Oedipal stage a male child, for example, will wish to be rid of his father so he may have his mother

solely to himself. I have never seemed to have half as much difficulty in understanding this theory as compared with some of my peers. The reason for this is because my brother did not successfully pass through the Oedipus complex. My parents decided to divorce when he was just five years old. During this period, the father is not really supposed to disappear, as is the child's wish. Instead, he is supposed to remain in the picture. The child should then receive the message that he can have anything he wants except Mommy. That is to say, only Daddy can be with Mommy sexually.

I did not have a similar experience, however, and possibly as a result, there is a great difference in our social/sexual activities. Whereas I grew up a bit on the cocky side, fun loving and extroverted, my brother grew up with a lack of self-esteem and was introverted. I see more neurotic tendencies in him than I see in myself. However, I am biased.

Related to the Oedipus complex, I did fail one stage most probably associated with it. Until recently, I thought I was alone in this feeling. I am a male, and I have always had a problem saying the phrase "I love you, Mom." I wonder, is it because I am unconsciously angry at her for the divorce? Or is it a fear that if I let her know I love her too much, she will disappear like Daddy? Regardless of the explanation, I know I do love her, but I still feel uncomfortable when I say it. I find myself more frustrated with this situation just after I tell my fiancée I love her with such ease. I anticipate by the end of the semester I will have a new set of tools to help me open up the "locker" which contains the correct answer.

I was in a large room of a private house with ten or twelve young boys. The area surrounding the house was desolate. The man who seemed to be in charge was very big. He was extremely mean and violent with the children. I was only a bystander. The man was constantly punching the children for no apparent reason. The boys seemed to be playing among themselves, and the man was not satisfied. His aggression could not be controlled. At one point, his wife begged him to stop hitting the children, and his response was a crack across her face as well. All at once, the whole cast was outside a private house on my street at home. We stood right outside of the park. A group of older boys was approaching. I thought the two groups of boys were going to fight, but I was very wrong. The older boys began beating on the man. The dream began to fade.

A present analysis of my dream deals with a part-time job I have at a school for emotionally disturbed children. I am working with male children ages seven to fourteen who are labeled juvenile delinquents. These children are basically from one-parent homes, and in most cases, it is the father who has faded from their lives. They are extremely hyper and aggressive. My feeling, however, is that these kids are simply deprived of attention and affection. Furthermore, I feel that labeling them delinquents is cruel and harsh. Their attitudes, I feel, are due to older people who are supposed to guide them, but instead the adults act as if there is no cure for them. They will always be "bad." This is portrayed in the dream when, even though the children are playing nicely, the man continues to beat them. They should not even attempt to be good.

This dream also brings back many past memories. I have a brother who is older than me. Both before and after my parents' divorce, we were subjected to my father's constant slapping. Something which really used to irk me when we went to visit him took place at the park down the block from our house. My father used to play ball with my brother for a real long time. When my turn came up, he would beat me very quickly and then call my brother back to continue playing with him. He got away with this until I was twelve. One day I tried something different. I asked him for a rematch. He denied already calling my brother over. I then told him, "Fuck off and die." He began to hit me. My brother was approaching. He grabbed my dad's arm and told him that if he did not stop, we would never see him again. Though my father had stopped at this point, I still have kept the promise my brother made that day.

The symbolism in the dream would appear to make the cruel man into my father. The young boys represented myself, while the older ones represented my brother. My mom could do nothing, for she was not really present. The scene was one from many years in my past.

I have been very carefully listening to the diaries pertaining to father-child relationships. I also wrote about my dad in one of the earlier diaries. Presently, however, I face a new issue pertaining to my father. When I get married next year, will my father be present to witness the ceremony, or will he continue to build the wall which reduces the chances of having a relationship each new day?

I have not seen my father in six years. In our last correspondence, he basically wrote of his hypertension, and I told him to seek psychiatric help. Not a very successful attempt.

I am not appalled by the idea of having him at my wedding, but he must be there as my father, not as a stranger. As a stranger, I could not afford to invite him. So how does he come as a father? I have decided to send him a brief note. It will read, "Hi, Dad, I am in every weekend. We should get together. Contact me if you agree at. . . ." At this point he has his chance to resume playing his mature (I hope) role. I do not plan on making it simple for him either. I feel that if we are ever to resume a relationship again, it must be now, before my life is settled. I do not need to hear from him when I'm thirty-five, married with two children, and living in a $500,000 home in Scarsdale.

I used to brag to classmates when I was younger about how great it was not to have a father around. You have only one parent to convince to let you do something, and you can't get hit as hard. What I didn't realize then was that even though my grandfather was young enough to do everything with me that my father should have done, I was still being cheated out of a complete family.

Finally, in one of my dad's letters from a few years ago, he mentioned that when in college I should take a course in "the family." I finished the course last semester, and I really got a great deal out of it. I would love to share with him the information I learned on the topic of father-child relationships. The guest sociologist said, and I'm sure Freud would agree, that "the worst mistake a man could make is to deny a relation-ship with his children." Sometimes I have a feeling my father already knows this.

Last week the following letter went out to my father:

Dear Dad,

Since our last correspondence, a great many changes have occurred in my life. Last year I completed a five- month study of the family as a social organization. I must say it proved to be a very beneficial course, as it has opened new doors of knowledge for me which were previously closed. I have to thank you for this experience, as it was your advice I had taken from a letter you wrote me some years ago.

To continue this correspondence in letter format would be nice if I were filling you in on two or three months of past activity. However, the last time we really spoke was prior to my thirteenth birthday. This leaves me not three months but eight years to catch up with. My point is, Dad, that I have finally aborted the idea that not having relations with a living father is acceptable. This view might have protected me through my adolescent years, but I can no longer be shielded by something I no longer believe. I think the time has come for us to meet again—or at least for us now to talk. I have been attempting this letter for six months or so. I finally sent it because I began to wonder if you shared similar feelings.

I am graduating in May. I am home a great deal on weekends, and I am leaving you with my school, work, and home phone numbers.

For now, I can only say that as life goes on, we all make changes to try and better ourselves. This is what I am attempting to do. I look forward to hearing from you. Until then, take care.

Pretty hefty shit, huh? I think my point was made clear. Though I only gave a family sociology course credit for this letter, I'm sure most of us know the real course from which such feelings arise. However, at this time my father doesn't need to be filled in on such special secrets.

Paul's diaries resemble those of the other five students in several ways. Without exception, they blame their fathers for the breakup of the family and for abdicating responsibility to the children. It is startling to see, in scores of parental divorce diaries written by men and women alike, how often students blame their fathers for the family's breakup. Most of these students have lost virtually all contact with their fathers. Paul is particularly resentful of his father for dropping out of his life. Anger invades his dreams, resulting in a nightmarish figure who symbolizes the father's violence toward the family. Paul observes that he became fearful of close relationships with other men because he believed that "everyone 'cheats,'" as his father did.

And yet once again we see important gender differences in parental divorce diaries. Unlike Mara, Rachel, and Tracey, who cannot mention their fathers without anxiously returning to their mothers, Ron, Michael, and Paul write very little about their mothers, although all three sons were raised almost singlehandedly by them. The portrayal of spousal abuse is also different. Tracey and Paul both refer to their fathers' physically abusing their mothers, but while the former dwells upon this, the latter treats it almost parenthetically. While all six children grew up largely without their fathers and still remain severely critical of them, the sons, not the daughters, express the wish to resume a relationship with them. Not only do the three sons return frequently to their fathers, but they also assume that they will achieve the professional and financial success associated with the male world. (Notice Paul's confidence that one day he will be living in an expensive home in a fashionable New York suburb.) Wallerstein's observation about the crucial importance of a son's identification with his estranged father is relevant here: "I was astonished to find that boys from divorced families experienced an intense, rising need for their fathers during adolescence—even if the divorce occurred ten years earlier. Divorced fathers play a heretofore unappreciated role in the lives of their sons at this juncture."[11]

GAIL
"The Sins of the Fathers Are Visited on the Children"

Mara, Rachel, Tracey, Ron, Michael, and Paul wrote about their parents' divorces from young adults' points of view. None of them was married or had children. Most college students are not parents, of course, and they can only imagine the experience of raising children. But how do older students, who are themselves parents, write about *their* parents' divorce? Are their stories similar to or different from those told by students young enough to be their children? Do we hear, for example, the same female voice in a mother's narrative that we heard in those narrated by the three daughters? Gail, a returning student in her forties, wrote five diaries about how the collapse of her parents' marriage affected her life as a child, mother, and divorced parent:

> The first class triggered thoughts of my relationship with my mother and son. I thought of the biblical admonition, "The sins of the fathers are visited on the children, even to the third and fourth generation." It made me have a fresh understanding of the commandment to honor your father and mother that *your* days may be long—this is the first commandment with a promise. Without the law and the promise, what protection would elderly parents have against their unhappy and perhaps vengeful children?
>
> I have a rotten relationship with my mother—much anger and unforgiveness. I, in turn, have been a terrible mother to my son. I wonder

whether his feelings toward me are similar to mine toward my mother and, by the same token, whether my mother's feelings toward me are similar to mine toward my son.

I have a lot of guilt toward my son because I was a bad mother and because I don't really like him and feel that I should. I think the basic reason I don't like him is because he makes me feel guilty.

I'm angry that a less-than-ideal relationship seems inevitable between parents and children. I don't get along with my son, but I love my daughter very much. I wonder if my children will ever feel as angry with me as I do toward my mother. I fear they will. It really bugs me when I see myself doing the same thing to my children that my mother did to me. Money (or lack of it) was always a problem when I was growing up. I can't tell you how many supposedly happy family occasions I have spoiled because I was afraid to spend money. I have passed on the same obsession with money to my children that was passed on to me by my mother.

Despite many other people writing diaries about their parents, I have resisted because I find that dwelling on all the past hurts only keeps them fresh and does not lead to healing. However, something happened this weekend which awakened all of my anger and resentment toward my mother, and I felt that I wanted to write about it.

I have a dear friend who, though she is only a few years older than me, has taken on the role of my mother. She, of course, would be very upset to know that I think of her that way because she considers herself to be my contemporary. I don't know if other people would see any resemblance. She is a much nicer person than my mother, not as self-centered, but still a very strong, dominating personality.

The situation is further complicated by the fact that she has a daughter with whom she is very close. When her daughter is not around, I become her daughter. We visit back and forth quite often. When her daughter is home, I no longer exist. I find myself feeling very jealous and getting very angry with the daughter, whom I ordinarily like.

It reminded me of my relationship with my mother. I was an only child for many years. When I was very young, I had a very close relationship with my mother. When I was eight, that changed. My mother left me in order to remarry, and she soon had a daughter with her second husband. During this time I stayed with my mother's older sister. I decided to live with her because she could be trusted. I didn't have ambivalent feelings toward her. I see now that much of my problem with my mother was that I always wanted her to love me more than anybody else. When I was very young, I felt that she did. But then she left me.

When my mother's second marriage fell apart, she told me that she had once sacrificed her happiness for me and said that if I didn't come and stay with her again, she would have nothing to live for. I left my aunt to stay with my mother. I used to dream that somehow my aunt would come to rescue me. When my mother married a third time, I didn't seem as important to her anymore. I became a problem to her. I got married to get away from her. I hated her. Then my mother had a son, who received all the love and attention I felt that I had never had from my mother.

Now history seems to be repeating itself. I don't want people to have power over me to hurt me. So I will be very angry with my friend and very angry with her daughter. Then, when the hurt is not so fresh, I will stop being angry and she and I will be friends again. I wonder if my mother and I will ever be friends.

I seem to have an inordinate need to be needed. The reason I married was because I felt he needed someone to give direction to his life, and I was there to give it to him. When it became apparent that there was absolutely nothing I could give him that he valued, the marriage fell apart.

I like for my daughter to need me. I love for her to get sick. Not deathly ill, of course, but a bad cold gives me the opportunity to dose her with cough medicine, smear her with Vick's VapoRub, and tuck her in bed all snug and warm. The other day she said to me, "Will you please stop hovering over me like a witch?" Is my need to be needed so strong that it overshadows everything else? Is my self-esteem so low that I feel I have no value except for what I can give?

I wrote my paper on *The Bell Jar*, focusing on Esther's relationship with her mother. As I wrote, I found myself feeling very angry at her mother. I noticed this especially when I wrote about how I felt Esther's mother had devalued her abilities. I wondered why and then suddenly realized that I felt my mother had done the same thing to me.

I had always assumed I would go to college right after high school. From the fourth grade on, I had been told that I had exceptional ability. My uncle was an English teacher, and I was particularly interested in writing.

Then, as I recounted in an earlier diary, I moved out of my aunt and uncle's home and rejoined my mother. I assumed I was going to college and did well in high school. Shortly after my mother's third marriage, she told me that I could not go to college because she couldn't afford it and insisted that I switch to a business course so that I could get a job when I graduated from high school.

How well I could identify with Esther when she talked about her reaction to shorthand! I would spend hours practicing and then invariably make the characters in the wrong direction. I had a course in business machines and walked out in tears more times than I cared to remember because I could not master any of the office equipment.

I completely lost interest in school after that. My guidance counselor tried to persuade me not to switch curriculums and suggested that I work my way through college, but at that point nothing seemed worthwhile to me.

Sometimes I think I could have ended up like Esther. I don't know why I didn't. I suppose it's because I have never let myself stay in a situation where I felt trapped. I've always found a way out. I sometimes believe that a guardian angel has watched over and provided for me.

I don't know why I am telling you all this. I only know that as I was writing, I became so overwhelmed with the desire for everyone to know about my life that I had to write about it.

I'm trying desperately to find something to write about. I've never written about my father.

My parents were divorced when I was two. My father was in the air force, and I grew up thinking he was very handsome and literally worshiped him. I had a fantasy that when he came home from overseas, he and my mother would remarry. Then I would have a normal family life like everyone else. In those days divorce was not common, and I was the only person I knew whose parents were divorced. When my father came home, I found out that he had already married and had a child. Nothing has ever hurt me as much before or since.

My father made the air force his career. I would travel to see him in the summer at the various bases where he was stationed. I would always get jealous of my stepmother and stepsister and want to come home long before it was time. Sometimes my father would drink, and I would get very upset. No one in my family drank, and I was not used to being around people who did.

After I graduated from high school, I went to see my father. I don't know what happened, but I didn't see him again for almost ten years. We completely lost track of each other. His brother wrote me once that he had heard from him and that he wanted to see me. I didn't want to see him because I just thought he would hurt me all over again. He would make promises that were sincere at the time, but then something would happen, and they couldn't be kept. The next year he came to see me. We had a wonderful visit. He got to see his grandchildren for the first time.

It was so good to be able to accept him as he was. He was very friendly but also very restless and moody. He and my stepmother loved to travel all over the country. I realized how well suited they were for each other and stopped resenting my stepmother.

We had quite a few visits back and forth after that. They were all good and drew us closer together with each visit. I formed a very good relationship with my stepmother. My daughter commented on how good it was to see a really happy marriage.

My dad died a few years ago. Shortly before his death my stepmother called to tell me he was ill and was not expected to live another month. When I traveled to their home, my stepmother said she wanted to give me an opportunity to be alone with him. Although he gave no indication of knowing I was there, I believe he did. I talked to him, hugged him, and sang to him. I kept stroking his arm and telling him over and over again, "You're my daddy and I love you." I watched him die.

I am so thankful that I was able to see my father again and love him. I'm so thankful I've been able to accept my stepmother. It doesn't really seem like he's dead, though. I loved my dad very much. This is the first time I've been able to write in detail about him since he died. Thanks.

P.S. My dad felt very guilty over divorcing my mother and being the kind of father he had been to me. When he lay dying, I had to assuage his guilt and let him know everything was alright. I hope that I was able to do that and that he died in peace.

We can hear the female voice of Gail's story: the inordinate need to be needed, the caretaker roles she ambivalently assumed with her husband and children, the low self-esteem from which she has long suffered, the necessity to renounce higher educational and career ambitions for more practical vocational goals. Her life illustrates the traditionally female belief that self-sacrifice is a higher virtue than self-development, a belief that rewards the male world which it benefits.

Yet, more positively, Gail's writings affirm the value of love and reconciliation. Her poignant description of the last visit to her dying father suggests that she has gained a degree of resolution to that conflicted chapter of her life. Moreover, her awareness of the intergenerational nature of parent-child conflicts may help her to achieve a degree of reconciliation with her mother and son.[12] The decision to return to college to complete her formal education also demonstrates her renewed commitment to self-development.

Gendered Voices

How do we account for these gendered stories of parental divorce? Why do women's diaries emphasize the intensity of the mother-daughter relationship and, by implication, family, interdependence, and self-sacrifice, while men's diaries reveal separation from the mother and affirmation of work, independence, and self-development? Why do Ron, Michael, and Paul wish to be reconciled with their fathers, while Mara, Rachel, and Tracey seem unwilling to resume contact with them?

In recent years, developmental psychologists and feminist scholars have turned their attention to the role of gender in an effort to answer questions such as these. One of the most influential writers has been Nancy Chodorow, who argues in *The Reproduction of Mothering* that, for a variety of psychological and cultural reasons, girls attach themselves more closely to their mothers than boys do. This heightened attachment has profound implications for identity development:

From the retention of preoedipal attachments to their mother, growing girls come to define and experience themselves as continuous with others; their experience of self contains more flexible or permeable ego boundaries. Boys come to define themselves as more separate and distinct, with a greater sense of rigid ego boundaries and differentiation. The basic feminine sense of self is connected to the world, the basic masculine sense of self is separate.[13]

In her book *In a Different Voice*, Carol Gilligan similarly maintains that the key to understanding women's development lies in the importance of attachment in the human life cycle. In Gilligan's view, culture plays a decisive role in conditioning men and women to perceive danger differently. Insofar as the male self is defined through separation, men see danger arising from personal affiliation and intimacy; the female self, by contrast, is defined through connection, and hence women see danger arising from impersonal achievement situations:

> The danger men describe in their stories of intimacy is a danger of entrapment or betrayal, being caught in a smothering relationship or humiliated by rejection and deceit. In contrast, the danger women portray in their tales of achievement is a danger of isolation, a fear that in standing out or being set apart by success, they will be left alone.[14]

Different Problems for Daughters and Sons

Student diaries suggest that parental divorce poses a different set of problems for daughters and sons. The daughters viewed themselves as continuous with their mothers; the intensity of the attachment led to love, intimacy, and protectiveness, on the one hand, and the threat of loss of autonomy and independence, on the other. Contrary to Gilligan's generalization, I have found that some female students, such as Rachel, expressed the fear of being smothered by their mother, a fear that is not limited to males.[15] Since the daughters experienced greater attachment to their mothers than did the sons, it was more difficult for them to resume relations with their estranged fathers, even when their mothers encouraged them to do so. The daughters, unlike the sons, did not assume they would follow in their fathers' paths to professional success.[16] Feelings of anger and hostility toward the father predominated in Mara's, Rachel's, and Tracey's diaries.

The sons, by contrast, viewed themselves as separate from their mothers; this distance led to autonomy, freedom, and self-development, on the one hand, and the threat of isolation, on the other. The sons were willing to reestablish contact with their fathers, never doubting they would follow their fathers' paths into the world and achieve professional success. Since they blamed their fathers for the divorce, however, the sons were wary of becoming too much like them. To be told that they resembled their fathers was distressing to Ron, Michael, and Paul.

The Sins of the Mothers?

The diaries demonstrate that daughters, in their closeness with their mothers, identify with maternal victimization. Mara observes that, because her mother sacrificed her own happiness for her daughter's, the latter now feels compelled to "lay down my life for hers if I had to." A variation of this may be seen in Gail's entry. "[My mother] told me that she had once sacrificed her happiness for me and said that if I didn't come and stay with her again, she would have nothing to live for." Rachel feels anguish and guilt over her mother's loneliness, while Tracey fears that her mother's health is being undermined by the effort to keep the family together. The daughters identify closely with their mothers' hardships following divorce, unlike the sons, who do not relate to their mothers' experience of victimization. Significantly, with the exception of Gail, all the students portray their mothers not only as victims but as essentially blameless for the divorce. It is striking to see how, in describing a subject as complex and problematic as divorce, the students exonerated their mothers from any responsibility for the breakup of the marriage. It may be that the reason students did not criticize their mothers in parental divorce diaries is because the "sins of the mothers" literally hit too close to home to discuss safely. Or perhaps students unconsciously perceived their fathers as in some sense having primary responsibility for the relationship.

Overcoming the Sins of the Fathers

All seven students stated in their final diaries that writing enabled them to begin a useful dialogue which they hoped would continue after the semester ended. They viewed writing—and hearing their classmates' diaries—as an opportunity both for cathartic release of pent-up emotions and for self-discovery. Some of them accepted my suggestion to send their diaries to their absent fathers in an effort to resume a relationship.[17]

Mara valued writing primarily because it helped her to put the relationships in her life into clearer perspective. The diaries allowed her to realize, in her own words, that "it's OK to be upset, happy, or depressed." She added that, although some of her diaries were so painful that she cried, she felt she was able to write more self-analytically when she was upset than when she was happy. Rachel was absent on the day when I asked the students to evaluate diary writing; instead, she devoted the last entry to describing her fears about graduation, which was only a few weeks away. "Leaving school and starting work is a frightening thought. It has been causing me severe anxiety. I didn't think I would ever finish school. It seemed to go on forever." She added in a postscript that she found the diaries read in class consistently thought-provoking and inspiring. Writing encouraged Tracey to express feelings she had never been able to speak about to anyone before, not even to her closest friends. The most memorable diaries, she said, were those about her mother. "I never realized how valuable she is to me until I wrote my diary. Why did I not realize sooner the treasure that was right in front of my eyes? Then I could have treated it delicately and carefully watched over it so that no harm could touch it." She concluded by saying that my comments made it easier for her to share her feelings with other people. "You accepted my inner thoughts and did not criticize them. You are like my diary, my secret friend who has breathed my thoughts and will treasure them forever."

Ron acknowledged that some of his difficulties with women had become clearer to him as a result of diary writing. The diaries did not teach him anything that could be included on a syllabus, but they did reveal important truths about himself. "To me, that makes for a much more valuable educational experience than any textbook or lecture could produce." The two diaries which had the greatest meaning to Michael were the ones about his father and the magical ring. He showed both diaries to his family, and the one about his father brought tears to his brother's eyes. Michael's final comment was reserved for his father. "I wrote in one of my diaries that I never forgave my father. I'm still not positive how that is going to turn out, but for now, I can face him. After all, he is only human. Someday I might even tell him I love him. Maybe." Paul remarked upon how many students in his class wrote about conflicted relationships with their parents. "Whether our parents were dead or alive, for example, we all found we had problems with them which had to be resolved. Until this course, I had never thought I would ever contact my father again. Two weeks ago, however, I sent him a letter asking him for some time to talk."

Gail was the only student among the seven who initially felt reluctant to write about past disappointments, yet she also came to value writing weekly diaries and hearing other students' entries. She was surprised that so many people in the class related similar family disappointments. "Growing up as a very unhappy child, I tended to believe that I was unique and that no one else could possibly have been treated as terribly as I was. Some of the diaries you read in class described horrors that I could not even imagine—and yet these people were functioning, and functioning well! This was good for me to hear."

4 / Hunger Artists

Just try to explain to anyone the art of fasting! Anyone who has no feeling for it cannot be made to understand it. —Franz Kafka, "A Hunger Artist"

Of all the stories I teach, none is more opaque to male students or more disturbingly transparent to so many female students than Franz Kafka's "Hunger Artist" (1922). Only ten pages long, the tale focuses on a performer who suffers the misfortune of living in an era which no longer values his unusual talent for fasting. Decades earlier, Kafka tells us, life was different. The entire town would turn out to marvel at the emaciated hunger artist sitting in his narrow straw-lined cage, dreaming of shattering his own world record. Rejoicing in the huge crowds gathered around his cage every day, the hunger artist would proudly extend his shriveled arm through the bars of his cage to allow children to feel its skeletal thinness. Despite his death-defying starvation, the hunger artist is never tempted to eat a morsel of food, not even when the permanent watchers at the circus, charged with the task of making sure he does not cheat, turn their backs on him, encouraging him to eat.

Indeed, the spectators do not know how easy it is for the hunger artist to reject food. Perfecting the art of fasting is the only desire in his life. Limited by an impresario's decision that he abstain from food for a maximum of forty days—beyond that period the public apparently loses interest—the hunger artist yearns to fast until the end of his days. "So he live[s] for many years, . . . honored by the world, yet . . . troubled in spirit."[1] When a well-wisher attempts to console him by pointing out that his melancholy is the result of his prolonged fasting, the hunger artist reacts violently, shaking the bars of his cage like a trapped animal. Although the impresario apologizes for these outbursts, attributing them to the irritation caused by fasting, the hunger artist knows that this explanation is a perversion of the truth. "What was a consequence of the premature ending of his fast was here presented as the cause of it!" (85).

To the hunger artist's dismay, the public eventually loses interest in the art of fasting, forsaking him for other performers. Forced to end his partnership with the impresario and hire himself to a large circus, he strives vainly to win a new generation of loyal followers. For a time the old excitement for professional hunger artists returns, and he is exhilarated by the possibility of fasting on and on, with daily placards announcing his record-shattering feat. But soon the fickle crowds tire of the hunger artist's act, his cage is abandoned, and he drops out of sight.

One day an overseer notices the cage and orders attendants to explain why it is standing unused with dirty straw inside it. The attendants poke around in the straw and discover the hunger artist lying in it, close to death. "Are you still fasting?" the overseer asks. "When on earth do you mean to stop?" The dialogue proceeds as follows:

> "Forgive me, everybody," whispered the hunger artist; only the overseer, who had his ear to the bars, understood him. "Of course," said the overseer, and tapped his forehead with a finger to let the attendants know what state the man was in, "we forgive you." "I always wanted you to admire my fasting," said the hunger artist. "We do admire it," said the overseer, affably. "But you shouldn't admire it," said the hunger artist. "Well then we don't admire it," said the overseer, "but why shouldn't we admire it?" "Because I have to fast, I can't help it," said the hunger artist. "What a fellow you are," said the overseer, "and why can't you help it?" "Because," said the hunger artist, lifting his head a little and speaking, with his lips pursed, as if for a kiss, right into the overseer's ear, so that no syllable might be lost, "because I couldn't find the food I liked. If I had found it, believe me, I should have made no fuss and stuffed myself like you or anyone else." (89–90)

Why does the hunger artist starve himself in order to feel fulfilled? Why does he ask forgiveness for an act that seems both voluntary and involuntary, and for which he wishes to be admired yet not admired? Why does he reach out to others—he almost kisses the overseer—only to spurn communication and connection? In what sense does his artistic performance mask a self-destructive wish? For what does the hunger artist truly hunger? In short, what is the psychology of the man who is, in the impresario's words, a "suffering martyr"—"which indeed he was," Kafka adds cryptically, "although in quite another sense" (84)?

As Kim Chernin has suggested, Kafka's "Hunger Artist" can be read, in part, as a parable on eating disorders, a prophetic warning of our cultural obsession with food and dieting.[2] The hunger artist's anorexic-like behavior will be familiar to anyone who has studied the paradoxical dynamics of this mysterious disease: the need to remain in control while demonstrating out-of-control behavior, the exhibitionistic wish to display one's body while expressing contempt for the corporeal, the effort to preserve the illusion of omnipotence and self-sufficiency while regressing to a state of total infantilism, and the quest for perfectionism while feeling hopelessly imperfect. The hunger artist is a deeply contradictory figure, a self-effacing performer who grandiosely believes he is the greatest faster of all time, a submissive man who reacts violently to those who fail to take him seriously, a loner who becomes irritable and depressed when the multitudes desert his act.

Violence against the body constitutes the essence of the hunger artist's form of expression, violence that reflects narcissistic injury, masochism, and passive aggression. Like his late nineteenth-century American counterpart, Melville's Bartleby the scrivener, the hunger artist "prefers not to." Food becomes the object of his protest, and the decision to stop eating symbolizes nothing less than the repudiation of desire. The cage in which he is imprisoned becomes a metaphor of his diminished body; his self-enclosure stands in sharp contrast to the robust panther which roams the cage after his death. Combining aestheticism and asceticism, the hunger artist finally succeeds in extinguishing his life, thus recalling another tormented Kafka protagonist, Gregor Samsa in *The Metamorphosis* (1912), who, upon hearing his family's lodgers noisily devour their food, sadly thinks: "I'm hungry enough . . . but not for that kind of food. How these lodgers are stuffing themselves, and here am I dying of starvation!" (43).

The Hunger Artist and Kafka

There are intriguing parallels between the hunger artist's and Kafka's own rejection of food. In the autobiographical "Letter to His Father," written in 1919, Kafka declares that many of the clashes with his father arose over food and drink. Kafka's earliest childhood memory involved a traumatic incident at night in which, whimpering repeatedly for water, he was commanded by his father to remain quiet. When the warning failed to have its desired effect, the father dragged his son out of bed, carried him onto a balcony, and left him there in his nightshirt, outside the shut door. The incident aroused feelings of terror and confusion in the youth; for years afterward he suffered from the tormenting fear that his father, the ultimate authority, would come into his room for no reason and humiliate him again.

In an even more significant passage in "Letter to His Father," Kafka reveals the extent to which his father's attitude toward food had a formative influence on his life:

> Since as a child I was with you chiefly during meals, your teaching was to a large extent the teaching of proper behavior at table. What was brought to the table had to be eaten, the quality of the food was not to be discussed—but you yourself often found the food inedible, called it "this swill," said "that beast" (the cook) had ruined it. Because in accordance with your strong appetite and your particular predilection you ate everything fast, hot, and in big mouthfuls, the child had to hurry; there was a somber silence at table, interrupted by admonitions: "Eat first, talk afterwards," or "faster, faster, faster," or "there you are, you see, I finished ages ago." Bones mustn't be cracked with the teeth, but you could. Vinegar must not be sipped noisily, but you could. The main thing was that the bread should be cut straight. But it didn't matter that you did it with a knife dripping with gravy. Care had to be taken that no scraps fell on the floor. In the end it was under your chair that there were most scraps. (194–195)

As a result of his father's dictatorial commandments, Kafka came to believe that there were three separate and distinct worlds: a world in which he lived as a slave, forced to obey laws intended only for him; a second world, infinitely remote from the first, where his father lived and governed as a god; and a third world, where everyone else lived happily, free from tyrannical rule. "I was continually in disgrace; either I obeyed your orders, and that was a disgrace, for they applied, after all, only to me; or I was defiant, and that was a disgrace too, for how could I presume to defy you; or I could not obey because I did not, for instance, have your strength, your appetite, your skill, although you expected it of me as a matter of course; this was the greatest disgrace of all" (195).

By rejecting food, Kafka repudiated his father's world of appetite, brute strength, and tyrannical rule. Fasting represented both defiance against his father's domineering control and self-punishment for harboring patricidal feelings. Unable to eat heartily or drink beer with his meals, as his father wished him to do, Kafka, the grandson of a Kosher butcher, became a vegetarian. Nevertheless, conflicts over food continued. "For years he suffered from his stomach," Kafka's friend and future biographer, Max Brod, wrote to Felice Bauer in 1912.[3] Kafka's most recent biographer, Frederick Karl, describes him as "very probably, a secondary anorexic, turning food and the experience of it into a form of warfare, which he could fight and win but at the expense of his well-being."[4]

Kafka's struggle with food appears in his earliest diaries, long before his scarecrow body was ravaged by the tuberculosis that finally consumed his life in 1924 at the age of forty. A fantasy recorded in a 1911 entry reflects the desire for bingeing and purging symptomatic of bulimia:

> This craving that I almost always have, when for once I feel my stomach is healthy, to heap up in me notions of terrible deeds of daring with food. I especially satisfy this craving in front of pork butchers. If I see a sausage that is labeled as an old, hard sausage, I bite into it in my imagination with all my teeth and swallow quickly, regularly and thoughtlessly, like a machine. The despair that this act, even in the imagination, has as its immediate result, increases my haste. I shove the long slabs of rib meat unbitten into my mouth, and then pull them out again from behind, tearing through stomach and intestines. I eat dirty delicatessen stores completely empty. Cram myself with herrings, pickles and all the bad, old, sharp foods. Bonbons are poured into me like hail from their tin boxes. I enjoy in this way not only my healthy condition but also a suffering that is without pain and can pass at once.[5]

A 1913 diary entry records Kafka's fantasy of being nothing more than a slab of meat, ready to be sliced for human consumption. "Always the image of a pork butcher's broad knife that quickly and with mechanical regularity chops into me from the side and cuts off very thin slices which fly off almost like shavings because of the speed of the action."[6] Given his rejection of food, there was a grim irony, as Ernst Pawel observes, in Kafka's final illness, during which he was literally unable to eat. "There is an element of rising savagery in the way in which he progressed from the avoidance of certain foods to what amounted to a self-imposed starvation diet, rendered pathetically ironic by the fact that in the end the very nature of his final illness—tuberculosis of the larynx—made swallowing all but impossible, so that he quite literally starved to death."[7]

And yet despite the parallels between Kafka and the hunger artist, it would be misleading to reduce the author to any of his characters. Whereas Kafka can create, from the depths of his extraordinary imagination, the character of the hunger artist, viewing him as a symbol of a martyred and misunderstood writer, the hunger artist can only starve himself, rejecting life rather than re-creating it through art, as his maker did. While the hunger artist undoubtedly reflects his creator's ambivalence toward art, the conviction that writing is both a blessing and a curse, Kafka insisted that art is the antidote to life. "Poetry is disease," he wrote to Gustav Janouch, "yet one does not get well by suppressing the fever. On the contrary! Its heat purifies and illuminates."[8] And whereas the hunger artist falls into oblivion and perishes, unnoticed by the world, Kafka achieved through his art lasting fame, creating imperishable stories that nourish the imagination.

Eating Disorders as a Cultural Phenomenon

"Fasting would surely come into fashion again at some future date," Kafka prophesies in "A Hunger Artist" (86), a prediction that has come true with a vengeance. The American obsession with dieting has now reached almost epidemic proportions, giving rise to an increased incidence of anorexia and bulimia among college women. Both of these eating disorders are surprisingly recent cultural developments.

In anorexia, victims starve themselves to the point where, in extreme cases, they take on the appearance of concentration camp survivors. Anorexia reflects a morbid fear of becoming overweight, a fear that persists even when body weight is 15 percent below normal. Psychologists have offered numerous theories to explain the dynamics of anorexia, ranging from the quest for control and perfectionism to the unleashing of violence against the self. Fear of awakening sexuality also plays a key role in a young woman's decision to stop eating. The anorectic frequently stops menstruating and, because of hormonal imbalances triggered by starvation, develops downy hair over her body and takes on a masculine appearance.[9] Although the symptoms of anorexia nervosa were first described more than a century ago—the illness was named by the British physician Sir William Gull in

1874—the disease became well known only in the late 1960s. "One might speak of an epidemic illness, only there is no contagious agent; the spread must be attributed to psycho-sociological factors," Hilde Bruch remarks in *The Golden Cage* (1978),[10] one of the first books on anorexia. Joan Jacobs Brumberg argues in *Fasting Girls* that anorexia is "clearly a multidetermined disorder that depends on the individual's biologic vulnerability, psychological predisposition, family, and the social climate."[11]

Bulimia is a newer phenomenon. Marlene Boskind-White and William C. White, Jr., two Cornell University psychologists who studied the bingeing and purging eating habits of female college students, coined the word "bulimarexia" in 1975 to describe the psychological dynamics of "perfectionism, obsessive concern with food and body proportions, isolationism, low self-esteem, and a strong commitment to please others, often at the individual's expense."[12] Most researchers now use the term "bulimia nervosa," or simply "bulimia," to describe this disorder.

Anorexia and bulimia have attracted increasing attention in recent years from clinicians, nutritionists, and feminist scholars (the vast majority of people suffering from these disorders are women), but a veil of secrecy persists. Few first-person accounts of anorexia and bulimia exist, and most anorectics and bulimics cannot bring themselves to speak publicly about their illnesses. When they do share their terrible secrets with a relative or friend, they often feel increased shame and isolation.

Breaking the Silence

One way to break this silence is to encourage students to write diaries about their experiences with eating disorders. "A Hunger Artist" is, of course, a perfect story to read in this context, as is Margaret Atwood's *Edible Woman*,[13] but anorexia and bulimia are so prevalent among college women that they generally submit entries on this subject long before we discuss these texts.

I want to focus in this chapter on five women who were members of the same class; four of them wrote about bulimic behavior, and one wrote about compulsive overeating. None betrayed the skeletal thinness of Kafka's hunger artist, but all discussed the extent to which eating disorders reflected larger conflicts in their lives. They gave me permission to read their diaries to the class, and their writings inspired entries from other students who had never before imagined the "art of fasting."

Diaries on eating disorders illuminate many of the reasons behind self-starvation, and as we shall see, the students offer a variety of explanations involving psychological, cultural, and feminist perspectives. The themes unifying the five women's writings are violence against the female body and the suppression of desire; a profound ambivalence toward food, which is symptomatic of larger issues in students' lives; the need to master inner conflicts and regain self-control; and the search for love, validation, and self-acceptance in a family that is often torn by conflict. Over the years, literally scores of women—but no men—have written diaries about suffering from anorexia and bulimia. Eating disorder diaries are thus female texts. The diaries have been a revelation both to the other students and to me, deepening our understanding of the vexing difficulties of growing up female in the United States.

BRENDA
"It All Started Innocently Enough, a Young Girl Being Concerned with Her Looks and Her Weight"

Brenda, a sophomore, was the first person in the class to write about an eating disorder. Like most of the other women who discussed bulimia, she said that she did not become aware of a problem until long after the onset of its symptoms. She turned in the following diary during the third week of the semester:

A problem which has been with me for over four years, which I had to enter psychotherapy for, is a disorder which affects many young women in our society. The problem became apparent in my sophomore year of high school, and the symptoms persisted until a little over a year ago. I have bulimia.

I don't know how or why it started, but I can remember as far back as eighth grade being overly concerned with my weight and going so far as to use laxatives to control it. The realization that I had an eating disorder never came until two years later, when my symptoms became impossible to ignore. It all started innocently enough, a young girl being concerned with her looks and her weight. However, some of us possess a predisposition toward letting it go beyond control.

I consider myself a somewhat neurotic or compulsive person to begin with; however, factors like my father's being an alcoholic and leaving me when I was very young surely contributed. As I look back, I see the time when I was in high school as being marked by my father's increasing demands to have me back in his life and to somehow be able to control my life. My problems with him, my stress level, and my bulimia all escalated throughout high school.

Sometime in my sophomore or junior year my mother had me put into counseling, which I hated. I stayed with this ridiculous therapist for six months until I declared myself "all better" so I didn't have to see him anymore. I don't believe I learned anything from that man. Within months, my symptoms were so bad that I missed volleyball practices, taking whole boxes of laxatives and bottles of ipecac on the weekends. My blood pressure dropped to almost too low to donate blood, and I started to become very frightened about what I was doing to myself.

The symptoms of the disease were dictating my whole life: I wouldn't go out with friends on certain occasions because I had planned an evening of bingeing and purging. No one but my mother knew. So finally I had to tell her that I would reenter therapy with another doctor. Everyone thought I was killing myself as I fell in and out of major depressions, my therapist occasionally suggesting antidepressant drugs. But gradually my symptoms became less frightening, and I discontinued therapy when I left for college.

Since I've been here at school, pressures have increased tremendously, my relationship with my father has gotten progressively worse (I refuse to speak with him ever again), I haven't seen a therapist since high school, and yet on my own I've managed to live without symptoms for the past year.

I don't really know how to end this journal. I can't thank anyone for the recovery (which I consider lifelong) but myself: my counselor was all right, my parents think I still make myself sick, and my father never cared. I do know that I have a new sense of confidence, and I feel much better about myself than I have in years. I'm a much more independent person than I ever was and feel much better equipped to handle difficulties in my life.

Brenda apparently has little difficulty writing about her experience with bulimia; she writes factually, without embarrassment, guilt, or shame. She closes the diary on a self-confident note, though not before venting anger toward her father, whom she views, as her next diary demonstrates, as a major source of her problems:

Unfortunately, this week I feel totally uninspired as to what to write about. I attribute that to the fact that I've had so much on my mind lately: I am more than behind in most of my classes, have been having the worst time trying to find a job, am in the negatives as far as my finances go, and have been thinking about how to deal with my father. OK, there's a topic—my relationship with my father. Unfortunately, that subject would require a book to cover, but I'll do my best to condense it.

To give you a little history, my parents got married at an early age. When I was a baby, my father left my family. Whether I did when I was younger or not, I don't hold his leaving us against him now. I feel very aware of that and feel that it has no influence on my feelings for him now, even though he thinks that's one of the reasons I resent him. Anyway, until I was twelve years old, he didn't make much of an effort to see me or my mom or my two brothers.

When he did finally try to become a "part of my life," I had already grown distant from him. He didn't just try to see me more often, but any time our plans didn't work out or I was busy one weekend, he projected his guilty feelings onto me by blaming me for the "horrible" way I was treating him and putting him off. For years I fell for this and actually felt guilty—not just with him, but I now have a chronic guilt complex about everything. Eventually, I caught on to what was happening and told him, with a lot of difficulty and a lot of retaliation on his part.

The poor man is a recovering alcoholic who never should have dropped therapy, because he needs it. To give you an example of his mental condition, I'll quote you a telephone conversation we once had:

ME: I only want a passive relationship with you. I don't know you and don't want you to interfere with my life, but I would like for us to be able to get along.

DAD: All you want is a passive relationship? That's your neurosis, Brenda. All of your relationships are passive!

ME: My neurosis?? How do you know about ANY of my relationships? You don't even know me. So, Dad, why don't you tell me about my neurosis and all of my passive relationships. . . .

DAD: No, you tell me, they're your problems and your relationships.

I don't know how to explain it, but the guy just doesn't have a grip. He keeps meticulous track of every letter I have ever sent him, and his computer remembers every letter he's mailed me. Maybe that's good for him, though, because he distorts the past, and he distorts facts to an unreasonable extent. You just can't argue with him when you're dealing from two different decks. He uses me, he abuses me, he promised to pay for college and then decided a month ago to withdraw his offer. Says he wants to be my father but doesn't know how to give or how to love.

I think the reason he's been on my case so much in the past three years is because my brothers refuse to have anything to do with him. The way it is all ending (I hope) is by my refusal to ever accept another phone call or letter from him.

Brenda's diary recalls those written by Mara, Rachel, and Tracey in the preceding chapter. We see the same anger toward the father, the same wish to separate her life from his, the same belief that she has nothing in common with him. Brenda's writings suggest that the sins of the fathers have been a major factor in her illness and that her father has exacerbated the situation by labeling her problems a neurosis. For this reason, Brenda can see no hope of reconciliation or compromise with him, no possibility of a useful dialogue. She closes the entry with the vow never to let her father back into her life. She never returned to the subject of her father in any of her later writings.

MARCY
"I Felt There Was Power in the Boyish Figure and Weakness in Girlish Curves"

During the same week in which Brenda wrote about her problem with bulimia, Marcy, a senior, turned in the first of four diaries about the difficulty of being a woman in a patriarchal society. She begins by referring to Freud's antifeminist concept of penis envy, insisting that women have been victimized not by anatomy but by culture:

Although I would be the first person to object to Freud's theory of penis envy and the notion that all women have an innate psychological wish to be a man, I must admit that I personally have always felt a certain dissatisfaction with my gender. I am quite certain, however, that this is entirely for social (not psychological) reasons.

I was a tomboy until I was thirteen years old. There are two incidents which I remember very clearly that served to confuse and upset my understanding and acceptance of my gender. The first of these events occurred on a very hot day when I was five years old and playing in a church playground. I was of course playing with the boys because the girls were much too boring (wearing frilly dresses and playing with dolls were not for me—athletics in the dirt were more my style). All the boys decided to take off their shirts because of the heat. So I proceeded to remove my shirt also. Well, you would think that a creature from another planet was standing there from the reaction these boys had. They pointed and laughed, saying, "Tits! Your tits are showing!" Having the limited experience of a five-year-old, I was quite sure that I had no idea what "tits" were. I remember surveying their bodies and then my own and not finding a single difference. I did not understand when they explained to me that since I was a girl, I was not free to cool off on a hot day.

The other incident that stands out in my memory is an argument that ensued between the boys and girls in the second-grade cafeteria. I was sitting at the boys' table as usual when the fight broke out. The boys were calling the girls "corroded," and the girls were telling the boys that they had "cooties." The basic premise was that girls thought they were better, and boys thought they were. There I was, right in the middle of all of this, not knowing which side to take. I knew that I was a girl by definition and that by insulting them I would be insulting myself, and yet I really believed that boys were better. I just sat there silent and confused.

I'm really not sure why I have chosen to discuss these particular things for this diary. I only know that I often still feel that familiar confusion. Why am I valued more if I am physically attractive than intelligent? Why am I expected to be domestic when inside I feel like any other bachelor living alone? The fact is that all women's psyches are messed up by the traditional sex-role stereotypes.

A good example of this is the lack of heroines in the movies. Women sit in movies theaters and identify with the heroes because the director created the movie so that the spectator would identify with the hero. However, at the same time, she knows that she is not like him and cannot be because she is a woman. The majority of the women she sees on the screen (or in the media in general) are portrayed as helpless passive victims who need to be rescued by men. They are also sexually exploited and shown as objects for the satisfaction of male scopophilia or voyeurism. Women then must identify themselves as objects. The internalization of these values can have a significantly destructive impact on the female psyche.

This is a very brief explanation of the psychological confusion I feel just from being a woman. I don't want to be an object or a victim. I want to be a hero, and I've always known I could be, but society keeps trying to tell me that I cannot. That is why I sometimes still wish I were a man. If I were a man, I would not have to face the confusion and the oppression. Sorry Freud, it's not for the penis.

Continuing these meditations in her next diary, Marcy reveals the ways in which women are victimized by a culture that reduces them to a sexual object—a thin object, she adds:

This week I am going to continue what I wrote about last week—that is, the female psyche in a misogynistic society. In particular I want to discuss body perception and eating disorders.

The reason I choose this topic is because it affects nearly every single female I know. (Although I'm not sure about the nationwide statistics, I'm sure this is indicative.) The main problem is the media. It tells us that women should be thin thin thin. Everything is dietetic, and only thin women are shown as models. But the fact is that women have naturally a good deal of fat on their bodies. The result of this dichotomy between media ideal and reality is a society of women obsessed with food and weight.

Perhaps this does not sound so awful. However, in addition to all the deaths caused by bulimia and anorexia every year, even the women who seem "healthy" are victims. All of the women who want that dessert so badly but gather all the willpower in themselves to say no, all the women who have dessert and then feel as guilty as if they had committed a sin, all the women who go to the gym everyday and sweat until they dehydrate—these are the victims as well. Even I am a victim.

I believe that my story is most frightening because if you've ever seen me, you know that I am very skinny. When I was fifteen years old, and I had just developed hips, I wanted to cut them off. This was obviously the product of my still wishing I was a male in a world that favored males. If I had hips and breasts, how was I going to deny my female sexuality?

So I set about to get rid of them. I tried all different methods. I would go a few days with no food and then have some soup or something. Then I found out that all you have to do is vomit afterward and you could eat all you want. So I did this for a while. And don't think I did any of this alone. Two of my close friends, both as thin as I, joined me in my weight loss attempts. An objective observer would probably think that this was a normal stage of development for young women. But obviously, it is not. It is the unhealthy and life-threatening reaction of women to the bogus beauty ideals created by men.

My best friend has a fabulous body. She is thin but not too thin, and she has nice curves. It is the saddest thing to see her grab a handful of her own flesh and look at it with such venomous disgust that you would think it was a cancer or something. You can see nearly every woman do this same thing if you go into the women's locker room in a gym. They get on the scale and pray that more of their bodies will be gone. They literally wish to diminish themselves. They learn to hate their female bodies so much that they will go to any pains to make them disappear. "I don't care if I kill myself doing it, I'm going to burn off those extra pounds." Sound familiar? To me it does.

I have finally learned to love my body because it is the only one I have, and so it is to me beautiful. I think all women need to learn to feel this way about themselves and to ignore the message from the media that says, If you're fat, you're no good. If it took me this long, and I happen to be skinny, how long will it take more voluptuous women? The prospects are bleak.

With each diary, Marcy extends her analysis of a patriarchal society's pernicious influence on the female psyche. In the first entry she explores the dangers of gender stereotyping; in the second she investigates the relationship between body perception and eating disorders; and in the third she responds to a question I had raised in one of my comments: to what extent does a woman's dissatisfaction with her body reflect a fear of sexuality? The question angered Marcy, but she continued to think about it, soon discovering a troubling pattern in her life: an attraction to "male chauvinists."

Whereas in the previous entry she identifies the "media" as the major cause of eating disorders, she now writes about a subject much closer to home—a father's sexist influence on his daughter:

In last week's diary you asked whether I was afraid of my female sexuality. My first response to this was anger. I was defensive. I thought to myself, "I have completely normal and healthy sexual relationships with my boyfriends, past and present." But then I realized that my fear is not on that level. What I mean is that privately, in the safety of my close relationships, I have no problem with my sexuality—in fact, I enjoy it. However, in public situations, in front of the whole world, it troubles me to be female. I guess this must be because of the many factors about misogyny in our society that I discussed in my previous journals, and also because my father is a big male chauvinist sexist man. I have resented his attitude, and only recently did I realize its effect on me.

And yet, when I think about the serious boyfriends I've had in my life, all are very different but share one trait—that is, they are male chauvinists. Consciously, I find it inconceivable that I would be attracted to a man who reminds me of my father, and yet here is this evidence. In fact, my first boyfriend reminds me exactly of my image of my father at his age. When I first met him, he was wearing his college football uniform. My father also played football in college, and in most of the photographs I have of him he is also wearing a football uniform.

There are other things about my boyfriend that remind me of my father as well, but I have never acknowledged the similarities. My relationship to my boyfriend was unusual too. He loved me much more than I did him; actually, I don't think I ever loved him at all. At times I was even sickened by him and his attitudes, and sometimes by his physical being. At the same time I liked being with him and being nauseated by him. When I think back, this is very self-destructive behavior. I wonder if this diary is making sense. Some things are easier to speak of than to write.

After hearing Brenda's and Marcy's diaries read aloud, other women in the class began writing diaries about eating disorders. Marcy was surprised by the number of these students, and in her fourth diary, written in tones ranging from righteous indignation to caustic sarcasm, she offers additional details of her obsession with thinness:

I was never diagnosed as having anorexia or bulimia, but I had, in mild form, some of their symptoms. As I mentioned in another diary, when I was fifteen years old my body started to change from boyishly skinny to round (but still skinny). I became very disconcerted. For reasons that I did not understand until later, I felt there was power in the boyish figure and weakness in girlish curves. I absolutely despised fat or flab of any sort. Fat people repulsed me. To this day I am very turned off by any flab on people, and I go out only with thin (some would say skinny) men.

Anyway, I decided to combat my developing body by controlling my diet. My most specific memories of dieting and purging were at sleep-away camp, where I could get away with not eating because no one would monitor me (like my mom would at home, who has always been telling me that I am too skinny). Now that I think about this, she gave me an awful lot of attention when the subject of weight and eating came up, and perhaps it was more of this type of attention that I sought when I tried to reduce myself further.

But I think the main reason was a fear of sexuality—a fear of turning into one of those objectified nonhuman things sprawled out all over the pages of dirty magazines and elsewhere. I guess I thought that if I turned into that, others would take over control of my body, and I would no longer have any control. I think that almost all women who starve themselves do so as a form of controlling their own life. It's something that certainly no one else can control, the "rewards" are visible, and sometimes people even comment on them. Sometimes women lose so much weight that they stop menstruating, thus having another visible sign of their own control over their bodies as well as accomplishing the feat of reversing the development of female sexuality.

I remember being really hungry and using willpower not to eat and telling myself to "fight" the temptation to eat. I also remember feeling victorious and powerful after a full day of not eating. When my stomach was so flat that it was concave and my ribs were sticking out, I was strong. I used to drink a lot of Diet Pepsi. I always had a can in my hand. I know this one girl who used to buy twenty kinds of diet soda, and that would be all she ate all day. She would pretend that the different flavors were a variety of fruits and foods.

I practiced regurgitating my food every once in a while when I felt that I had eaten an unearthly amount of food, like a whole pint of ice cream. I think I would have done it more, but I really found it to be most unpleasant, so I used that technique only for emergencies. Many times after I ate a big meal I would feel bloated, and I would hate my body and think it was too big. And yet my whole life people, both family and strangers, are constantly telling me how skinny I am. In fact, I have often heard men say of me, "She would be attractive if she gained ten pounds," or "Yuk! she's way too skinny." And I am never offended by these remarks.

In a way, they give me a sense of freedom because I think, "OK, I'm not fat now and I can even enjoy a few good pig-outs and people will still think I look all right." But I know that I will not be happy with myself if I gained ten pounds, even if the whole world told me how good I looked. I just feel more comfortable in a skinny body. Sometimes I even feel sorry for women with a big chest and a big belly or thighs, but I guess some of them are used to it, and I really believe that they should and could learn to love their own bodies. Maybe not, though, with all the "thin is in" propaganda.

I heard a comedienne do a funny routine. She was talking about how it used to be fashionable for women to be all flabby and fat, like in the classical paintings. She said, "That must have been great. All we women had to do was sit around and eat pastries and get painted. If anyone told us we were gaining a little weight, we could say, 'Damn straight, I'm posing for Rubens this afternoon, now pass me a cannoli, you piece of shit!' "

I don't use food as a means of control anymore. Now I try to eat healthily without gaining or losing weight. But when I hear the diaries of other women who still have these problems in severe ways, I feel really bad for them. I know that a part of it is due to the media images of ideal women and such. I also know that they must have other problems in their lives to contribute to this disorder.

I wish I could help them, but I don't believe that I can. I think that part of the reason that my condition never got really serious was because my best friend had severe anorexia and was in the hospital for most of our high school years. She almost died from it, and I may have wanted strength or attention, but I did not want to die. She is better now, and I think that therapy helped her a lot. But she still watches her weight and diets. It is sad. That is all I can say. It is very sad.

LAURIE

"It Is My Deepest, Darkest, Most Painful Secret"

Unlike Brenda and Marcy, Laurie, a senior, was still caught in the binge-purge cycle. Bulimia was an ongoing problem, creating intense guilt and shame as well as ominous physical symptoms, and she found it painfully difficult to share her secret with anyone. The two diaries she wrote on being bulimic contained an urgency apparent to everyone:

> I don't mean to bore you or overemphasize a subject that so many students have chosen to focus their diaries on. In fact, I hesitated to put these thoughts on paper because what I'm about to discuss is something I've kept locked up inside of me for so long; it is something I seem unable to control. None of my friends, housemates, or even my boyfriend knows what I am suffering from and what I'm struggling to overcome every single day. It is my deepest, darkest, most painful secret.
>
> In many ways, hearing that I am not alone with my problem and realizing that others can comprehend what I'm going through gave me the courage to write this journal. If you are still in the dark as to what I am talking about, it is bulimia, more accurately called bulimarexia. It is an extremely destructive and horrible eating disorder that I have been battling for over five years. More than being an embarrassing addiction, bulimarexia is life threatening, and though I am fully aware of this fact, it still is a problem I am incapable of conquering. If people can understand how strong an addiction smoking, biting your nails, or drinking is, then they can understand the seriousness of being bulimarexic.
>
> It starts out as something innocent, a few girlfriends discovering this great weight-loss plan where you can eat as much as you want and never gain weight. What an ideal way to stay thin—thin being the only way for women. Unfortunately for me, this seemingly innocent weight-loss plan progressed into a sick obsession that began to rule my life. Food became an enemy as well as my closest friend; it was something that could make me feel so good and so at ease, yet it was also something that could make me feel ugly, inadequate, and miserable.
>
> I don't know exactly why this problem began. I know it has strong connections with low self-esteem and the desire to be perfect. The media only serve to perpetuate eating disorders, for television, magazines, and billboards brainwash women into believing one needs to

have a beautiful face, a beautiful figure, and beautiful hair to be desirable, to be loved, to be accepted. So much emphasis is placed on appearances and thinness in our society. Women are constantly bombarded with messages that they are too fat, too ugly, too wrinkly, too flabby, too greasy: the list is infinite.

I learned early on to internalize and believe these messages sent out in our society. I learned to hate my body, and I learned to take extremely drastic measures to change and improve myself.

I want so badly to overcome this addiction. I desperately want to love and accept myself as I am, with all my flaws and imperfections. To say reaching this point is difficult is a total understatement. Recently, I began group therapy with about nine other girls approximately the same age as I am; we are all suffering from the same eating disorder. We have all admitted that we want to be perfect; we all want so deeply to be that ideal woman whom the media promotes. We all come from similar backgrounds, and all of us have excelled as students. One girl just graduated from Barnard and another from Smith. So, it is quite obvious that bulimarexics are not idiots; most of them are bright, hard-working, ambitious women who simply cannot accept themselves as they are.

I hope that together we can sort through our problems and help each other win this terrible battle. I don't want to die, which is a fear I think about every day. I don't want to go into cardiac arrest or have all my teeth rot and fall out of my mouth. I'm so tired of living with this addiction and hiding it from everyone I am close to. I pray that I can overcome it. I want to be normal; I want to love me as me.

The diary that I handed in two weeks ago, which was read aloud to the class, about "my deepest, darkest, most painful secret," was the first time I have ever discussed my problem with anyone outside of my immediate family, my therapist, and my therapy group. Finally writing about my eating disorder and letting people know about my secret life was a catharsis for me; it felt as if some huge weight was lifted off my shoulders. I honestly cried as I wrote it, realizing just how hard it is coping with bulimia. I cried at how pathetic I am, bingeing and purging day after day, knowing that it can eventually kill me or at least destroy my body.

My therapist had always recommended writing in some sort of journal or diary as a way to help me overcome bulimia. She told me that writing your thoughts down on paper would help you understand yourself more fully and would also help you understand your problem. I never took the time to write, however. I didn't believe keeping a journal would change anything. Writing that diary made me realize how important keeping a journal is; I can "see" myself better, and it just feels good in general to release your pain, fears, and thoughts on paper.

I felt it was important that my diary be read aloud to the class primarily because this problem that affects so many women is frequently misunderstood. I also wanted the other women in the class who may suffer from the same eating disorder to know that they are not alone; I feel for them, I know how deep the pain runs, I know how frightened and helpless they feel. After class a few weeks ago I heard one woman tell another person that she was the one whose diary on bulimia was read aloud. I give her so much credit for having the courage to reveal her identity. I do not feel that I am ready to let people know that I am also bulimic. I'm too scared. I suppose I'm too concerned about what people will think of me.

I wish more people would be aware of this horrible addiction and understand how extremely difficult it is to stop. My brother always says to me, "Why would anyone want to throw up? Puking is disgusting. Why don't you just control yourself?" Believe me, I desperately wish I could control myself. But as I mentioned in that diary, bulimia is an addiction as strong as being addicted to cocaine, cigarettes, or alcohol. It's not something you can just stop without help. I used to think I could stop whenever I wanted. I never thought I needed professional help. Shrinks are for crazy people.

After the problem started getting worse and I found myself completely dominated by bulimia and the whole evil binge-purge cycle, I knew I needed help. I didn't want to acknowledge the fact that I had this sickness, that I was a full-fledged bulimic, so I kept ignoring my parents when they told me to get help. My dad would leave phone numbers of therapists in my bedroom, but I wouldn't call.

Do you know what finally made me give in and call and get help for myself? I went to the dentist, and I had nine cavities. He told me that the enamel on my teeth had been worn off. The same week I had gone to the dentist, one of my teeth shattered from biting into a sandwich. I mean, I never used to get cavities. Like a lead brick it hit me: this was just one sign of how I was destroying my body. I was literally terrified that I was going to lose all of my teeth.[14]

The next day after my dentist appointment, I called the doctor. Something had to be done—enough was enough. I don't want to die! Seeking therapy is an essential part to conquering eating disorders. I do not believe people can cure themselves on their own. I hope all of the women in the class are involved in some sort of therapy now. If not, please go. I know how difficult it is coming to terms with the fact that you have a problem. Just do it. I'm glad I did.

Since I wrote that diary, certain things have changed in my life. In a way, opening up in the diary gave me the courage to open up to my boyfriend. He and I have been dating for over two years. Though we've been together for so long, almost living together for a year, he has never been aware of my problem with bulimia. I kept it a well-hidden secret, and that was no easy task. In fact, he had no idea that I was in therapy twice a week.

I constantly had to lie to him about where I was and what I was doing. The fact that I had to lie to him used to eat away at me; I walked around with a guilty conscience all of the time as well as the fear that one day he would catch me. I wanted to tell him; I wanted to share this ugly part of my life with him, but I could not. I was too ashamed. I didn't want him to think that I was crazy or mentally ill or unstable. I wanted him to think he had the greatest girlfriend, who was "all together" and had her head on straight. I thought if he knew about my problem, he would end things. He would think I was too weak a person to date if I was seeing a therapist.

Last Saturday I was in a miserable mood all day. I had spent two hours talking to my therapy group about bulimia and about hiding it from my friends. I knew I had to tell my boyfriend; I couldn't keep lying to him and deceiving him. It was driving me crazy. Driving to go out to dinner one night this week, I said to him, "There's something I haven't told you that I've wanted to for so long." He grabbed the wheel so tight. He thought I was going to tell him that I cheated on him. When I came out and told him that I had an eating disorder, he seemed relieved; bulimia was easier for him to swallow than infidelity.

When it sank in, he was rather surprised. He wanted to know for how long I had the problem, what I am doing about it, can I stop it, and why didn't I tell him sooner. Well, to make a long story short, it was the best thing I ever did telling him. He was so compassionate and so caring. He said he would help me get through it, that he loves me too much to give up on me now. He even asked me if he could come to therapy with me to learn more about the eating disorder. It feels so good not to have to hide it from him any longer, and to know that he still loves me. I think telling my boyfriend and talking about my eating disorder via these diaries are helping me move closer to conquering the problem. More than anything I want to be normal and eat normally. I want to learn to love and accept myself, no matter what I look like.

Laurie's preoccupation with food shows up in her similes and metaphors. Lying to her boyfriend used to "eat away" at her; when she tells him the truth, while driving to a restaurant for dinner, he feels relieved, since bulimia is easier for him to "swallow" than infidelity. And in disclosing her obsession with self-starvation, Laurie feels "as if some huge weight was lifted off my shoulders."

JORIE
"I Am Not as Ashamed of My Bulimia As I Am of the Reasons behind Being Bulimic"

Jorie, a senior, wrote three diaries about growing up in a troubled family. She saw her problems with bulimia and drug and alcohol addiction as part of a larger pattern of self-destructiveness. She viewed the decision to enter therapy twenty months ago as a turning point in her life:

> When we were discussing Kafka's *The Metamorphosis* and "The Judgment," I could relate strongly with both Gregor and Georg and how they felt about their families. The one aspect that I could relate strongly with was Gregor's wish to hurt his family because of the way they had hurt him. I feel, like Gregor, that had my parents maybe showed me love instead of constant abuse, maybe my own actions would not have been so severe.
>
> One of the first acts of defiance that I remember was running away from home. I was thirteen and had been using drugs for about three years. My aunt and uncle lived two hours away from home, and I knew that they understood my situation with my parents and would let me stay with them. I left my home and started to hitchhike to their home.

Some woman picked me up and lectured me the whole time that I was in her car about the dangers of a young girl hitchhiking. She dropped me off about a half hour away from my relatives' house. As luck would have it, my uncle was on his way to my parents' house. He picked me up, and I begged him to let me stay in his house. He agreed, knowing what it was like for me in my house. He said I could stay for a week, and he would work on cooling my parents off.

When I returned home, there were no hugs, no asking if I was all right, just glares from my parents. My uncle and aunt left the house quickly because they knew what was going to happen. My aunt later told me that she could feel the hate radiating from me. She said that it frightened her that I could be so angry at such a young age.

I seriously contemplated suicide throughout my pre- and early teens. I felt that there was no way that I could live up to my parents' expectations. I felt, however, that if I could hurt them as much as they had been hurting me, then just maybe they would wake up and realize what they were doing. My actions to hurt them involved a lot of drug use. I could not commit suicide because I could not risk my uncle and aunt's finding me; I was not out to hurt them, just my parents.

Instead, I became a drug addict. Addiction is a slow suicide. I was definitely out to kill myself. I am also bulimic. Although my excuses for bingeing and purging were to stay thin, it was just another way that I could be self-destructive. The whole time I was active in my drug and food addictions, I copped an "I'll show them attitude." I wanted to make my parents sorry for the rotten way they had been treating me.

I could relate to Gregor's metamorphosis. All my life I was reminded what a nothing I was. As a result I became a severe isolator. My favorite thing to do, when I couldn't get high, was to go to my room around 7:30 at night, crawl into bed, and daydream until I fell asleep. This started when I was about ten and ended when I was sixteen. My lack of self-esteem led to my actions of self-destruction. This is definitely apparent in my drug addiction and bulimia. I am also a defeated perfectionist. I will start a project and never finish it, or I will not start a project because I know that I cannot do it perfectly. This is self-destructive because it prevents me from accomplishing anything.

Therapy has done wonders for me as far as my awareness goes. Because my parents' actions were what they were, I have the responsibility to recover from this abuse. I have also come to realize that they are sick people. In a way, I am getting even with them because they will have to live with their miserable little selves while I have the chance to recover. However, like Gregor and Georg, I do love my parents.

Last week when reading Franz Kafka's "Letter to His Father," I felt tears welling up in my eyes. I could really relate to the letter, how Kafka felt toward his father. My father carries many of the same characteristics that Kafka's did.

When Kafka discussed the family dinner table etiquette, I had a rush of memories and feelings. Dinner was always a stressful time in my family. We were not allowed to sing, and God forbid we act the least bit "silly." Though those were the expected norms, hardly ever do I remember a meal in my family that did not end up in a screaming, raging fight. These fights were either between my mother and father, my mother and me, my father and me, or my sister and me.

I could identify with Kafka's father's double standards at the table. While we were expected to act like little adults, my father was allowed to make any racist or misogynistic statement that he felt like making. If my sister criticized Mom's cooking, she received a verbal reprimand, I would receive a verbal and/or physically abusive response, and my dad's criticism was, of course, ignored.

Like Kafka, I never felt capable of living up to my father's set of laws for me. For one thing, I was very feminine. The only thing worse, to my father, was not being a boy. I could understand Kafka's pain regarding the annoyance that he felt he caused his father. I always felt that my father thought I was an annoyance. He was in his late forties when I was born. I was not only unplanned by my parents, I was also another girl.

I have a lot of shame-based issues involving my father. I feel that the only way that I can be at peace with my father is to resolve the shame that is so binding. Like Kafka, I need to hear my father say that I am not guilty. Then, I think, my shame (some of it, anyway) will start working its way out of my feelings. I know I am not guilty, but at the same time I am willing to accept what guilt I actually own.

This week my diary is on eating disorders. I never thought of my eating disorder as a topic of interest; I see it as something I am stuck with and have to deal with on a daily basis. I have always been hung up on my weight. My earliest memory of being self-conscious of my weight is when I was six. I remember the school nurse saying what my weight was, and immediately I felt inadequate, fat. I believe that my eating disorder is a disease, and I will always have it.

I have been abstinent from my symptoms for about fifteen months, but I am still bulimic. I was active in my eating disorder from the time I was ten to the time I was twenty. I am not as ashamed of my bulimia as I am of the reasons behind being bulimic. I don't really remember bulimia being a deep dark secret, but I guess it was because I felt so relieved when I finally admitted it was a problem for me.

Before I was in recovery, I was really embarrassed about my food consumption. I did try to conceal it from my friends. I come from a food-addicted family, so my consumption did not have to be hidden from them. I didn't really have to hide my purging. My purging was a starvation that lasted anywhere from a week to six weeks. I would stop eating. It's scary now, but at the time everyone used to compliment my willpower to stick to my "new diet."

My parents found out about my eating disorder after we had been in family counseling for my drug addiction. Our counselor explained to my parents that it is more common than uncommon for women drug addicts to be bulimic and vice versa. My bulimia isn't as painful as the underlying issues. I have been in therapy for almost two years now. It has not been easy, but it's worth every ounce of pain I have been through. I would highly recommend therapy to anyone.

The origins of my eating disorder are multifold. People will have an eating disorder as a result of being sexually abused; it keeps the bulimic in control of how attractive her body is. People will also be bulimic as a result of the lack of control that they feel regarding their bodies. I was physically and emotionally abused and was never (rarely) allowed to make my own decisions. People will live what they learn.

I come from a dysfunctional family; everyone is addicted either to food or to some other drug. Until I started recovery, I had negative self-esteem. Today it is slowly being rebuilt. My sexuality took a beating. For a long time I was asexual. As my disease progressed, so did my screwed-up sexuality; I also became addicted to sex. The longer I am in recovery, the clearer my sexuality is becoming. My relationship with my parents still has a lot of kinks, but they are being straightened out.

I originally wrote a diary on the subject of addiction, not specifically mentioning bulimia, because they are the same thing. I wrote about it because it is easy to analyze them in a Freudian perspective. I can see a lot of parallels between myself and Kafka's hunger artist. I have a misconception of the word "perfect." I also have a lot of issues with my dad. Psychoanalytically, by starving himself the hunger artist is indicating that he does not like sex. Being the good bulimic that I am, I am addicted to sex. Just like with food, I indulge, then feel guilty.

I don't remember how I felt when I first wrote the diary about my eating disorder. Knowing that other people in the class have the problem doesn't affect me. I am secure in my support system already, so when I hear other people mention that they are also bulimic, I can relate, but it doesn't have the soothing effect of relief. It was easy to write about the eating disorder because of the guaranteed confidentiality. I don't know if I would have been disappointed if you didn't read my diary in class.

I have been as honest as I am capable of being when writing about the experiences. My experience in recovery has been that war stories are just that—war stories. Bragging does not get me better, honesty does. The audience for my diaries has been me. Writing is very therapeutic for me; it helps me get past my shame barrier. I am really glad that there is the confidentiality when reading the diaries. I would feel awkward if people in class knew who I was.

PAULA
"I Binged and Binged but Never Quite Made It to the Purge"

Paula, a junior, wrote about the relationship between masochism and the search for love and attention. Her problem with overeating made her almost wish that she was "naturally" anorexic or bulimic. In her early diaries she wrote about her ambivalence toward her father, whom she resented for divorcing her mother and withdrawing from his family. In the first of three entries included here, Paula reports how she began to inflict pain upon herself in order to gratify a self-destructive urge:

I wonder, is masochism uncommon? Not masochism in the context of deriving sexual pleasure from self-inflicted pain, but just plain old pleasure from experiencing pain one purposefully inflicts on oneself. I am a masochist. There is sometimes an ulterior motive for my masochistic tendencies—attention. It's strange to admit this, but I have before, and probably will again, hurt myself to gain the attention of someone else.

The first time I did it was when I was in high school, and I remember being angry at my dad for spending too much time with his wife, with whom I did not get along. It wasn't so much the time he spent with her, it was the time he didn't spend with me, and the fact that he was in some ways becoming very much like her and seemed to want to push me away.

While I was at work one afternoon during a weekend I was visiting him, I picked up a single-edged razor blade and started slicing up the backs of my hands. Nothing worthy of stitches, but I did draw blood. My dad did eventually notice at some point during the weekend, and I shrugged it off as being bored at work. Funny, I don't remember if I achieved the desired effect—more attention from my dad.

I repeated this hand-slashing action a few times during high school and my first year of college, primarily as an attention getter from my parents. Sophomore year, I remember trying to cut myself with a plastic knife, which didn't work too well as far as breaking the skin, but it was painful, and the pain made me feel better about whatever it was that was troubling me.

Another time I cut myself was when I thought my boyfriend was becoming attracted again to his old girlfriend, who was in one of his classes. Her presence most certainly threatened me, and I needed reassurance that he loved me and not her. One afternoon at work, where I have access to single-edged razor blades, I decided that cuts on my hands would make me feel better and command attention from my boyfriend. This time it worked—not only did the pain make me feel better, but my boyfriend became very concerned and started to show all the things he said he felt about me. Why does this kind of pain give me pleasure? If it were just the guilt I mean to impose on others, it would not be as difficult to understand. At any rate, it would be interesting to see what Sigmund Freud would make of this case study.

Like the other women in the class, I obsess over my weight. I was always overweight as a child, and as I grew older, my weight always bothered me, but never really enough to do much about it. After my weight peaked in my freshman year of college, I decided to do something drastic—go on a liquid diet. I stuck to it very well and lost fifty-five pounds, and I actually felt good about myself; many of my depressing moods were gone, and I was much happier.

Going off the diet was scary at first, being a noneater for a period of four months, but eventually I got over my fear of eating (actually, fear of gaining weight, fear of waking up one day just as fat as when I began) and basically lived like a normal person again. Over a course of months I noticed I was gaining a little weight, especially after I began using a prescription medication with a side effect of possible weight gain. I didn't gain all of the weight back, not even half, but I returned to the constant state of depression and unhappiness, and everything around me was falling apart. I tried on my own to lose the extra weight, weight that was not even really noticed by any of my friends, but I had a very difficult time losing it, despite the fact that I was sticking to a low-calorie, low-fat diet.

So I called a nutritionist in the office of the doctor who had supervised my liquid diet and made an appointment to see her, thinking that I would appeal to her to let me return to the diet. All the time I knew that in the long run I was actually avoiding my problem by taking the easy way out, but it was the only thing that I felt I could do to make me mentally stable and not on the verge of being suicidal. The nutritionist agreed with me about the avoidance thing but saw how emotionally distressed I was and agreed to let me return to the program.

I did very well on it a second time, but one thing strange seemed to be occurring: I kept dreaming that I was eating. It started with my housemate, who told me she had a dream that I was eating ice cream—one of my favorite foods. I laughed and forgot about it, until I had a dream that I had eaten more than just ice cream. I woke up in a cold sweat because I thought I had actually cheated on the diet but then realized that it had just been a dream.

I had another dream that I ate ice cream, and then a third dream that I ate a meal. If I found myself desiring food at a conscious level, I can understand how I might dream about eating it. But on this diet I do not experience hunger or desire for any food—which is one of the reasons why it is so easy for me not to cheat, or even want to cheat. If I longed to eat when I smelled food, or saw food, I could understand why I might dream about it. But I can certainly say that I am lacking any desire for it.

I can go out to dinner with people, look at a menu, and plan out what I would eat if I were eating: it's kind of a joke with my friends, who are used to this. I can sit through a meal and watch people eat without any problems. I don't even desire ice cream, which could very well be my favorite food, and watch my housemate eat it almost nightly. So why am I dreaming about it? I know that dreams are manifestations of unconscious wants, but in this case it doesn't even make sense why I would want food even unconsciously. I must lose weight, and I am in the mind-set for it. Why am I having these dreams?

Sure, I've had an eating disorder—I always ate too much. I binged and binged but never quite made it to the purge. Being a fat person was never fun. I always wished that I was naturally anorexic or bulimic; I used to think, "Boy, how could being too thin be a problem? I would kill to have their problems!" I always envisioned eating disorders as purely physical problems, but after hearing the journals for the past few weeks, I now understand that there are psychological and emotional components to the disorders, and not just physical symptoms.

I must admit that part of me still maintains a desire to have the physical attributes of anorexia or bulimia, but that is largely a reaction to this culture's emphasis on being perfect. I feel guilty for my ignorance of these disorders, which caused my many jokes about them.

Hearing the journals did make me feel uncomfortable, because I have essentially been poking fun at something that should not be taken lightly. I can certainly relate to the feeling of containing a "deep secret" about their disorder, for I did the same thing, except my secret was that I was eating almost whatever I could but pretending that I wasn't. I would deny eating junk food that mysteriously disappeared and would try to carefully rearrange the remaining food so that it looked like it hadn't been touched. I always felt miserable after I binged, but I guess that feeling lifted before I felt the need to get rid of the food I had just eaten.

I have since participated in a rapid weight loss program and have lost a lot of weight, and people who never knew me fat can't even picture me that way, but I still have no problem picturing myself as fat. I am in a constant struggle to keep my weight down, and if I gain weight, I get very depressed. To stay thin I must constantly watch what I eat and make sure that I do not lapse back into my old eating habits—which is sometimes very hard to do. In this way I can certainly understand why an anorectic or bulimic is never satisfied with her appearance, because I suffer from the same complex. I only hope that hearing the journals of others with the same condition has helped them in some way, and that my journal does not sound like I am reducing their problem, or even encouraging it, but serves as another viewpoint of someone who can understand a bit of what they have experienced.

Brenda, Marcy, Laurie, Jorie, and Paula recount different stories in their diaries, yet each would agree that culture plays a powerful role in compelling women to reduce their bodies in order to satisfy patriarchal notions of beauty. Anorexia and bulimia are cultural illnesses, rarely seen in developing countries where food is scarce, and rampant among middle- and upper-class women in developed countries. For all five women, the impulse toward fasting had less to do with the rejection of food than with the craving for another form of nourishment—love, approval, validation. Violence against the body represented their response to the weighty conflicts in their lives.

Although researchers such as Janet Surrey suggest that women with eating disorders have problematic relationships with their mothers,[15] none of the five students revealed this in her diary—perhaps because, by criticizing their mothers, the daughters feared cutting themselves off from a major support system. Instead, four of the five cited a troubled relationship with their father as a serious problem in their lives. The diaries portray the fathers as alcoholic, sexually or physically abusive, controlling or neglectful, and noncommunicative. Like Kafka, who unsuccessfully sought his father's approval— "My writing was all about you," he admitted in "Letter to His Father," "all I did there, after all, was to bemoan what I could not bemoan upon your breast" (219)—the women believed that they could not establish a meaningful dialogue with their fathers.

Other Diaries on Eating Disorders

The five women were not alone in writing about eating disorders. Three other female students wrote about being anorexic or bulimic in the past, one of them requiring hospitalization for several weeks. Other students said that, although they themselves did not suffer from eating disorders, they knew people who did. One woman, exasperated by what she felt was an abnormal emphasis upon anorexia and bulimia in her classmates' diaries, wrote about how a recent experience confirmed what she was hearing in the classroom:

> Last week as I sat in class and listened to the other diaries being read, I couldn't believe my ears. The very first day of the semester I walked into the classroom and observed my new classmates. Everyone seemed fairly normal. Who knew that I was sitting in the midst of bulimics, drug addicts, sex fiends, and some very disturbed individuals? I don't mean to sound degrading or anything. I understand that many people have different kinds of problems. It's just that I've never known anyone with such serious problems—or at least I never knew about them. My eyes were opened to this fact this weekend.
>
> I learned something that was very disturbing to me. I had gone to a really great party Saturday night where, of course, like countless other college gala events, grain alcohol was served. My best friend at school became violently ill and vomited all over the backyard. I stood with her and tried to comfort her, telling her that getting sick was no big deal and that it happens to people all the time. It was then that she decided to reveal her deep, dark secret to me.
>
> You guessed it. She told me that she used to be bulimic. I was shocked. Even after hearing the countless journals of bulimic girls in class, I was horrified to learn that one of my closest friends felt that she had to hurt herself this way just to have a good body. She also told me that everyone in her family is heavy. She must've been afraid that she, too, would be cursed with love handles and cellulite—so afraid that every night she stuck her finger down her throat as insurance that it wouldn't happen to her. She was very drunk that night, and I don't even know if she remembers that she told me. I've been afraid to bring it up. I guess it's because I really don't know what to say to her.

The Prevalence of Eating Disorders

The last diary raises three important issues that must be addressed. First, how can a class that seemed "fairly normal" on the first day of the semester contain so many "disturbed" individuals? Was this a representative class?

Second, how did Brenda, Marcy, Laurie, Jorie, and Paula evaluate the experience of writing about food conflicts? Finally, how did the other students in the class, particularly the men who had never given much thought to eating disorders, react to these diaries?

To begin with, a majority of the women and *all* of the men were astonished by the number of people who wrote about having eating disorders. Many of the afflicted women were also surprised by this. To determine how many people identified themselves as having an eating disorder, I sent around an anonymous questionnaire at the end of the semester asking male and female students to evaluate their eating patterns. Based on the results of the questionnaire, eight out of the twenty-five women in the class, or 32 percent, believed they had exhibited anorexic or bulimic behavior at one time or another—a figure that is almost double the average percentage of students (17) who write about eating disorders in my other classes. Of the remaining women, six indicated that they knew another person, usually a relative, friend, or roommate, who suffered from an eating disorder. Only one of the ten men in the class wrote about having a problem with food—nighttime overeating.

How do these figures compare with the national statistics on eating disorders? The question is difficult to answer because there have been few good epidemiological studies. The revised edition of the American Psychiatric Association's *Diagnostic and Statistical Manual of Mental Disorders* (DSM-111-R) estimates that anorexia affects from 1 in 800 to as many as 1 in 100 females between the ages of twelve and eighteen; about 4.5 percent of women may be bulimic.[16] These figures may be too low, however, because of narrow diagnostic criteria. *DSM-111-R* defines bulimia as a "minimum average of two binge eating episodes a week for at least three months," but there are many women who could be considered bulimic, even though they binge less frequently than this. Marcy noted, for example, that she resorted to purging only during emergencies. In addition, *DSM-111-R* measures behavior rather than attitude; someone who is technically not bulimic may nevertheless remain obsessed with the bingeing and purging cycle. There is a consensus among researchers that anorexic and bulimic behavior is widespread among college women.[17]

The American obsession with dieting is, of course, well known. Self-report studies suggest that between 50 and 75 percent of American women consider themselves to be overweight and are dieting at various times. A 1982 pilot survey of eating patterns at Wellesley College estimated that 22 percent of the women in the study had a serious eating disorder. Although the question-naire concluded that most students were close to their ideal weight, there was an "exaggerated level of psychological concern relative to the actual weight loss desired."[18] On the basis of these studies, the 32 percent of the women in my class who identified themselves as having eating disorders would seem to be a fairly accurate reflection of American college students.

Writing about Fasting

Without exception, Brenda, Marcy, Laurie, Jorie, and Paula concluded in their final diaries that writing was helpful in confronting and working through personal conflicts. Although their diaries reflect different degrees of self-analysis and self-disclosure, all five women were able to look at themselves more objectively and identify conflicts they wished to resolve. They were also gratified that their entries emboldened others to write about similar experiences. Three of the five women expressed reservations about diary writing, however, and their reservations are worth noting.

Brenda, the first person to write about an eating disorder, tried to organize a self-help group in her dormitory for anorexic and bulimic women, but when she received no response, she became discouraged. She was especially annoyed at those people who "suffer, complain, and yet do nothing" about their problems. "It doesn't make a bit of difference to me," she wrote in her final diary, "whether you use my journals in your book. Sorry, but I'm rather indifferent about it. Go ahead."

Brenda may not have realized how difficult it is for most people to write or speak about something as painful as bulimia without the safety of anony-mous diaries. Eating disorders are a source of humiliation for many people, and they are not easily convinced to join a self-help group. The ease with which Brenda wrote about bulimia may have prevented her from anticipat-ing how hard it is for others to be self-disclosing. Ironically, as the semester progressed, she asked me not to read her diaries aloud, a pattern that con-trasted with the increasing openness of the other students.

Marcy, who wrote four entries on the difficulty of being a woman in a patriarchal society, expressed ambivalence in her final diary over the per-sonal nature of her writings. She viewed the diaries as a "temptation" which she found herself resisting, and she remained suspicious of the opportunity to "purge the self of all the problems that have been building and festering within." She did not want to yield completely to this temptation, she said, because she was a private person. She concluded that while she did disclose a great deal about her life, she held back most of the "good stuff."

Marcy's cautionary note reminds us that, as self-revealing as we may wish to be, we are also self-concealing. We all have a need for privacy, for drawing boundaries between that part of the self which we wish to give to others as a gift and that part which we need to hold back for self-protection. Even Kafka, who was unusually self-revealing, observed that writing means "revealing oneself to excess."[19] If, as the psychoanalyst D. W. Winnicott observes, artists experience both "the urgent need to communicate and the still more urgent need not to be found,"[20] then how much greater may this need for self-privacy be among nonartists?

Diary writing allowed Laurie to express her pent-up feelings and take charge of her life. Of all the entries on eating disorders, Laurie's contain the most desperation; bulimia was an ongoing emergency for her, with an uncertain outcome. "I wanted other people to know how frightened I am that I'll never get better, that it might kill me, and how embarrassed and ashamed I am that I have an uncontrollable eating disorder." She singled out as particularly valuable the dialogic nature of classroom diary writing; just as she learned from students who had overcome their eating disorders, so, she hoped, would other students benefit from her knowledge.

Writing encouraged Jorie to explore childhood experiences, helping her to "get in touch with the child within me that I thought had died, or I guess never knew existed." She observed that many of her diaries expressed bitterness toward members of her family. "I know a lot of my diaries were directed at the anger that I feel toward my father, but because I was able to express it and have it validated, I began to start healing from it."

Paula, who wrote about slicing the backs of her hands with a razor blade in order to attract attention from her father, felt that diary writing became tedious during the second half of the semester. She attributed this both to the necessity to type the diaries and to the competition to write compelling diaries that would be read to the class. At first she felt that hearing the diaries was interesting, but after a while it seemed that "everyone was 'competing' to top everyone's problems, as if everyone was going to class to see if *this* week's problems were more intense than last week's."

Male Responses to Eating Disorder Diaries

Only two of the ten men in the class commented on the eating disorder diaries read in class. One wrote that before hearing the diaries, he had never realized the prevalence of eating disorders or understood why so many women were willing to damage their bodies in order to remain thin:

> I had a huge meal last night, and I tried to envision what it would be like to stick my index finger down my throat. Just the thought made me almost vomit, let alone the act. I see so many attractive women in this class, and I just cannot imagine why they would even think of losing or rather of torturing off this weight. I've thrown up before from drinking, and that is a nightmare, as anyone in this class can attest to. To do this on a consistent basis is a very frightening thought.

The other man remarked that the diaries sensitized him to the experience of growing up female in a patriarchal culture. "I think that I speak for many of the people in this class when I say that the reading of these diaries has helped to open up our eyes and has given us a chance to learn and experience something that could never happen in a normal classroom setting."

As the semester ended, I asked the students to comment on whether they felt, as a result of hearing so many entries on eating disorders, like the amusement seekers in Kafka's story, who take an early interest in the hunger artist only to turn away in disdain and boredom. Additionally, since we were reading Sylvia Plath's poetry, I inquired whether they viewed themselves as part of the "peanut crunching crowd" in the confessional poem "Lady Lazarus," who "shoves in to see / Them unwrap me hand and foot— / The big strip tease."[21] That is, did they feel part of a voyeuristic audience deriving crude entertainment from the artist's anguished cries? A few students acknowledged feeling morbid fascination while listening to the diaries, but most shared the point of view expressed by the following man:

> I really don't think any of us in this class has participated in exploiting the others. There have been times when I have chuckled over a particular phrase in a journal. But I have *never* laughed at any of my classmates' misfortunes. Since I have been lucky to avoid some of their misfortunes, I can only pray that I will never experience what they have experienced. The fact that they have faced their problems and have shared them in

class has shown great integrity and courage. I hope that my classmates will never encounter any more tragedies or misfortunes for the rest of their lives. They have had more than enough for one lifetime.

In offering sympathy and understanding, the class thus responded to the female hunger artists differently than the amusement seekers reacted to Kafka's starving character. Insofar as voyeurs lack empathy, the students were not morbid onlookers but caring, attentive listeners. They discovered that Kafka's story, and those of the diarists, have profound psychological, cultural, and feminist implications; and they became more aware of the violent forces directed against the female body and spirit. They grasped the truth of two of Kafka's most startling observations about the power of writing: first, that "a book must be the axe for the frozen sea inside us";[22] and second, as he wrote to Max Brod, "Writing is only an expedient, as for someone who is writing his will shortly before he hangs himself—an expedient that may well last a whole life."[23] Writing about their own experiences as hunger artists, the students came to understand Kafka—and themselves—a little better.

5 / Suicide Survivors

There is but one truly serious philosophical problem, and that is suicide. Judging whether life is or is not worth living amounts to answering the fundamental question of philosophy.
—Albert Camus, *The Myth of Sisyphus*

Like many people who study suicide, I do so out of a need to understand a personal tragedy—in my case, the self-inflicted death of an admired college English professor, a man who entered my life in 1963 when I was a freshman and soon became my mentor and best friend. He was, apart from my parents, the most formative influence on my adulthood, awakening my love for literature, stimulating my curiosity in psychoanalysis, and encouraging me to become a teacher. At a time when I felt like an impersonal number at the large state university where I was studying, he showed special interest in me, enriching my life in a multitude of ways.

Len approached teaching with unsurpassed intensity, and he had an uncanny ability to make literature come alive to his students. Imbued with the activist spirit of the 1960s, he believed that literature could transform the world and change his students' lives. When asked to elaborate on his approach to teaching, he wrote the following comment, which I subsequently framed and placed on my office bookcase:

> You have accurately discerned that I am not interested in the usual things English teachers are concerned about. . . . I want, in short, to change your life. But I don't feel this is at odds with the aims of literature. You see, it's my sincere belief that the function of literature is to change lives—and to let people know a lot more about themselves and the world. I am not a religious missionary because I am not religious.

But I will agree that I am a kind of missionary. Yes, I want to make the world a nice place, but I am also desperately in love with literature. And I try to combine my deepest cares by teaching literature and making sure that I indicate how that literature speaks to every person in the classroom (including me). Literature, and art in general, is nothing if it is not a criticism of life. Writers are men, not distant "authors," and they write about people, not "characters." If I didn't care about and love my students, I wouldn't take the trouble to get into painful self-searching.

I had no idea how painful that self-searching would become in time. I was eighteen when I first met Len, twenty-three when he died, and though I have dwelled upon his life and death for a quarter of a century, I still do not know why he committed suicide. I am now twice as old as I was when he died and realize that I know him half as well as I once thought.

"Tell Me Why I Shouldn't Kill Myself"

An early and outspoken critic of the Vietnam War, Len believed that the United States was heading toward an apocalypse. That he was heading toward a personal apocalypse, I realized only slowly. The growing social and political turbulence filled him with a premonition of doom. Depression darkened his normally ebullient spirit. Idealism gave way to skepticism, then pessimism. Inside the classroom, he remained lively and engaging; outside the classroom, he seemed deflated and apathetic about his life. Hired as a lecturer, he never finished his Ph.D. dissertation on the American critic Edmund Wilson, despite completing all his research. When his contract was not renewed, he lost faith in himself, concluding that his academic career was over. He was also despondent over his wife's failing health, irrationally blaming himself for the incurable degenerative disease from which she suffered. Ironically, the deterioration and eventual collapse of their marriage aggravated her illness, deepening his guilt.

I was a graduate student at Cornell University in Ithaca, New York, when Len phoned me from his parents' apartment in Brooklyn, a five-hour drive away, on Labor Day 1968, to tell me, in a voice eerily composed, that he had just taken an overdose of sleeping pills. He was not calling, he said, because he wanted me to talk him out of his decision; rather, he asked me to say good-bye to his family and friends. He was not angry at anyone, he added, and hoped that no one would be angry at him. He felt that suicide was the right decision and that he would no longer be a burden to others. He believed that he had accomplished nothing in his life, had disappointed his family and friends, had ceased to be a good teacher, and had made a mess of things. He was convinced that everyone would be relieved by his death.

Panic seized me, but I knew I had to remain calm and proceed deliberately if I was to help him. He refused to disclose where his parents' apartment was located or when they would be home, nor would he reveal where his estranged wife was living. When I asked how many pills he had swallowed and what kind, he replied that he had taken forty or fifty chloral hydrate tablets—more than enough, he assured me, to do the job. I did not doubt for a moment the seriousness of his suicide attempt, for in the preceding months he had often called me in the middle of the night, awakening me with the stark question: "Tell me why I shouldn't kill myself?" The telephone calls were always unnerving, even when I grew to expect them, and each time I urged him to speak to a therapist; he refused, believing that his problems were insoluble.

In what turned out to be a self-fulfilling prophecy—or, more accurately, an example of life commenting upon art—Len had given me a copy of Camus's *Myth of Sisyphus*, with its bold assertion that suicide was the one truly serious philosophical problem. I argued that Camus's existential heroes were on the side of life, aware of the fragile nature of existence and determined to live every moment of it in full consciousness and revolt. I quoted to him Camus's passionate words—"It is essential to die unreconciled and not of one's own free will. Suicide is a repudiation"[1]—but Len was not convinced. To him, Camus's tragic death in 1960, when he was killed in a car accident at the age of forty-six, only seemed to confirm the absurdity of existence.

I could not disguise the fear in my voice as I implored Len to call an ambulance or the police, a plea he adamantly refused. I found it impossible to carry on a reasonable conversation with a person who had set into motion his own death. The longer I spoke, the more I feared his life was slipping away. I found myself choked with emotion, unsure what to say or do. After several minutes I told him that if he did not hang up and call for assistance, then I would. Later, in reflecting back upon the event, I realized that I should have kept him on the phone while my wife, who was with me throughout the crisis, rushed to another phone to call the police. Lacking hindsight, I pleaded with him to go for help, and when that failed, I hung up and dialed the operator.

Just as I succeeded in getting through to the operator, Len somehow got back on the line and, in a controlled voice, reprimanded me for making—the words are etched indelibly in my memory—the "conventional response." The second call was a repetition of the first, and when I exhorted him once again to summon help, lest I would, he responded: "Then I'll go somewhere else to die." Grief-stricken, I hung up for the second time, phoned the operator, who connected me to the police, and breathlessly explained the situation. A few hours later a police officer called with the news that they had broken down the apartment door but found no one inside. The next day Len's body was spotted in his old Plymouth outside the apartment, his wrists slashed. He was thirty-one.

The Aftermath of Suicide

Suicide creates intense, long-lasting guilt, grief, and anger among family and friends, and Len's death overwhelmed me. By literally hanging up on him, cutting him off, I felt like I had betrayed his friendship. He had forced me into a Catch-22 situation; had I remained on the phone, as he urged me to do, listening without intervening, I would have respected his wishes but felt greater disloyalty, blaming myself for not having done everything in my power to save his life. Years later I discovered that my situation was by no means unique: approximately one in four suicides occurs in the presence of another person or while the suicide victim is speaking over the telephone—a phenomenon that emphasizes the interpersonal nature of suicide and the crucial importance of the role of the other.[2] As Edwin Shneidman, a leading suicidologist, has remarked, "The concept of the 'significant other' has its sharpest operational meaning in a case of suicide where another person seems to be both the life-sustainer and the last straw, at any rate, the focus of the victim's life and the precipitating reason for the death."[3]

I am convinced that, notwithstanding his stated wishes to the contrary, Len wanted to be talked out of death.[4] Surely he must have known that I would not only disagree with his decision in the most emphatic terms but also do everything in my power to come to his aid. This was the position I had maintained during all our conversations on suicide, and he knew how strongly I felt about this subject. A basic assumption in suicide prevention is that most people who attempt or commit suicide unconsciously wish to be rescued and thus leave clues to their anticipated deaths. Suicidal behavior is highly ambivalent: one wishes simultaneously to live and die. If Len did not want me to intervene, he could have simply written a letter explaining his actions.

Following the death, Len's family and friends mourned the tragic waste of his life, feeling that part of their own lives had also been destroyed. If, by committing suicide, Len was offering a "gift" to his loved ones, they felt less relief than horror and reacted as if his death were an act of aggression—which suicide often is. As the psychoanalyst Wilhelm Stekel noted as early as 1910, *"No one kills himself who has never wanted to kill another, or at least wished the death of another."*[5] While there are other motives for suicide, including the desire to escape from pain, the wish to be reunited with a loved one in death, and the belief that death will magically solve one's problems, suicidal individuals tend to be profoundly aggressive.[6] Len's wife went into shock upon learning of his death and had to be hospitalized immediately. She died one month later, on his birthday—a death that may have also been self-induced, a retaliation for his abandonment of her.[7] His friends and students were also horrified by his death, wondering how someone who was once so full of life, so determined to transform and humanize the world, could perish by his own hand. Many of us felt intense anger and hurt, along with guilt that we had not done enough to save his life.

Suicide Survivors

In the weeks following Len's funeral, I remained emotionally numb and confused. Suicide always comes as a shock, even when it is not entirely unexpected, and there is probably no form of death that is more difficult for survivors to mourn. There were no self-help groups in those days for "suicide survivors," a term that now refers to relatives and friends of people who terminate their own lives. Suicide survivors share many characteristics:

> marked distortions in time, especially the inability to remember the date the relative or friend died; difficulty in responding to direct questions about the number of people in one's family; emotional estrangements from other family members; a sense of foreboding; a pessimistic outlook on life, including the suggestion of an early death; overtly suicidal ideas and less overt self-destructive behaviors.[8]

Although I have never been suicidal, I have found myself in the situation of other suicide survivors whose lives have been changed irrevocably. Suicide survivors have fewer support systems available to them than survivors of other tragedies because of the stigma of suicide and because of the tangled emotions arising from the act. Perhaps the most painful realization is that one often does feel a degree of relief over a loved one's suicide, along with anguish and remorse. In my own case, Len's nightly telephone calls had become unbearable, and while I never took the telephone off the hook, there were times when I was tempted to do so. Suicide survivors are burdened by self-reproach, making recovery problematic.

For months afterward, I could not talk to anyone about Len's suicide, not even to my wife, who was as close to him as I was and no less devastated. We both felt a gaping void in our lives. I kept asking myself what Len was thinking and feeling during the final moments of his life; each time I visualized him alone in his car, I felt heartsick. Unable to find an outlet for my grief, I could not, to cite Malcolm's lines to Macduff in *Macbeth*, "give sorrow words. The grief that does not speak / Whispers the o'er-fraught heart, and bids it break."[9] I immersed myself in my graduate studies, hoping to avoid brooding over the past. Yet even as I tried to concentrate on life, I remained preoccupied with death.

Serendipitously, I was taking at this time a graduate seminar on Joseph Conrad and William Faulkner, taught by Walter Slatoff. Early in the semester Professor Slatoff mentioned, almost as an aside, the discovery of new biographical evidence indicating that, in a moment of depression, Conrad had shot himself deliberately in the chest as a young man. He later mythologized the wound in the semiautobiographical novel *The Arrow of Gold*. A telegram that Conrad sent to his uncle, elaborating on the details of the self-shooting, helps to explain the high suicide rate among his fictional characters, including those with whom he strongly identified, such as the eponymous hero of *Lord Jim* and Martin Decoud in *Nostromo*.

Obsessed with Len's suicide, I found myself gravitating toward Conrad's suicide attempt, hoping that an understanding of the latter would shed light on the former. One of the characteristics of suicide survivors, I later discovered, with a shock of recognition, is the constant search for an explanation of suicide. I began studying the enormous body of literature on self-destruction and plunged into psychoanalytic theory, which made sense both theoretically and experientially. The result was my 1971 Ph.D. dissertation, entitled *Joseph Conrad and the Self-Destructive Urge*, which was published in 1977 as *Joseph Conrad: Writing as Rescue*.[10] By studying the psychodynamics of suicide, I acknowledged to myself the paralyzing emotions arising from Len's death: the guilt, anger, and anguish that are the legacy—or illegacy—of suicide. It was a relief to know that I was not alone in feeling burdened by these emotions. I also joined a suicide prevention organization in Ithaca, which trains volunteers to assess the suicidal risk of callers and then decide on an appropriate course of action, ranging from counseling to emergency rescue procedures. In 1980, after receiving tenure at the State University of New York at Albany, I began three years of psychoanalytic training in New York City, an experience that has broadened my understanding of mental illness and health.

"The Nightmare of My Choice"

In retrospect, I can see why, following Len's death, I was so drawn to Conrad's stories, particularly to *Heart of Darkness*,[11] a novella that had curiously failed to move me when I first read it in high school. I regarded Len in the same way that Marlow views Kurtz at the beginning of the story—as a "very remarkable person" (19), an "emissary of pity, and science [in Len's case, literature], and progress" (25), a person who had "enlarged my mind" (65). Both Len and Kurtz had immense plans, vast energy, lofty humanitarian aims, and an extraordinary gift for expression. Paralleling Marlow's relationship to Kurtz, I idealized Len and, despite our closeness in age, transmuted him into an admired father figure, whose approval meant the world to me. Like Kurtz, Len defined himself as a missionary, and his belief in the humanizing and transformative power of literature elevated him into a heroic figure.

And yet something terrible had happened to Len; some deficiency had been revealed which rendered him, like Kurtz, "hollow at the core" (59). I pictured Len's dying words as "The horror! The horror!" (71). Marlow's observation about depression seemed to describe Len's last months—"Even extreme grief may ultimately vent itself in violence—but more generally takes the form of apathy" (44). Just as Marlow defends Kurtz and is prepared to risk his own life if necessary to protect Kurtz from the forces of darkness, only to draw back at the last moment, unwilling to plunge into the abyss with his dying friend, so too did I retreat out of self-preservation. After his death, I could not help but judge Len in the same oxymoronic way in which Marlow judges Kurtz: as a man of "exalted and incredible degradation" (67). And Marlow's dazed reaction to Kurtz's death anticipated my own reaction to

Len's death: "It was not my strength that wanted nursing, it was my imagination that needed soothing" (73).

This is, of course, a literary construction, an interpretation of a real character as seen through the veil of a shadowy fictional one. It may be objected that I am being overly self-conscious and literary. To regard myself like the stalwart Marlow must seem grandiose. I can hardly read a road map without getting lost, much less undertake a heroic and perilous voyage into the deepest recesses of Africa. To compare my "psychic" journey with Marlow's is like comparing (to paraphrase Mark Twain) a lightning bug with lightning. Nevertheless, to the extent that readers identify with fictional characters, I saw myself as Conrad's captain, permitted to retreat nervously from the brink of death and compelled to narrate the story of a man who will remain forever, as Marlow describes Kurtz, the "nightmare of my choice."

For suicide survivors, life is never the same, even when one has more or less come to terms with the experience. I still feel vague anxiety when the phone rings late at night or when I hear a student casually say that he is going to "kill himself" over a grade. It has taken me a long time to recognize that I was not responsible for Len's death and that it is the victim who must bear the responsibility. It is easier to realize this intellectually than emotionally; for example, even as I was writing earlier drafts of this chapter, I could see that I was more self-blaming than I was consciously aware of. This is the first time I have written about Len—and the most painful writing I have undertaken. I don't know whether I have penetrated any of the veils of his life or death; as Marlow observes in *Lord Jim*, "It is my belief no man ever quite understands his own artful dodges to escape from the grim shadow of self-knowledge."[12]

Self-Analysis and Psychoanalytic Theory

For me, the grim shadow of self-knowledge has been illuminated in part by psychoanalytic theory, particularly the repetition-compulsion principle. In *Beyond the Pleasure Principle* (1920), Freud postulates the existence of a "compulsion to repeat" which contradicts the pleasure principle. Freud's famous example is the *fort-da* (gone-there) ritual enacted by his eighteen-month-old grandson in response to his mother's temporary disappearance.[13] By throwing over his bed a wooden reel with a piece of string round it, the child symbolically makes his mother disappear; by pulling the reel onto his bed again, he makes her magically reappear. The game of disappearance and return enables the child to endure his mother's absence. Although Freud interpreted the repetition-compulsion principle as confirmation of a "death instinct," contemporary psychoanalysts regard it more plausibly as a reflection of the need to relive and master traumatic experiences.

The repetition-compulsion principle has been striking in my own life. By converting a passive situation into an active one (becoming a psychoanalytic critic and doing research on self-destructive writers), I have gained a degree of control over a frightening situation. One of the driving forces behind my teaching and writing, I now see, is a reparative fantasy in which, by attempting to "rescue" fictional characters, I replay my discussions with Len and strive for a more positive outcome. Although I cannot bring Len back to life or journey into the heart of his darkness, I can play the role of significant other to my students, especially to those whose lives have been touched by suicide or by other traumas and who are still burdened by their own private albatross.

Writing as Rescue

The theory of writing as rescue which I explored in my work on Joseph Conrad applies to other authors who write out of the need to exorcise the specter of self-destruction. Creative writers as diverse as D. H. Lawrence, Ernest Hemingway, Sylvia Plath, and William Styron have all remarked upon the mysterious healing power of self-expression. Writing cannot be reduced to therapy, but it promotes both self-mastery and self-healing. "One sheds one['s] sicknesses in books," Lawrence wrote in a letter, "repeats and presents again one['s] emotions, to be master of them."[14] Hemingway's Robert Jordan dwells upon a similar thought in *For Whom the Bell Tolls*: "My guess is that you will get rid of all that by writing about it. . . . Once you write it down it is all gone."[15] Sylvia Plath experienced psychological relief through writing poetry, noting in her *Journals* that "fury jams the gullet and spreads poison, but, as soon as I start to write, dissipates, flows out into the figure of the letters: writing as therapy?"[16] And William Styron has commented in *Sophie's Choice* on how his fiction may be viewed, psychobiographically, as an effort to work through personal conflicts. "I realize now . . . how my writing had kept serious emotional distress safely at bay, in the sense that the novel I was working on served as a cathartic instrument through which I was able to discharge on paper many of my more vexing tensions and miseries."[17]

There are many reasons why writing is conducive to psychological health. To begin with, writing enables artists to confront and master, if only temporarily, potentially self-paralyzing conflicts and fears, purging toxic emotions. Writing allows artists to descend within themselves and impose order upon chaos, defining the indefinable. Writing encourages exploration of multiple points of view and promotes greater self-detachment. Writing is an act of creation, a validation of the effort to leave part of oneself to posterity. Writing is also a way to memorialize loss and achieve a victory of sorts over death, the "love and care lavished upon the work of art serving," as David Aberbach remarks, "as a permanent testimony to the artist's attachment to the lost person."[18] Finally, writing strengthens the artist's connection to the community, thus helping to offset the solitude and struggle associated with the creative process.

Admittedly, neither the "talking cure" nor the "writing cure" is a panacea for fictional or real characters. Cathartic relief, if and when it comes, may be short-lived. Despite Lawrence's belief that some writers shed their illnesses in books, we know that other writers may repeat and re-present their conflicts without mastering them. Ironically, many of the strongest testimonies of the healing power of writing have come from novelists and poets who later perished by their own hand. Both Hemingway and Plath committed suicide, the former in large part because of the recognition that his creative powers had been exhausted, the latter notwithstanding the extraordinary burst of creativity in the months preceding her death. Nevertheless, for every artist who has failed to be sustained by his or her own art, there are numerous others who have affirmed that writing has been crucial for their psychological well-being. I know that writing about suicide has been therapeutic for me, as it was for Conrad—and for the many students who have similar stories to tell.

Coming Out of the Closet

"The suicidal person leaves his psychological skeleton in the survivor's closet," Edwin Shneidman has observed.[19] The number of these closets is startling. The American Association of Suicidology estimates that there are at least 30,000 self-inflicted deaths each year in the United States. Many authorities believe that because of underreporting, the true figure may be closer to 100,000 deaths. It has been estimated, moreover, that each suicide directly affects at least six other people. There are thus millions of people in the United States who are suicide survivors, and their numbers are increasing by at least 180,000 per year.

Not only is suicide the second leading cause of death in young adults (next to accidents), but suicidal thinking and suicide attempts have become a fact of life for an astonishing number of people. According to the national school-based Youth Risk Behavior Survey,[20] sponsored by the United States Centers for Disease Control, 27 percent of all high school students thought seriously about committing suicide in 1990; 8 percent of all students actually attempted suicide; and 2 percent of all students sustained injuries in the course of a suicide attempt serious enough to warrant medical attention. The study, which surveyed 11,631 high school students from every state in the country, estimated that over a quarter of a million high school students made at least one suicide attempt requiring hospitalization in the preceding twelve months. The CDC also noted that the suicide rates for adolescents 15–19 years of age have quadrupled in the last forty years, from 2.7 per 100,000 in 1950 to 11.3 per 100,000 in 1988. The CDC concluded its study by recommending a variety of strategies to reduce the suicide rate, including educating youths about the warning signs of suicide and the availability of suicide prevention services.

Literature courses offer an excellent forum in which to talk about suicide because the subject appears both in the earliest classical plays and in the latest poems, novels, and autobiographies. Twentieth-century literature is preoccupied with suicide,[21] and it is scarcely possible to read a modern novel without confronting a self-destructive character. To speak about a fictional character's suicide is to inquire into the motives and, hence, the psychology of suicide. Over the years I have used several literary texts that focus on suicide: *Hamlet*, Ibsen's *Hedda Gabler*, Dostoevsky's *Brothers Karamazov*, Kafka's "Judgment" and *Metamorphosis*, Conrad's *Heart of Darkness* and *Lord Jim*, Woolf's *Mrs. Dalloway*, Miller's *Death of a Salesman*, Plath's *Bell Jar*, Joanne Greenberg's *I Never Promised You a Rose Garden*, Mishima's "Patriotism," and Salinger's *Catcher in the Rye*. I have discussed many of these texts in *The Talking Cure* and *Narcissism and the Novel*.[22] Suicidal literature is not necessarily depressing or morbid; the writer, like the physician, is interested in illness in the larger context of healing and health. Literature reflects, as one critic has expressed recently, "*gestures of healing*—reparative acts that permit writers to feel whole and to make some link, other than alienation, with the world."[23] Even if these gestures of healing are temporary or incomplete, they point the way toward health for writers and readers alike.

Prevention and Postvention

In my psychoanalytic classes I usually spend a few minutes talking about Len's death. I emphasize the warning signs of suicide, the psychological dynamics, the common misconceptions of suicide, the different theories as to its causes, and the various treatments available. I stress how important it is for students to realize that help is readily available. And I tell my students that although it is difficult to talk about suicide, it is more difficult not to talk about it.

Diary writing is especially helpful to students who are either suicide survivors or in a suicidal crisis. For suicide survivors, writing promotes the bereavement process, first, by allowing them to accept the reality of their loss, and second, by enabling them to confront and master the chaotic emotions arising from a loved one's suicide. Suicidologists use the term "postvention" to describe the process of helping the bereaved come to terms with suicide.[24] For students who may be actively suicidal, writing creates a powerful bond to a supportive community. These students feel a sense of relief when their diaries are read—they know they are being heard. They also derive the comfort of knowing that others have survived suicidal crises and that help is available. For students who have not been exposed to suicide, learning about prevention and postvention becomes a valuable part of their education.

Befriending Skills

It is particularly important for teachers who receive suicidal diaries to respond as empathically and nonjudgmentally as possible. They must display what one psychologist has called "befriending skills": being compassionate and humble; sharing a person's pain; listening instead of offering advice; and providing acceptance, empathy, and caring.[25] Teachers must respect a student's need to grieve, and they must remain calm and reassuring, allowing students to write openly about suicide and express their feelings. Students who write about suicide require compassionate and understanding readers; a teacher's empathic failure obviously has serious consequences. Teachers must guard against countertransference responses such as projecting their own guilt, anger, fear, or disapproval onto students. Teachers, like therapists, must recognize their own limitations when dealing with a potentially life-threatening crisis. As psychoanalysts John Maltsberger and Dan Buie observe, "The three most common narcissistic snares [for the therapist] are the aspirations to heal all, know all, and love all."[26] Finally, teachers must suggest outside help when they feel it is appropriate.

The Limits of Confidentiality

Confidentiality is essential for classroom diary writing, but in certain situations the need for confidentiality is outweighed by moral, ethical, and legal considerations. If, for example, a student writes a diary revealing the possibility of an impending suicide attempt, it is incumbent upon a teacher to notify the university's counseling or medical service. I have never been in a situation where this has been necessary, but I can conceive of the possibility. There are at least two compelling reasons to seek outside help: first, a teacher, like a psychologist or lawyer, can be held liable for failure to disclose information that a person may harm another or himself or herself; second, a student's disclosure of an impending suicide attempt is a cry for help that should not go unheeded.

Talking and Writing about Suicide

There is a common misconception that talking or writing about suicide heightens a person's vulnerability. The opposite is almost always true. People are usually relieved when they have the opportunity to express suicidal feelings, and they feel less lonely, stigmatized, and withdrawn. There is no evidence to indicate that a classroom discussion of suicide will plant an idea in a student's mind that will later culminate in a self-destructive act. The only time a classroom discussion might become dangerous is if a student over-identifies with an author who glorifies suicide. Following the publication in 1774 of the confessional novel *The Sorrows of Young Werther*, a rash of suicides occurred, all apparently copying the death of Goethe's youthful romantic hero. (Writing the novel proved more cathartic to the author than reading the novel proved for many of Goethe's followers.) In 1978 the film *The Deer Hunter*, which graphically depicts Russian roulette, provoked a spate of real-life suicides. By refusing to romanticize either real or fictional suicides, literature teachers can avoid contributing to the Werther effect.

Suicide prevention and self-help groups are effective precisely because they enable people to express themselves, to enter into reciprocal relationships with others who may have similar problems, and to avail themselves of the treatments that have worked for others.[27] For the same reason, I have found that students are relieved when, in response to a vague suicidal observation in a diary, I ask them if they are indeed suicidal. The question encourages them to talk about their feelings and find solutions to their problems.

Suicide Diaries

Students who write suicide diaries generally fall into one of two groups: those who write about a relative's or friend's suicide or suicide attempt, and those who write about feeling suicidal themselves. Students in the first group generally do not understand why a person would wish to take his or her own life, while students in the second group offer explanations for their actions and describe how they felt during a particular crisis. Students in the first group usually write only one or two diaries on suicide; those in the second group often write several diaries. Of the students whose diaries are included in this chapter, all but the last two, Terry and Ruth, fall into the first group. Predictably, suicidal students experience much more resistance in writing about their feelings than nonsuicidal students. Their diaries are more intense, and they pose greater challenges to the teacher, who must decide when to read—and not read—their diaries to the class.

Almost without exception, students who write about another person's suicide or suicide attempt express shock, confusion, grief, guilt, and anger—the same emotions I experienced after Len's death. The closer students are to the deceased, the greater their devastation. A relative's suicide is generally more traumatic than a friend's, unless the friend was a former lover. The death of any relative or friend produces sorrow, but if the death is a suicide, the sorrow is tinged with anger and guilt. The tension between sympathy and judgment is particularly striking in suicide survivor diaries.

Suicide has the uncanny ability to cast a wide net, ensnaring friends, family, and even distant acquaintances. Undergraduates who write about suicide are still young and have another forty or fifty years ahead of them, but they believe that the event has irrevocably altered their lives—a conclusion supported by research on suicide survivors. Suicide calls into question so many deeply ingrained assumptions about life, defies so many social and religious taboos, and shatters so many lives that virtually no one can write about it dispassionately. Many suicide survivors have never spoken about the subject before, not even with those people who have been most directly affected by the event. Consequently, the diaries reveal their first effort to write about this experience and share it with another person.

ELAINE
"Death Is Hard Enough to Deal with, but Suicide Is Entirely Different"

Suicide is different from other deaths, and coping with it is much more problematic, as Elaine reveals in her diary:

> Suicide. That word stirs up many different emotions inside my head. Taking your own life. Why would anyone want to do such a thing? It is very hard for me to see why anyone would simply lose the will to live, to just give up. Sure, things get bad sometimes, maybe things even get downright awful too, but to commit suicide is a permanent solution to a temporary problem. When the subject of suicide was brought up in class last week, I thought, "That would probably be a good topic to discuss in my journal." But having personally known someone who succeeded in taking her own life, I started to reconsider writing about it.
>
> Why did I reconsider? Probably because I was being selfish because I did not want to face that terrible occurrence in my life again, or even because I wanted to deny the fact entirely. But I know that I can't ignore what happened to my best friend's mother. I've never really talked about her death and how I felt about it. That's because I knew I had to be strong for my best friend. Maybe writing about it now will help me to deal with my friend's pain a little better. In any event, here is my story.
>
> Joan and I have been friends since childhood. Her mother was a close friend of my family, and I used to call her "Mom" because that was just how our relationship was. Joan's father, who was much older than her

mother, was very strict in his ways, and as a little girl he frightened me terribly with his gruff voice and massive stature. Joan seemed fairly happy growing up, until her father lost his job and couldn't find another one. Joan and her mother worked very hard at looking after him and taking care of the house as well as each other. Her father's presence at home and subsequent depression were a major setback in Joan's life, but she was always a strong person, bright, witty, and always smiling. Joan doesn't smile much now that her mother's gone.

When Joan called me that Monday night at midnight, I immediately knew something was wrong. Little did I know what she was about to tell me. When I asked what was wrong (I knew not by the tone of her voice, for that was pretty calm, but by the hour of the call), Joan simply said, "My mom died." Death is hard enough to deal with, but suicide is entirely different. Joan told me that at six o'clock that morning she woke up with a start (she did not know why) and heard something fall in her living room, so she got up to see what had dropped. There, lying on the floor, was her mother, with a gun by her side. She had shot a hole through her head, and Joan was the first to find her.

I cried when Joan called to tell me what happened. Why did her mother do it? Things in her life seemed all right. She left no note behind; her death will always be a mystery. The way she chose her death infuriates me. Who did she expect to find her? How could she do this to Joan? Why didn't she just up and leave? I think that would have been easier for Joan and her father to deal with.

Were there signs? Thinking about it now, I would have to say definitely yes, for the last time I saw Joan's mother was when Joan and I went shopping before returning to college, and I dropped Joan back at her house when we were done. Her mother came to the car to say hello, and before I drove away, I remember her saying, "It was nice knowing you." Yes, I found this strange, but at the time suicide was the furthest thing from my mind. Joan said that for months before her mom's death, she would tuck Joan into bed at night, and she would say, "Remember that I'll always love you, no matter what."

At first Joan found this strange, but she just thought her mom was expressing her feelings, and that was nice. I'll never forgive her for taking her life. I think it was a selfish thing to do. Was she subconsciously killing someone else? I don't know who that person would be—

she didn't have ill feelings toward anyone I knew, and I knew her pretty well. Wherever Joan's mother is now, I hope that she is happy, but I also hope that she can know just how terribly she affected the lives of those who knew her, and how angry we are.

Many students write similar diaries about important signs which were either missed or not taken seriously at the time, perhaps because of the mistaken belief that those who threaten suicide do not actually go through with it. The truth is that every suicide threat should be taken seriously. Few people attempt or commit suicide without first revealing their intentions. One of the main values in reading aloud diaries written by suicide survivors is that they aid in suicide prevention. Warning signs include, as listed in the American Association of Suicidology publication *Suicide & How to Prevent It*: suicide threats or similar statements such as "I won't be around here much longer" or "You won't have to bother with me anymore," prolonged depression, dramatic changes of behavior or personality, giving away prized possessions, withdrawal from family and friends, abuse of alcohol or drugs, and making final arrangements for one's death.[28]

Much of the guilt felt by suicide survivors derives from the realization that they overlooked crucial signs or failed to act decisively on them. To ignore these clues or make light of them is to miss the opportunity to save another person's life, yet this reaction is very common, as the following students indicate in their diaries.

DOROTHY
"The Signs of Suicide"

Just recently an old friend of the family committed suicide. It was a strange feeling that came over me when I found out. When you spoke about the signs of suicide, it made me realize that all the signs had been there. His family was and still is devastated by his death. His brother found him in his bedroom on the floor with a bullet hole in his forehead and the back of his head gone. After the initial shock the family fit together many of the events that occurred the week prior to his suicide.

He had apparently told his brother to find a new best friend in case something happened to him. He also asked him to take care of his dogs should anything happen to him. His brother unfortunately thought nothing of these statements and thought he was having a bad day. A friend told the victim's parents that the night before his death he had said that he was thinking of killing himself, but they thought he was joking. The actual process by which he worked out the act was well planned. He had apparently spoken to two different gun shops about ammunition. He had called up his girlfriend and asked her to pick him up in the afternoon to go to work. When she got there, she found his brother running from the house in shock. It is very unfortunate that someone had not spotted the warning signs. The pain and devastation of the event can be seen on the faces of the entire family, and I'm afraid the scars will never heal.

WAYNE

"What Would Happen If He Had Killed Himself?"

Some years ago, a good friend of mine became extremely upset and angry with his parents and threatened to kill himself. They were all gathered in the living room and treated his announcement with skepticism. Enraged, he ran into the kitchen, pulled out a carving knife, and returned to the living room. He put the knife to his throat and repeated his intention to kill himself. His parents mocked him and told him to put the knife down and stop acting like an idiot. Humiliated, he threw it down and went to his room.

He told me this story two days after it had happened. I was in his room. I asked him if he still felt the same way, and he proceeded to open his dresser and pull out a noose he had made for himself. Not realizing that things had gotten that bad, I told him to destroy the noose, as if by erasing the symptoms of his depression, the cause would also vanish. At this point his brother entered the room. He saw the noose and asked where his brother was going to hang himself. When he pointed to the track lighting fixture on the ceiling, his brother answered, "You idiot. All you'll do is tear the track lighting off the ceiling and break it, and then Dad will really kill you." This comment managed to defuse the situation, and we began to talk of other things.

Despite this depression, my friend abandoned this suicidal urge, and while he has been depressed since then, to my knowledge he has not attempted suicide. What his own private thoughts are, I cannot guess.

While this incident had a positive outcome, I still feel guilty that I was not able to provide him with some sort of advice at the time. The truth was, when confronted with something of that gravity, there is very little to say. I told him not to kill himself and gave him all the typical reasons why he shouldn't, why it was a wrong and shortsighted solution, but I knew deep down, from his perspective, that none of my words meant anything compared with the pain he was feeling. And I can't help but wonder what would happen if he had killed himself. What portion of the blame would be mine?

Wayne's feeling of guilt and helplessness reflects the attitude of many students who notice the signs of suicide yet find themselves unsure how to respond, as we can see from the next diary.

RALPH

"What Will I Do If She Does the Unspeakable?"

What I am about to write is very distressing to me, but I haven't been able to think about anything else.

My ex-girlfriend and I are talking for the first time after a messy breakup. I am glad that we are able to be friends again because I still care about her very much and very deeply. The details of why we broke up aren't important, but let's just say that it was a very intense relationship and seemed to run out of control of all reason and sense. She had been abused for her whole life—emotionally abused by her parents, sexually abused by a neighbor, emotionally and sexually abused by so-called boyfriends.

When she was going out with me, it was the first time she had ever had a relationship where the other person involved thought of "us" before "me." She didn't know how to handle it. She was always looking for some other reason for my behavior; for instance, if I bought her flowers, she wouldn't think that I was buying her flowers simply to buy her flowers, but instead thought that I must be buying them because I expected something in return—sex, in other words. I was amazed at this because I did things for her innocently. I never had a relationship like the abusive ones she had experienced in the past, so I couldn't even fathom the idea.

Anyway, that has all passed for me. Now we are talking again, and it looks like we will be friends. I really enjoy her company, and I love talking to her and just being with her. I realize that she can't handle an emotional relationship because she has to come to terms with her abusive past. I am proud to have her as a friend. She is a very special person.

This next part will be difficult.

Thursday we went to a movie and then back to her apartment. We were sitting on her couch when I noticed a red, irritated mark on her wrist. I immediately became concerned because I had a cousin who was suicidal and have seen those marks before.

I asked her what the mark was.

"Just a scratch," she said.

"A scratch from what?" I asked.

"I scraped it on the table."

Although I knew damn well what the mark really was, I left it at that—partly because I could tell she didn't want to tell me, and partly because I really didn't want to know the truth. I really wanted to believe that she had scraped her wrist on the table.

About half an hour later she suddenly told me that she was lying before about scraping her wrist. What really happened was that in a fit of depression she started to dig at her wrist with a key until it started to bleed. When she saw how upset I got when she said this, she said not to worry, she would never really do anything, she wasn't stupid enough to commit suicide. She is always telling me not to worry about her.

Right now I am very frightened for her. She said that she would never do anything, and the attempt did not cause any serious damage except for a few dig marks in her wrist, but what if she has a more serious fit of depression and tries to do something more permanent to herself?

I am very confused. I have emotions swimming around inside of me that I do not know how to deal with. Writing this, I am almost in a state of panic. Sometimes I wish I could just make all of her pain disappear with the wave of a wand, but I know it's not that easy. She's abusing herself because all she has ever known is abuse. I wish I could show her that there is something else out there, that love doesn't have to be abusive—in fact, shouldn't be abusive. I wish I could be there so that she doesn't attempt it again, but it's impossible to be with her every minute, and that wouldn't be good for either of us anyway.

A part of me knows that she would never commit suicide. Is that part just denying the obvious? What if leaving her to work out her problems is the wrong thing to do—then what? What will I do if she does the unspeakable?

I wish I had the answers.

MARGARET
*"If I Didn't Listen to That Chilling Feeling
Inside Me, My Mother Would Be Dead"*

Most students who write about suicide indicate that crucial signs were missed, with disastrous results; only once have I received a diary in which an accurate premonition averted a suicide, as Margaret reports about her mother's near-death:

> I have so many mixed feelings about suicide that it's hard to put them into one diary. I think the first time I ever thought about suicide I was fifteen. It seemed such an easy way to escape what I thought was a horrible life as a nonexistent teenager. The only problem was . . . I didn't have the guts. So I put it out of my mind . . . sort of.
>
> Life continued on as it always had, and I tried to pretend I was happy. It worked, on the outside. Instead of trying to end my life, I ate. I ate and ate and ate until I weighed over 200 pounds. Anyway, that's a different story. I continued to think of suicide as an unacceptable solution to my problems because I couldn't push out of my mind what killing myself would do to the other people in my life. It really hit home one summer day at my grandmother's house.
>
> My mother, my sister, and I were all living at my grandmother's house. No, actually I think my sister was still living with my father. Anyway, my mother was drunk, and she was very upset. This all happened so suddenly. I mean, one minute we were laughing and joking, and the next minute, my mother's crying her eyes out, saying my grandmother never wanted her. They started arguing and I couldn't stand to hear it, so I went for a walk.
>
> I didn't even get halfway down the road when I got this feeling that just shook me to the bone. I had no idea what it was or where it came from, but I knew I had to get back to the house. I didn't know what was going on; I just ran. When I got back to the house, my grandmother was sitting at the table stirring her coffee like nothing was wrong. When I

asked her where my mother was, she said she was upstairs. My voice filled with panic. I went running upstairs, and I didn't know what to expect. What I saw will stay with me till the day I die.

There was my mother, with her hand overflowing with pills, and she slammed the door in my face as I tried to force my way in. I couldn't believe what was happening. I ran back downstairs and told my grandmother what was going on. (At least I think I did.) I called the police or the hospital to try to get an ambulance, and I was put on hold!! Can you believe it? Here I am, sixteen years old with my mother upstairs taking God knows what, and they put me on hold!!

It took about forty-five minutes for anyone to show up at the house. By this time, I had called a neighbor friend of mine. He was upstairs trying to get Mom to open the door, and suddenly he came running down asking us for all the towels we could find. I was totally out of control, and my grandmother was pouring coffee; I guess it was her way of dealing with the situation.

The police were the first to show up. They wouldn't let me upstairs. I was so mad!!! That was my mother, and they wouldn't even let me up the stairs to see how she was. I didn't even know if she was alive or not. I did the only thing I could think of to do. I climbed up on the roof to try to see in the window. As a result, I almost got arrested! The police actually tried to arrest me for trying to see if my own mother was alive!

When the ambulance finally came, they said they couldn't take my mother because she refused to go to the hospital. Well, of course she refused; she was trying to die. They said it was some kind of law that they couldn't take her against her will. They were able to find out that she had taken some of my grandfather's heart medication (he had already passed away) along with some type of pill that makes medication go into your bloodstream faster. She was in clear danger of dying, and they wouldn't do anything.

Finally, my mother passed out, and they were able to take her to the hospital. Of course, the police were pretty pissed off at me, so they wouldn't let me ride in the ambulance. I had to go with my grandmother. She had my great-uncle drive, and (unbelievable as it may seem) he decided to stop to get gas on the way. When we got to the hospital, my mother had so many doctors in her cubicle that we couldn't go inside. Instead, we gave all the bullshit information they always want in the middle of a crisis. We weren't really allowed to see my mother for over four hours. During this time, I had the pleasant task of calling my father's house at three o'clock in the morning to inform my sister of the situation.

Finally, I just couldn't take it any more. I barged into the emergency room, only to find my mother's bed empty. I thought she was dead and that they were just waiting to tell us. No, she was in intensive care. She was going to live. Later I learned that she had actually died in the emergency room and was brought back to life. Regardless, she lived and had no permanent damage.

That was my first real experience with suicide. That taught me more than I will ever need to know. I saw how many people were potential victims of my mother's act, and it convinced me that suicide would never be an option for me. My mother still thinks about it sometimes, but I think if she had been on the other side of that emergency room door, she would have a different perspective. It's too bad I can't take her through what I went through. We have talked about it, but somehow she will always remain on the outside of my experience. I will always know that if I didn't listen to that chilling feeling inside me, my mother would be dead.

Few events cause more devastation than suicide or lead to more unresolved grief. As researchers have noted, suicide is usually sudden and unexpected, often violent, and occurring in families that are often experiencing other stress. Suicide may also compromise traditional mourning rituals. Some religions deny a suicide victim burial in consecrated ground, although a priest or rabbi may circumvent this prohibition by claiming that the deceased was insane at the time of the act. In addition, suicide leads to harmful expressions of unconscious anger and to distorted communication patterns; many parents and children continue to deny that a loved one's death was really a suicide. Following a suicide, many of the usual support systems may be withdrawn.

JUDY
*"Although He Chose to Kill Himself, He Also Killed
Her in So Many Ways"*

Whereas Elaine could not decide whether Joan's mother committed suicide in order to hurt her family, there is no doubt in the Judy's mind about the hostility implicit in the act she describes:

Hearing your story about your friend this week brought back memories of a few years ago when my best friend's boyfriend committed suicide. I have known Myra since high school, and we are very close. Jason was also from our high school, and he and Myra continued to be boyfriend and girlfriend until college, when they were separated for the first time. He was nice enough, but he drank a lot and smoked pot. He was nice to Myra, it seemed. I truly believed she loved him and he loved her. In their freshman year of college they began having problems. She wanted more freedom, and he wanted to get married. They broke up, and Myra began dating many other guys. Jason kept in touch with me, and I knew at the time he was partying more and more. During summer Jason began following Myra around and said he wanted her back. She was reluctant. She missed him but felt she needed more time to herself.

In September, one day before Myra was to leave for college, Jason shot himself in the head. He and Myra had just had a big fight, and he was really drunk. He first cut himself with a razor and wrote in blood the words "I love you" in a letter which he sent to her. Obviously he had been planning this—Myra received the note two days after his death. He added "ed" to verbs so that they would be in past tense. In accordance with your discussion of suicide in class, I believed then and believe now still that he killed himself instead of killing her.

Myra was devastated. Still is devastated. She left home immediately and went to college. She felt great hurt and anger. She did blame herself, as Jason had wanted. Although he chose to kill himself, he also killed her in so many ways. When she came back home during Thanksgiving, she was a mess. She wore black and covered her room with memories of Jason, gifts he had given her, pictures of him, etc. I felt so uncomfortable in her bedroom. I never knew what to say, so mostly I said nothing but, "Myra, I understand." I didn't really understand, but I grieved his loss. I told her not to blame herself that Jason was just really wasted at the time and couldn't handle things.

None of this helped her really. I felt sorry for her—exactly what she didn't want. This was such a great strain on our friendship. I watched her losing control and suggested she seek professional help. This really pissed her off. The next year I shall never forget. The emotions she felt were so intense and even scary at times. I was afraid she might kill herself. She must have sensed this as she kept telling me she would never do that. Myra is still today haunted by Jason's death. She couldn't return to college the following year—it was too much for her. This year she has started again. She still has an ominous way about her, though. She will probably never be able to retain a mental state as before Jason's death.

What has plagued me, as well as Myra, is what could have been done to stop Jason—if anything at all. In a sense, Myra feels as if she failed him, and so do I. I feel anger toward Jason for changing my relationship with her forever. Myra's recovery or reconciliation with Jason's suicide is a day-by-day thing with her and with me also. We are still in touch regularly. Part of Myra has died with Jason. I hope she can live with the rest.

The subtle verbal ambiguity in Judy's last paragraph reveals the psychological ambiguities of suicide. "In a sense, Myra feels as if she failed him, and so do I." Does Judy share Myra's belief that Myra has failed Jason, or does Judy believe that she too has failed him? Jason is the one who pulled the trigger, yet both women seem to believe that they should have been able to stop him. Myra ended her relationship with Jason because she sought more freedom, but now she seems wedded to a dead past, married to suffering.

ROSA
"I Will Never Forgive Myself for This"

For students whose former lovers commit suicide, guilt may become unbearable, particularly when they feel responsible for having broken off the relationship. Even when students realize that their guilt is irrational, they find it difficult to make peace with themselves, as Rosa indicates in her entry:

> Suicide is such a baffling thing to me. I cannot understand how anyone could take their own life. I have thought about suicide many times for many different reasons (not committing suicide, but just the concept of it). Every time I think about suicide, though, I think about how much I love life and all the things I have to look forward to. I cannot imagine how bad things would have to be for someone to kill himself.
>
> For many years suicide was just a concept to me. I knew what it was, I had heard of people doing it, but it was never very real to me—at least not until a few years ago, when someone I had been friends with for years and also dated killed himself shortly after I ended our relation-

ship. This was one of the hardest things I had to deal with in my life. The guilt was overwhelming. Maybe I wouldn't have felt so guilty and so responsible if he didn't get down on his hands and knees and beg me to go back out with him. But I wouldn't. I told him he was too much of a compulsive liar and that I couldn't deal with him anymore. I will never forgive myself for this. I would think, Why wasn't I able to see that his lying was a cry for help? Was I too self-absorbed? That couldn't be it, could it? I never thought of myself as a "me" person.

I felt guiltier everyday. I wanted so badly to be able to turn back time. If I did this, if I did that, IF, IF, IF. Then WHY, WHY, WHY? It was a never-ending cycle. I would feel guilty then angry, guilty then angry. I thought it would never stop.

To this day I still haven't forgiven myself, but I don't think about it quite as often.

CECILY
*"He Was Ultimately Convicted for His Illegal
Activities but Never for His Emotional Battery"*

The cycle of guilt and anger seems to be almost universal among those who have been affected by suicide. Each student may describe the cycle slightly differently, but it is rare for anger and guilt not to predominate in a diary. Some students, like Rosa, cannot forgive themselves for another person's death; others, like Cecily, focus their anger on the person attempting suicide:

When I was sixteen, a close friend of mine attempted suicide. He was sixteen too. We attended the same high school; however, he ran around with a different group. He was a "burnout," as we used to call "those" kids in high school, yet he and I had somehow broken our label-enforced barriers and become friends.

They told him the next time they caught him selling, they'd put him in the "real" place. We guessed they meant no more juvenile delinquent homes—after all, he was sixteen.

Before I heard of the arrest, two policemen visited my home. They sat with my parents and me in our living room. They told us that he had been caught selling to the junior high kids a week earlier, resisted arrest, and simultaneously tried to slit his wrists. When he was brought before the judge, he announced that the next free moment he had he would, in fact, succeed in killing himself. They called him psychologically unstable and immediately placed him in a psychiatric ward for troubled adolescents. Two days later he somehow escaped and hadn't been heard from since. Did I know where he was?

No, I didn't, not then at least. I don't think they believed me; neither did my parents, his parents, the school principal, the hospital, or the courts. I was summoned to each and every one of these places until he finally showed up. I knew he'd be back when he got lonely or ran out of money or was bored. I knew he wasn't lying dead somewhere like everyone said. I knew that suicide bit was all a ploy, a selfish and cold-hearted ploy. The remainder of the story is irrelevant to my point except to say he was ultimately convicted for his illegal activities but never for his acts of emotional battery.

Though this may not be your average suicide attempt, if such a monumental tragedy can ever be referred to as average, it remains representative of all suicides *in my mind.* That may be immature or ignorant or even self-centered, yet I cannot listen to another speak of a suicide without this story taking over my thoughts.

From a general intellectual or psychological perspective I do believe that suicide attempts and/or suicides are cries for help. I ache for those who feel their lives are worthless and hopeless enough to prematurely end it. I wish I could fix it—make all the bad go away and give them the will to live again. But, when I put aside the textbook and hear of a real suicide or suicide attempt and see the toll its ruthless acts have taken upon those around the person, I am transformed into a bitter and angry critic. When this transformation occurs, I question my career goals and even my own humanity.

When I was sixteen, I had my first introduction to suicide (thank God it was in the form of a failed attempt), and as a result of that six-month episode in my life, I chose to major in psychology with the intention of focusing on adolescent drug abuse and suicide. However, four years later as I sit in on an intense discussion of suicide, I clench my fists and bite my tongue in fury. How dare he! How dare he attempt to take his life, to give up, to leave *me* behind to pick up the pieces! How dare he! How dare *your* friend take his life and leave you feeling helpless and guilty? How dare he!

And in my own sad conclusion, how dare I judge so harshly and selfishly and then hypocritically say I want to make their salvation my life profession?

CATHERINE
"I Reserve My Sympathy for Those I Think Deserve It"

Sometimes students write about their anger toward a suicide's parents. Because of Catherine's experience with two children who died tragically, she had little sympathy for their parents, whom she viewed as responsible for their deaths:

I believe that my lack of empathy toward most people stems from being exposed to a little too much hard reality at an early age and then at a later date. Jonathan was eleven and I was eight. He lived near me, and his role in his family was that of the black sheep. His brother and sister often taunted him and ganged up on him. His parents were indifferent to his sufferings. They were and still are wrapped up in their own world and their images. He is involved with politics, and she is involved with the church.

Jonathan did not fit into their neat and tidy life. He was wild, beautiful, and sensitive—always full of dirt and mischief. He used to hide from his family under the willow tree in my front yard. My mother tried to take care of him and give him the love he did not receive at home. No one saw the problem in its ugliest light. He needed his family's love and was shunned. I remember seeing him huddled under our tree, dirty and shivering like a dying animal. He never cried.

One day I went to his room to get him, and I found him hanging in his closet—dead. I hate his parents to this day. They deserved no pity and got too much. Their tears were wasted after his death. They were the tears that Jonathan never cried, and the tears that he will never cry because he never knew real joy or real love, and at the age of eleven he died for it. I will never forget his blue lips and his eyes. It is not a lie that strangulation causes the eyes to bulge in an inhuman way. I live with that image in my eyes and still cannot forgive his pathetic parents for putting it there.

Two years ago a nine-year-old boy died a violent death in my arms. I still have scars on my hands from his little terrified nails digging into my flesh. His parents were narcissists too. They expected him and his sister to fulfill all the dreams they had failed at. When his sister turned out to be less than perfect, he was given that burden. His first failure came when he did not make a sports team and his father told him to go live somewhere else. He was missing for two weeks when his sister found out that he was living in an alley with a bunch of drug addicts and abused kids. We went to get him, and he lay in a corner shaking. His sister wouldn't go near him.

I picked him up and barely recognized his face. He grabbed me around the neck and started screaming about the colors that were killing him. I held him in my arms, and we ran to my home. His lips were cracked and bloody, and his angel face looked possessed by insanity. He dug his nails into my skin until I was bleeding, but I didn't feel it. His body jerked violently in my arms. He laughed and screamed the whole time and then began to vomit all over me; then he stopped fighting, smiled at me, kissed my hand for a minute, shut his eyes, and never opened them again. He was dead when I carried him into my house—his parents cried useless tears.

It is hard for me to have empathy for people who do not know what problems are. People who live in a sugar-coated world—for parents who can't love their children because they love only themselves. Some people think I am a bitch because I don't comfort my housemates who cry because they let men use them and get depressed over not being able to afford $800 skis. There are too many problems that cause too much pain, and I reserve my sympathy for those I think deserve it.

Suicide creates so much anger among survivors that it may be hard for them to remember that other survivors deserve sympathy rather than censure. Catherine, for example, seems unwilling to believe that the parents of the two deceased children are also grieving. And yet as the authors of Suicide and Its Aftermath observe, "Of the over 200 families we have seen, we have yet to encounter a family or a family member with anything suggestive of malicious intent or even neglect. We believe that suicide occurs in all types of families: the functional and the dysfunctional; the very good, the not so good, and the just good enough."[29]

WARREN

"How Do I Associate Stu's Death with the Holocaust?"

For some students suicide is so catastrophic that it seems analogous, on a personal level, to the Holocaust—a comparison that Warren makes reluctantly, not wishing to trivialize the word.

> The closest my family has ever come to tragedy has been our experience in dealing with the Holocaust during World War II. While some of my parents' family survived this extermination, many did not. As a Jew living nearly fifty years after these events, I have found it an interesting process trying to deal with what happened to my family and to the Jewish people as a whole. On one level, it does not touch me at all. How can I grieve for people that I never knew, people I have never met and never would? On another level, I am constantly grieving, not for my family but for the Jewish people as a whole. The Holocaust helps me temper my life. It shows me that no matter how many personal problems I may have, there is always a bigger picture.
>
> I have known only one person my age who has died. His name was Stu, and he was in my high school graduating class. Stu was one of the most cheerful and expressive persons I have ever known. Last summer, for reasons unknown to me, he jumped off the balcony of his apartment building and died. How do I associate Stu's death with the Holocaust? Well, to me the Holocaust is about death, plain and simple. Death had been an unknown factor to me until Stu's suicide. Now I am able to associate the Holocaust with the one personal death that I know of. On a realistic level, I realize that his death is nowhere nearly as tragic as the Holocaust, but on an emotional gut level, I feel that the tragedies are equal. Both are so horrible, so devastating that they seem to balance each other out.
>
> Death comes in many forms. Every day I live with the weight of the Holocaust on my shoulders. In my dreams I walk through the muck and stench of the death camps. I stand naked to the world as I await to be herded into a shower of poisonous gas. In my dreams I am falling from a great height, in panic of what I will meet below. For a second I fly, but then I just fall. Did Stu feel like he was flying? I mean just for a second? I hope so. I really do. So, to answer the question what Stu's death has to do with the Holocaust, the answer is nothing and absolutely everything.

ALISON

"I Am Running Away from My Brother's Fate"

Just as Warren's recurrent dreams of falling from a great height indicate, in his view, an identification with a deceased friend, so does Alison interpret her dreams of her brother as an attempt to resist sharing his fate.

One night last week I was extremely depressed. I mean, I was really low; I was awake but felt like I could feel nothing. It just felt like a void. My friends who know me and love me know that there are just times when I am feeling down. I may go out at night but just can't seem to have fun. I may just complain or talk in detail about how awful I feel. These moods always pass, and I can snap out of it just as fast as I snapped into it. I hate when I am in a depressed phase. It is almost physical pain. I cannot just stop feeling it. To others it sometimes looks as if I am feeling sorry for myself, and maybe that is true, but I just can't help it.

Anyway, as I mentioned in a previous diary, my brother committed suicide. I really am not going to go into the details, but basically he felt so low that he died from it. One night last week I was sort of thinking about him and thinking how he felt depressed and hopeless. I was feeling depressed but not hopeless. I have never felt hopeless and have never thought of suicide because I know that the feeling will pass.

That night I had the scariest dream I've ever had. I was on someone's front lawn near the woods by a nearby neighborhood. I don't remember too many of the details, but I do remember that there were two killers who were going after us. (I don't remember or didn't even know at the time who else was there with me.) I was standing on the sidewalk, and two people on the lawn were being killed. I saw them get an ax through their heads and get their arms cut off. I was standing on the sidewalk and didn't think I would be able to get away, but somehow I had already heard the story and knew that someone got away, so I started to run down the block. I was terrified but kept praying that I was the one who was going to get away. The whole time I kept thinking that I really hope it was true that I got away. I woke up scared and sweaty.

I interpreted this dream as meaning that I am running away from my brother's fate and know that it won't happen to me. But I still have some fears that maybe it will.

TED

*"Parents Are Supposed to Love Their Children Enough
Not to Leave Them"*

Probably no suicide is more wrenching than a mother's. In most families, the mother is the chief caretaker and nurturer; consequently, the threat of maternal loss is overwhelming to the children. Even when students observe that they have more or less come to terms with the event, their writings indicate otherwise.

Diary writing is particularly valuable for students who are despondent over parental loss and unable to grieve. Ted, a junior, wrote four diaries about his mother's death, which occurred when he was twelve years old. His diaries reveal a structure of expanding disclosure. The first entry begins with a haunting dream of her death; the second entry, written in response to a discussion of early parental loss, indicates how alone and frightened he felt during the class; the third entry, a moving account of the last time he saw his mother alive, discloses that she was a manic-depressive; and the fourth entry, in which he uses the word "suicide" for the first time, records the impact of maternal loss on his life.

> The last dream I can remember I have tried to interpret ever since. I'm sitting on a huge dark crystallized rock form. I am wearing all white, and I can feel a certain stirring of enormous power within me. This power within me suddenly erupts, and I can see past thoughts leaving my mind. These thoughts are represented by a wide spectrum of colors. All of a sudden the colors stop, and I feel an unfillable void take the place where mind previously was. I start to scream, then I see my mother's face, and I start to calm down. Then the horrible uneasiness feeling calms [sic] back, and I find myself alone on a rowboat in the middle of a bright blue lake. Then I wake up quite scared. I just looked back at a previous sentence and saw a Freudian slip I committed—"calms" back.
>
> This dream I have not yet been able to fully interpret. I do think the leaving of my thoughts represents the uneasiness and hard time I had dealing with my mother's death. For when I see her face, the feeling begins to leave. But then again I am alone. I believe this dream has to do with me having to deal with the permanence of my mother's death.
>
> The last class, although I enjoyed it, depressed me more than any single class that I have attended. There were about thirty other people express-

ing their relationships with their parents, while I sat there in a state of loneliness sprinkled with the fear that my fate is sealed because of the loss of my mother at an early age. I realize that anyone reading this will say I'm full of self-pity, for who the hell has a perfect childhood? Mine, of course, wasn't that bad; I was not poor or abused and was loved deeply by my father, but when discussing the integral part one's mother plays in one's life, I can't help but feel alone and frightened. After having lost my mother at an early age, reading about how important a part a mother plays in one's development fills me with uneasiness.

You asked in class if people blame their loved ones for dying, and consciously speaking, I honestly can say I don't. For some reason beyond her control my mother was unable to deal with the world, be it her childhood or a chemical imbalance. I still love her. I just wish I could have been able to venture into the depths of her mind.

Have you ever read *Breakfast of Champions*? Vonnegut clearly expresses the belief that mental illness is caused by chemical imbalance. At this point in my life I do not see any real damage done by being raised by a mother who happened to be a manic-depressive. By the way, I hate that term because it gives anyone who gets it the same characteristics as anyone else who is afflicted by it. It kills the uniqueness of being slightly insane. I don't really regret her death; I think I have come to accept it— of course not totally. However, it still makes me uneasy when other people my age talk about twenty years or so of a relationship with their mothers, when I have only twelve years to talk about.

Rain dripped from my hair as I walked into my mother's darkened room. She looked at me and tried to smile. Her eyes, raccooned from mascara, looked as lonely and desolate as a vacant lot. I hugged her, and at the time I was unaware of how desperately she needed that hug. She told me she loved me and then gave me money for ice cream. I bounded out to the pavement, the coins jingling in my wet palms, unaware that I had just heard the last words my mother would ever say to me.

I returned two hours later quite proud after having played an excellent game of Dungeons and Dragons. I was not greeted by Mom but rather by a policeman. He told me my mother was in the hospital. I was not worried because I thought my mother just had another nervous breakdown. Quite an unusual thought for a twelve-year-old, but I was not your average child. Although only a child, I had a slight indication of my mother's illness. My mother was a manic-depressive, which meant at times that she was bountiful in her love and energy, while at other times she was caged in by self-pity, unable to leave her bed.

A week later I found out that the last time I saw her she had either just eaten an overdose of Valium or took them right after she saw me. This overdose put my mother in a coma for a month. I never did get to see her in the hospital and was truly hopeful that one day her arms would be able to shelter me. I kept that dream for an entire month until my father came home early one day and I knew. I won't try to describe my feelings in words, for they are and always will be a part of me that I need not share with another.

This was the hardest thing I have ever written, even though it is poorly written. I don't know what possessed me to write this, but it sure made me relive the utter hopelessness I felt at the age of twelve and many, many times since.

I would like to discuss depression in this journal. Depression to me is uncontrollable and complex. For me it usually doesn't last longer than a day and always varies in intensity. For the most part I consider myself a relatively happy person, yet I still at times cannot control depression. It starts in the brain and flows through my entire body. It attacks every aspect of my life when it comes—relationships, family, friends, my sex life, my hopes, dreams, and aspirations. What puzzles me is that one day I believe I am doing well and I continue to feel great for a while, and then depression starts. I don't know what starts it. I always try to fight it. So what if not everything is going perfectly—no one's life is.

What I want to know is, Which perspective is correct—the conscious one you have of yourself, or the unconscious one you have? I tend to believe in the conscious view as being the more realistic, for it is backed up by evidence. Yet, during depression my conscious perspective of myself takes a beating, along with my self-esteem. I am usually unable to fight, even by bringing out things that make me happy.

I wonder how often the majority of people get depressed. I am truly amazed at the effect depression can have on people. Some people are overwhelmed and possessed by it. I guess the only reason I am worried about depression at this present moment is because I am depressed right now, and because my mother committed suicide. That troubles me a lot, for parents are supposed to love their children enough not to leave them. It is not really that I think she left me. I think what puzzles me more is what made her believe her life was so miserable. What depressed her, and why couldn't she deal with it?

Am I going to be able to deal with life? Most of the time my answer would be yes, but at this moment I would have to say I don't have a clue. Depression is so strange because it represses certain thoughts that make you happy and replaces them with a feeling of helplessness. Well, I'm babbling to no end right now, so I'd better stop typing. Writing this journal really made me feel better—I'm not bullshitting either.

Just as Alison remains depressed over her brother's suicide, fearing the same ending, so does Ted draw the conclusion in a gloomy moment that his "fate is sealed" because of his mother's suicide. The two students use the identical image to describe depression, the feeling they are in a "void." The identification with their deceased relatives is so strong that they seem to identify with the suicidal depression, too. One can feel in their diaries intense anxiety and almost paralyzing inertia. By reliving the "utter hopelessness" of his mother's death, Ted acknowledges the existence of two perspectives from which he alternately sees the world: a conscious one, in which he sees himself as a basically happy person, in control of his life; and an unconscious one, in which he battles the gorgon of depression and low self-esteem.

Because a parent's suicide increases the risk of a child's vulnerability in later life, it is especially important for the child to receive love and understanding from family and friends. And indeed, in other diaries that are not included here, Ted describes the comfort he received from his father, whose support has never wavered. Writing has also been a comfort, despite the anguish of dredging up painful memories. While none of the conflicts about which he writes is resolved in the end, there is relief in expressing them and hearing others respond empathically.

For Ted, writing about his mother's death has brought to life his memories of her. "In many of my diaries," he observes at the end of the course, "I talked openly about my mother's death, which I haven't done in years. This remourning, so to speak, made me feel closer to my mother than I have in years. I was expressing my feelings about a subject that most of my family members seem unwilling to discuss with me." The value of writing about his mother's suicide, Ted later told me, persisted long after the course ended.[30]

TERRY
"You Asked Me Why I Was Angry"

The process of remourning also takes place among those who write about their own suicide attempts. Most students who write these diaries are women, reflecting the fact that women attempt suicide much more frequently than men do. Indeed, women make three out of four suicide attempts, while men commit three out of four suicides. Researchers believe that, despite overlap, there are distinct differences between suicide attempters and suicide completers.[31] Men generally choose violent methods to commit suicide, such as a gun, while women often overdose on drugs. Over the years many students have written about suicide attempts; significantly, no one has ever expressed regret that the attempt was unsuccessful. In the remaining pages of this chapter I shall focus on two women, Terry and Ruth. Both wrote several entries which they allowed me to read to the class—and both wrote letters to me, years after the course ended, in which they evaluated the experience of diary writing.

A quiet, self-effacing young woman who betrayed little emotion in class, Terry wrote diaries that contained more anger than I have ever come across in a student's writing, anger which she aptly compared to a violent hurricane. A sophomore, she wrote five diaries in her summer school class, four of which are included here. The first entry opens with an obscure aggression fantasy directed against a woman who has apparently aroused Terry's fury. I commented upon the diary's angry tone and invited her to elaborate on her feelings—an invitation she accepted, angrily:

Aggression Fantasy!!!!!!!! Must admit Freud got this right on the mark with me! When I am angry, it is so overpowering because I do not feel in control over it. Note, I rarely act upon it other than to yell hysterically—and those few times when I do something a bit more rash, it's never even close to what I fantasize doing.

INTENSE! When I am angry, my pulse soars, my skin tightens, my muscles contract till they shake, and my teeth remain unclenched only when I'm yelling. Even the mere thought of something that once provoked me to this state of frenzy can evoke these symptoms almost anywhere (in the middle of a class, for instance).

Though I don't always yell.

Often I sit, encaptured in the intense feeling throughout my body. I shift limbs, tightening and flexing, yet the hurricane inside me cannot be let free. It may very well be my most painful emotion, one which usually paralyzes me with fear and awe of myself.

Intense. Even that word is too soft for the emotion.

When I first read works of Poe, including "The Cask of Amontillado," I couldn't help but notice how similar his words were to my thoughts, with one exception. Poe's actions are never sick or torturous enough to give me serenity and peace of mind.

Bury someone alive with a few skeletons, big deal!

At this moment I am furious with this little bitch who deserves only INTENSE pain and suffering; I would wish her death, but the worst that could happen would be hell, and that is not near enough punishment for this waste of being.

Oh the satisfaction that I would encounter witnessing her eat live waterbugs and maggots. And to have pins thrust inward over every inch of her body and then quickly thrust out and in again over and over till her skin falls off. AND to have every hair on her body plucked out one by one—EVERY hair—EVERYWHERE!

Right now I am not too angry, so that will be sufficient—FOR NOW. It is only a matter of time before my muscles tighten, and then nothing will give me inner peace. Yet usually all I ever really do is talk. And sometimes not even that.

You know—be a good little Christian girl! Forgive! Forgive! Turn the other cheek! YOU WANT REPRESSION!!!!!!!

I believe in my faith too. So I can't even blame it on habit. But the things I could do with electric shocks! Yet even as I speak, I know that if the tables were turned, if tomorrow she was put in my situation and I in hers, I would not do the mean thing she has done to me. Even now.

REPRESSION!!!!!!!!!!

Fuck this diary. You want repressed anger, I'll show you repressed anger—unrepressed.

I DON'T WANT TO DO THIS FUCKING DIARY!!!!!

Since when is the psychoanalysis of my life anybody's business other than mine? I'm sick of this shit. All my life I get these assignments in school—autobiographies, personal essays, "anonymous essays" (this is my personal favorite—the person at the front of the room reads everybody's essay, since everybody has put their name to it, yet they call it anonymous). Is the teacher supposed to be God or something? Yes, yes I know the purpose of the assignment isn't to be nosy, and I believe each and every teacher I've had, but at this point I really don't give a shit.

What is the purpose of this assignment? If I remember correctly, it was to help the student see Freud's theories in his/her life a little more clearly. Well, I have begun to see a lot more of Freud in my life, but I haven't written about it in my diaries—or else I've watered it down so that it's boring yet safe.

And then I feel selfish because this is the first class that I've had the guts to say, "NO!—That's personal—It's mine, you can't have it." In this class EVERYBODY spills their guts, even the professor!

But I don't care. I could never say no to anyone, especially "authority." It feels almost like rape sometimes—the teacher knows they are in a position to ask you to do this type of assignment, you can never come up with anything good unless you're sincere, and you're forced to give a part of yourself that you consider personal—sacred. And for all you know, this person could hate your guts, be indifferent, who knows? He/she's probably not God, though.

Think I'm paranoid, lazy, whatever, the answer is NO!!!! I don't want to give you any part of me this week, and I don't see the point in embracing any bullshit essay I create as being a part of me. (In a tone from your class, any shit other than my own authentic shit I find I'm repelled by, and I am attached to my shit because it is a part of me.)

Please understand that I do realize the purpose of the assignment, I don't necessarily disagree with it, and I do think about how the ideas discussed in class influence my life. Please also understand that this has nothing to do with you personally, it's your timing more than anything. Please also understand that I may change my mind next week.

[The next sentences are handwritten.] Rereading this a day later, I have realized how angry this sounds. I'm not trying to sound cocky; if you want me to re-do this diary, I will. But it will be insincere and "made up." My Freudian experiences this week are too personal to share.

I certainly did not want Terry to rewrite her diary, since it was the spontaneous, passionate anger, so vividly described it almost leaps off the page, that makes her writing powerful. By wishing to hold on to her anger, nurturing it secretly, she was understandably protecting herself from her enemies. I did not want to become one of these enemies, much less a "rapist." (The difference between the rapist and therapist, Nabokov observes mordantly in *Lolita*, is a matter of spacing.)[32] Others had forced her to be self-disclosing, with disastrous consequences.

At the same time, I sensed that Terry wanted to share her experiences with the class. Central to her opening diaries was fierce rage which I did not want to invalidate or trivialize. If she could express this rage, releasing the hurricane within, she might be able to defuse much of its terrifying force. Before she could do this, however, she had to overcome her mistrust of me; other authority figures had exploited her in the past, and she had no reason to believe that I would be different. I felt she was testing my willingness to allow her to unleash her fury at me. If I became angry or hurt or fearful, I would prevent her from resuming her story. Just as therapists need to be aware of their countertransference, particularly feelings of malice or aversion when treating suicidal patients,[33] so do teachers need to be aware of similar responses when receiving diaries from students writing about past or present suicidal crises.

And so I told Terry that if she wanted to write about why she felt ready to explode, I would be ready to listen. I promised her that I would read her diary to the class if she gave me permission, adding that I thought the students would be able to understand and empathize with her experiences. And I praised the power and honesty of her writing. The volatility of her diaries concerned me, yet her prose sparkled with sarcastic humor, she seemed to enjoy writing, despite ambivalence over self-disclosure, and she appeared to be on the verge of revealing something very important in her life. The next week she turned in the following entry:

It is very hard to write this diary. Last time I wrote that I really felt that this stuff was too personal. All my life I have been forced to confide, and sometimes it is hard to say no when I'm asked to say something personal. Yet now that I've said I wasn't going to talk about the past, I almost have regrets. I like the people in this class. As I look around the room, I feel something almost like a bond with each of my classmates. There is not one student in this class I dislike. In fact, as I look around the room, I find myself wanting to get to know each and every person a little bit deeper. I don't know if it is the diaries that are read in class each week or just pure luck that the computer came out with a class list without one asshole on it. Maybe arrogant bitches and dicks don't want to spend their summer evenings learning about Freud.

So I change my mind and decide to answer the question Prof. Berman wrote on the bottom of my last diary—"What are you so angry about?"

Then again this is supposed to be a two-paged diary.

This is hard to write. When I was fourteen and had just started high school, I realized that I needed professional help. I had been feeling very depressed, had been crying a lot, and had been thinking about suicide, among other things. I had asked my mother to get me help repeatedly, but of course she didn't—that might imply I'm not perfect. However, luckily for me a kid committed suicide in my neighborhood about this time, which scared my mother, since suicide is an even bigger embarrassment; besides, who would she live her life through if I was dead? (Please don't misinterpret—my parents love me, but it's a conditional love, to an extent.) So my mom went up to school to one of those meetings that schools hold to make everybody feel better but that never attempts to solve the problem. It was here that she met my first shrink.

This shrink was actually good, but as head of the department, he only referred.

My next shrink would sit and roll her eyes as I talked. If I wasn't thinking about suicide when I walked in, I was thinking about it on my way out. Yet I stuck with it, as I had begged my mother for this, and because I figured maybe it was supposed to hurt.

After a while I asked her why she rolled her eyes—she told me I dragged on too much. I didn't realize I was supposed to be entertaining. Around this time I was hospitalized. I then got a shrink who told me, "Oh, give me a break. You're not really depressed. It's just adolescent melodrama." Yet I continued to pour out my heart to this condescending bitch; I was determined to get well.

During the time I was in the hospital, my father, who had promised me not to tell his mother, went and told her anyway. So much for trust.

In my second hospital I was placed with an intern because he needed the experience of working with an adolescent. To date he is probably one of the most arrogant assholes I know. After he interrogated me during my first three hours in this place, I finally said that it was getting too painful and I didn't want to go on. As punishment I was put on constant observation, along with a severely retarded person who got stuck in this ward, and with somebody else who kept yelling at and threatening me. For the rest of my stay there the staff continually told my parents that they were bad parents and to please leave me alone—the staff would fix the damage. After begging my parents night after night to take me out (as I had no say in the matter), I was finally discharged against medical advice.

By now I was on medication, and everyone at school knew of my problems, even my most bitter enemies. Privacy was a privilege I no longer had. All my teachers knew too—how else do you explain all my absences?

I was now put in my third hospital, and I still had not learned. I was open with everyone, not knowing that "you weren't supposed to be open your first week," that this was the week when everyone on the staff was "hard on you" to "make sure you tried." On my first day of group the ENTIRE group said that they literally hated me. Yet I returned the next day to make amends. The end of the week I was evaluated. Rather than tell me to keep hanging in there, I was told that I wasn't trying hard enough, which I later learned was pretty much procedure.

I ran away, was found, brought back, put in full body restraints to prevent me from running away again, and injected with Thorazine. I was kept on Thorazine for quite some time, as its drowsy effect, along with the fear I would get sick if I stopped taking it rather than getting weaned off it, gave the staff a wonderful control device. The rule in this hospital is that no one has any privacy—anything said to anyone could (and would) be told to every other staff member, and again I was forced to reveal myself to everyone, including both staff and patients who openly disliked me.

I could go into more details, but this is painful enough.

You asked me why I was angry. The arrogance, lack of compassion, and feeling of superiority I have seen in the average mental health worker have caused me to feel bitterness to anyone exercising these traits. As I want to torture (and I mean TORTURE) many of the workers in those hospitals, I get the same desire to torture anyone I see display these traits to me.

I don't know if this is Freudian or not, but it shows plenty of repressed anger and explains both why I am angry and why I did not feel I could do a diary last week.

[The next sentences are handwritten.] I cried throughout writing this diary, as it brought back lots of painful memories I could not share. I realize that I didn't go into how anger affects my life today as well as I should have. Maybe I will next week, but I answered your question, and I am too mentally exhausted to continue.

In the beginning, Terry found the idea of a required weekly diary onerous, and she was unwilling to reveal any personal material that could be used against her. But as the summer progressed, she found herself revealing more about her life than she had intended earlier. Her ambivalence over self-disclosure gradually lessened. Once she was able to overcome her mistrust, words poured from her pen. She began to feel a bond of kinship with the other students in the class, and though she was writing about a past rather than a present suicidal crisis, the act of writing was a kind of lifeline, linking her to her classmates. Through their supportive diaries, which they allowed me to read aloud, the other students were able to heighten Terry's trust and mirror her self-esteem. The contrast between the growing closeness she felt toward the class and the alienation she experienced in various psychiatric hospitals was striking. In the hospitals, she had no privacy and felt both invaded and ridiculed by staff and patients. Indeed, her diaries evoke the nightmarish world of Ken Kesey's antipsychiatric novel *One Flew over the Cuckoo's Nest*, in which Randle McMurphy falls victim to the horrors of the Therapeutic State.[34] Kesey's benumbed characters are stripped of their free will and forced to confess during "Pecking Parties," in which they are then ripped apart and humiliated. By contrast, the safeguards surrounding class-room diary writing enabled Terry to determine in advance the content of her entries and to control the degree of self-disclosure.

In her final entry, Terry describes the feeling of bringing up so much private material. She still has doubts about whether she can cope with the flood of emotions, but there is affirmation in her voice as she closes:

I am presently writing this diary at 4:18 in the morning because I cannot sleep and realize that I'll probably be tired during the time I allotted to write this diary.

I think it's really funny about your book, since I was planning to spend a major portion of this diary suggesting that you write it. I like the idea a lot; actually, I sort of wish you could just put all the diaries in a book and not say anything. Not that I think you don't have anything else to say . . . well, maybe, I don't know. Let me try to explain because now that I think of it, the class can't really be dropped here. Maybe it would be easier if I said what I got out of the class first.

What did I get from the class? I started out by calling Freud a pervert, and despite everything, that has not changed. But I learned a lot from Freud that I could relate to my own life, like anxiety stuff—repression stuff too. And a lot of things I wouldn't admit for anything. I wrote a lot more than five diaries—I wrote at least twice as many—and they've all focused me into thinking about things I like to keep repressed and that have put my present life in turmoil. I remember once being so angry from just thinking (that happens a lot) that I kept saying, "I hate those diaries!!!! What does he care! Some things are better off left repressed! SOME THINGS ARE BETTER OFF LEFT REPRESSED!" But it's all coming out now, so I have to deal with it. And it sucks, cause I don't know how.

Then again, I liked listening to the diaries in class more than anything else. I remember one time a girl had written about chronic depression, and I felt so less alone. Reading *The Bell Jar* was good too because it was really quite real. But it was kind of painful; I had to keep putting it down so I could cry. It was hard when we discussed it in class, too, because I kept seeing all my problems in Sylvia Plath, especially when you told the class that she wrote her mom every day—my mom and I talk nearly every day, and it's such a similar relationship.

It really meant a lot to me to have my diaries read in class. It's such a relief to get stuff off my chest. I'm really jealous of those people in your spring and fall classes who get to do twelve diaries. I feel like I've got too many diaries left, and writing them to myself isn't the same.

I like listening too. I like to think there's good in everybody, and I always thought that if you could see a person's pain, you could see beyond any fault. It's a nice theory, anyway, since I generally think people are jerks. Maybe I've just met a lot of jerks in my life—though I've met a lot of good people too. I really wish I could have gotten to know some of my classmates better. The diaries have helped, but I still think maybe this class draws in nicer people. I'm trying very hard to see good in everyone, and so I like to look at these things as proof; however, someone once told me, "I'm lovable, God doesn't make junk," and the first thought in my mind was, "But what about my roommate?"

The diaries really force you to look at Freud in your own life, which makes him much more credible. It's a very lifelike course—you walk away from it knowing that you'll use what you've learned somehow. Most courses don't do that. Listening to the diaries is a sigh of relief, too, since you don't feel so alone.

One more thing—please don't underestimate the contribution to the class that is made by the professor. Your sharing makes it easier to trust and examine ourselves. In addition, you're pretty approachable, which is necessary for this course. Also, you're very provoking in class, which forces one to think.

Finally, the positive feedback you give on the diaries makes them less frightening.

The most eloquent response to Terry's diaries came from another student who wrote about having been suicidal in the past and who, echoing Terry's words, remarked that the pain felt by high school students doesn't hurt less because adults fail to take it seriously. "Pain is pain, and while its cause may seem unimportant to one person, it still hurts the other person who is experiencing it. 'Adolescent melodrama' is a terrible phrase, one of the most cutting to those it is aimed at." Years later Terry recalled, with appreciation, her classmates' empathic response to her entries.[35]

RUTH
"I Am Constantly Fighting Depression and My Self-Destructive Habits"

Unlike Terry, who had to overcome intense anger and mistrust before she was willing to disclose past suicidal feelings, Ruth, a junior, was willing to write about her experiences. Because her class was particularly large, I did not have the opportunity to read aloud any of her early diaries. She experienced these unread entries as a personal rejection—a key theme, it turns out, in all her writings. In the nine diaries included here, Ruth offers a week-by-week account of her efforts to deal constructively with serious problems: low self-esteem, periodic depression, drug addiction, compulsive overeating, and promiscuity. Many of these problems, she tells us, are now under control, though they still demand constant vigilance.

Ruth introduces a theme in her opening diary to which she returns in many of her writings: conflicted feelings toward sexuality. She is especially ambivalent toward her present boyfriend, who makes many demands upon her. She evokes in the first entry the childhood night terrors, or fear of being "stuck for eternity in a black void," which she interprets as the beginning of her preoccupation with suicide.

There is less overt anger in Ruth's diaries than in Terry's but more sadness, insecurity, and self-reproach. Occasionally she allows her anger to surface. In one revealing passage, she expresses bitter disappointment with her parents, concluding that as a child she deserved to be treated with love and respect—a conclusion that the more self-deprecating part of her immediately challenges.

As stressful as her present life is, Ruth feels more in control now than she did two or three years ago, when she was hospitalized for a serious eating disorder and dependency on drugs and alcohol. Compared with those past problems, the present ones seem less frightening. Now she is more academically responsible too. Therapy has helped her, and she has learned to deal more successfully with depression and self-destructiveness. Writing about her experiences also seems to be helpful. She admits in the fourth diary that she has lost some of her enthusiasm for writing, but two entries later she observes that, as a result of hearing other students' entries, she feels less self-conscious about her problems, less alone.

Amid this increasing self-confidence, Ruth's ninth diary records a serious setback which, she notes with embarrassment the following week, might have had grave consequences:

Lately I have been thinking about the Oedipus complex and have come to the conclusion that sex, my boyfriend, and my father seem closely related. I like it when my boyfriend treats me like a little girl. Sometimes he says things like "Come to Daddy" and "Be a good girl." I also like it when he spanks me when we have sex. When I was growing up, my dad was always short with me and hit me. I think that my present behavior with my boyfriend is somehow connected to how my dad treated me.

My dad's love for me is intense and has sexual overtones. When I visit him, he hugs me for a long time, pressing his whole body against mine. I don't like it. Last month I had a dream I was having sex with my dad. All of these events and feelings cause me shame and confusion. I feel like I am disgusting and dirty.

For the next journal I'm going to write down my dreams and my interpretations of them. I remember at least one dream for every significant period of sleep. Basically my dreams are about sex, my family, present or past boyfriends, and/or school. I don't dream about anything else.

When I was a child, I used to have night terrors. These are dreams in which I often walked in my sleep, screamed, cried, and was terrified. Half of the time I would not remember the dreams. Everyone else in my house woke up because of my screams. In my dreams I would be in blackness. There would be no floors, walls, ceilings, people, objects, light, or anything. I would just be stuck for eternity in a black void. Perhaps this blackness represented my fear of death. I thought often of suicide as a child, so maybe the dreams were a representation of my subconscious being too afraid of the unknown to carry out my death wish.

For our last class, I was uncomfortable for much of the time. When we began to talk about contradictory feelings people have toward their parents, I felt guilty and a little sad. I felt this way because my feelings toward my parents don't seem to be as ambivalent or contradictory (i.e., love-hate relationships) as Freud's or the other students. I basically feel only negatively toward my parents. I feel like I am wrong or twisted because I really don't love or even like my mom and dad. These class discussions facilitate the surfacing of some painful memories or realities, and I have a difficult time sitting through class.

In my previous journal I said I was going to write down and analyze my dreams. Well, I remembered a good chunk of the many dreams I had this week and figured out what I think they meant. Mostly the dreams were about wanting to have sex with my boyfriend and the need to break up with him because he does drugs and is a bad influence on me, since I have a long history of drug use. Perhaps my boyfriend represents my dad to me, because I certainly have a love-hate relationship with my boyfriend.

The readings that were due this week all had to do with money and careers. The readings brought up feelings of anxiety and sadness. I am concerned with my future as an "adult." I am just beginning to realize reality (i.e., that I have limitations both physical and mental). Silly as it seems, I have recently come to the conclusion that I am not all-powerful. I have a lot of sadness surrounding this realization. I am afraid that I am not going to be competent enough to support myself in the manner I desire. I feel very inadequate in the realm of the professional and personal world. I have problems with drugs and alcohol, so there are situations I cannot put myself into, such as most bars, some parties, and a few people.

My boyfriend and I broke up this week because he smokes pot every day, and his smoking bothers me. I am sad about this breakup. I need love and affection more than any amount of money. I didn't feel loved and secure with my parents in my childhood, so attention and love from other people are extremely important to me. Although I continually crave affection and love, I feel unable to deal with the problems that come up in relationships. I am confused about sex. I like sex and fooling around but often feel like I am pressured into it.

I am a little upset that none of my journals have been read in class yet. I feel like I am uninteresting or something. Perhaps my journals are not good enough, that is, about psychoanalytic material, long enough, proper grammar, etc.

Anyway, this week I feel no different than last week. I feel weird telling Professor Berman about my personal life, so this week I'm going to talk about someone else. I have a friend who is very similar to Tommy Wilhelm in *Seize the Day*. She is always looking for people to "carry her." Forget it, the "she" is me. I'll just be frank. I usually only like to go out with guys who are very responsible and energetic about life. Presently I am attempting to "carry myself." I am becoming more concerned about my well-being, and not relying as much on guys.

This may be happening because my present boyfriend can hardly take care of himself. The fact that he cannot support me financially or emotionally makes me angry sometimes. I get depressed every time I have to write one of these diaries. I wonder why this is so. I was at first enthused about keeping diaries for this course, but now I am having difficulty thinking of things to say.

I feel depressed when I sit down and think about or do creative writing. I don't particularly like what's in my head. I am very obsessed with my boyfriend. I go through withdrawal whenever I am not with him. I have to concentrate on doing activities, so I won't eat a ton of candy, mope around, or do other negative things. I think he is an ass-hole for doing drugs everyday, and I see a lot of myself in him. I hate it when he is stoned. I'm not even sure I like him more than a friend. I guess I am addicted to him. I worship him, though. I would do anything for him. He is really affectionate to me, and I crave affection and love. Maybe that is why I stay with him. I guess I really like him a lot, but it is really scary liking him because he is such a bad influence on me. I am quite impressionable, and I don't want to go down with him.

I am going to write about a question I have concerning my sexual relationship with my boyfriend. I am beginning to feel less and less interested in fooling around with him, French-kissing him, and having intercourse with him. I am sometimes not only indifferent to him if we are sexual or not, but lately I have begun to feel repulsed by the thought of any kind of sexual intercourse with him, or with any one else for that matter. I still like him as much as I did when I met him almost a year ago.

I wonder if it is possible to like someone, as a boyfriend, but not to be interested in him sexually. I think that maybe I don't really like my boyfriend that much, and this is the way my body is telling me. On the other hand, perhaps I am going through a number of serious changes right now and am too overwhelmed to be in a sexual relationship with anyone.

Besides feeling repulsed and confused, I also feel guilty and insecure. I don't want my boyfriend to feel frustrated all the time, and I don't want him to leave me because he is sexually unsatisfied. One thing I am sure of is that I am going to concentrate on saying no when I don't want to have sex with him. When I say yes when I really mean no, I feel disgust-ing and depressed afterward. I am going to try to be true to myself from now on.

Today I was having a stressful day, but I didn't do anything destructive. It used to be that if things were going wrong in my day, I would not deal with the problem but would escape through various methods. I used to sleep, overeat, drink, do drugs, watch TV, read books, or have sex. Now

I am trying to take life less seriously and not stress out so much. If I am not stressed out, I feel less inclined to cope with destructive behavior.

I have been really down on myself lately because I think that I am not a high enough achiever. But realistically, I have improved in the area of taking care of myself and being happy. This is the first semester in four years that I have missed only a few classes. I am doing all my homework and classwork this semester. I have also stopped all my bulimic activity finally. I cannot believe so many people in the class are bulimics. From the other journals, I feel a lot less self-conscious knowing that I am not alone in this problem. I feel much less inferior.

On the subject of my boyfriend, I am becoming much more true to myself in the area of saying no to sex, even though I feel guilty when I say no. When I said no to him, he was very nice about it, although he felt there was something wrong with him.

I have just finished reading my journals from the previous weeks and realized I have written about my boyfriend in all but one. I suppose this evidence means that I think about my boyfriend more than any other thing in my life, or that he is the most important thing in my life. I believe that my dependency on him makes me a weak or a lesser person. I wish I did not judge myself so harshly, for it is quite painful. I look down on myself often. Perhaps I judge myself so severely concerning my boyfriend because I have doubts whether I should be continuing the relationship. The word "should" is self-defeating.

My mother is coming to see me for the first time in a long time. I am afraid, not only because I am always afraid to see her, but also because we are jointly meeting for a session with my therapist. I feel so much ambivalence concerning my mother, and when I am with her, I cannot even identify my feelings half the time. Usually I feel slightly frustrated or angry with her, and I am almost always on the brink of tears, if not actually crying. I even get teary eyed or cry when I just talk to her on the phone.

I don't know exactly what we are going to talk about in my session, but I know it will be about my past, my childhood. I am going to try not to think about it until she comes on Friday. Just thinking about it causes me to feel trapped, upset, and afraid. I do not remember much of my childhood and always feel like I am exaggerating when I verbally re-member parts of it to my therapist. For some reason, I feel like I am a liar when I talk about anything with my therapist. Surprisingly, a significant part of me is excited to see my mom, since somewhere inside I do miss her. Go figure.

My whole teen and adult life I was trying to get away from my mother. I guess when I was a little girl, my mom blew me off a lot. My mom was often short and verbally abusive to me. I never thought there was anything wrong with calling a ten-year-old a slut, or with refusing to talk to your child for hours when she misplaced a 98-cent bathing cap, until I saw other friends' families treating their children differently. I thought my friends' siblings were spoiled because their family was listening to their feelings and not screaming or hitting the children when they did something other than what the parent wanted them to do.

Thinking about these things makes me feel a little sad but also angry. How could God have allowed me to be raised by two parents who were unable to be patient and continually loving to me? But then when I think that thought, the critical parent part of me says, "How could you be so stupid to think you deserve to be treated like a princess?" Perhaps some hostility and anger are necessary in bringing up a kid.

I think that idea is bullshit, and as a little girl I deserved to be treated with love, kindness, and respect. I am still having enormous difficulties, though, believing that the grown-up me or at least the college-aged me deserves kindness, love, and respect.

I am surprised that so many people have eating disorders. I believed I was the only one. I have always felt that I was a freak or something. My eating disorder does not always take the form of starving (i.e., anorexia nervosa) or bingeing and purging (i.e., bulimia). I would merely binge and not get rid of the food but become depressed. I would constantly think of how fat I was, when in reality I was about the right weight.

Eventually I became so depressed and miserable that I admitted myself into a hospital specializing in eating disorders. In the hospital I found out I was a drug addict. When I came back from the hospital, I could not get a handle on my eating habits until I stopped using drugs and alcohol.

This diary is a very simplified version of the last three years. Since I was a sophomore, I have been unhappy, apathetic, and preoccupied with thoughts of suicide. I would never have admitted I had such problems with food, alcohol, and drugs if I wasn't in such extreme emotional pain.

I have to be very careful how I take care of myself, since I always feel very close to another wave of depression. I am constantly fighting depression and my self-destructive habits. I need to keep a constant vigilance over my need to harm myself either emotionally or physically.

Ways in which I help myself are going to a psychologist, talking to friends I can trust, not isolating, praying, sitting through the bad feelings, reading, writing, and, most important, going to support groups almost every or every other day. It is not appropriate to print the names of these support groups in your book, Dr. Berman, but you can mention them in class. Groups that help me are Overeaters Anonymous, Alcoholics Anonymous, and, most especially, Narcotics Anonymous. Usually I dislike these meetings every time I go because they are sometimes boring, but more often they show the truth about me.

Seeing the truth about myself is very painful because I have lived in a fantasy life for so long. I was never able to deal with the pain of life from an early age, so to protect myself I made up an imaginary world in my head. I believed that to be happy all I had to do was be as beautiful and thin as possible, and party. I thought drugs, drinking, and bars were the best thing in the world, and for a while they were. But eventually I stopped having fun partying because the charade was just not working anymore. I was using drugs to escape life, not enhance it.

I have been going to these meetings and been in therapy for about a year and a half, and just now I am starting to understand that bingeing on food, drugs, and alcohol are not the answer to my problems but often the root of them. The process of becoming a healthy person and learning the truth about myself takes a long time to accept and put into action. I am still resisting the fact that I use men to solve my problems, but one thing at a time. Maybe in another year or so I will begin to tackle that area of my life.

Today I realized that I have been having sex and fooling around with various boyfriends and having one-night stands, even though I did not want them at all, for seven years. I think I have been subconsciously prostituting myself for free with many of these males. I realized the situation when I was writing a short story about a friend I have in New

York City who is a mistress for hire. My friend has, generally one at a time, rich older boyfriends. My friend usually feels nothing romantic for these older men and is often disgusted by them. She goes out with them because they buy her clothes and take her on exotic vacations. She usually has a boyfriend or two on the side who she really cares for.

I have been thinking an awful lot about my friend and her livelihood of selling her body. I do not see much difference between how I feel when I have sex with people and how a prostitute would feel. I don't really enjoy sex and often need to grit my teeth to get through it. Sometimes it is painful, and sometimes I am so conscious of feeling like a prostitute that I have to fight back the tears. I think blow jobs and hand jobs are disgusting, yet I do that stuff to my boyfriend when he asks for it. I don't even like it when he touches me.

This afternoon my boyfriend asked me if I wanted to have sex, and I said no and told him that I was sore. He said, "All right" and went to sleep. A few minutes later he opened his eyes and said, "I really want to have sex." I said, "We can't," thinking, doesn't he remember that I said I am in pain? He answered, "Yes we can [have sex], I have a hard-on." Usually I might have considered having sex with him and bearing the pain, but I guess I am wising up. I said to him, "Well, aren't we selfish," and he replied, "Do you remember last night?" (Last night he didn't sexually come on to me and hugged me for ten minutes.) As if because he did that I owe him sex.

One other boyfriend I used to have wanted to have sex at least twice a day, which is not a big deal if one is in the mood and not exhausted, but the summer I was going out with him I worked about fourteen hours a day and was often really tired when I came home to see him. He wanted to have sex anyway, and I can remember falling asleep while he was on top of me pounding away. I have also cried while giving one of my old boyfriends a blow job because I did not want to give him one.

There are countless other examples of having sex or performing sexual favors, even though I was in pain emotionally and/or physically. Why have I done this to myself for so long? How come I just realized it now? I feel very sad. I know I am often extremely unhappy and depressed and lonely, but I don't think sacrificing myself for a man's sexual desires has helped, in the long run, to alleviate any of these feelings.

Perhaps one of the reasons I have not been able to say no is because I was terrorized by my father and mother much of my childhood, and perhaps I am afraid that if I say no to a man, he will become angry and strike out at me physically or emotionally like my father did.

At other times in my life I have sensed that having sexual relations with some of these men was somehow not sitting right with me, but I have had enormous difficulties saying no. I feel so empty and miserable when I do not have a guy hugging me. I thrive on male affection and their compliments. I did not realize how messed up I am in this area until just today. I always sensed there was something wrong with me in the area of sexuality, but I never could put my finger on it. I just don't seem to have any self-esteem at all and must be trying to get it from men instead of from within.

Last Sunday I swallowed all the pills in my house. I was feeling very depressed, alone, and hopeless. I would not say I was trying to kill myself; I merely no longer wanted to feel painful feelings. I thought I could just fall asleep for a couple of days or something, but I ended up having to go to the hospital to have my stomach pumped.

The hospital thought there might be something wrong with my kidneys because of the amount of drugs I swallowed, so they kept me there for four more days. The entire stay I could not believe what I had done and was very embarrassed.

Now, a week after the incident, I am still unhappy with my actions, but I understand a little more about why I did it. I had been seeing a psychologist, but I stopped a few weeks ago because of financial reasons. I did not think this really bothered me, but I guess it did. I have also been taking life too seriously, I think. I cannot seem to take a joke and feel very nervous if the slightest thing goes wrong in my life. I have been feeling overwhelmed much of the time and think maybe I have been pushing myself too hard.

This school year has been the first since I was fourteen that I have not coped with life by drinking, doing drugs, or compulsive overeating and bulimia. It is not very easy dealing with life straight on when I have been using substances as a crutch for eight years. I have been taking twelve credits for the last two semesters and going to all my classes, getting OK grades, and I have just started working. I guess things were too much and will probably get a less demanding part-time job. I feel bad about myself because I keep looking at other people around me and see they are dealing so well with life, and how I can only do the minimum.

I am trying to give myself a break and not be so hard on myself, for there was once a time when I could work forty hours a week, have a serious boyfriend, and do OK in school, but I guess during this certain period in my life I cannot perform at this high a level anymore. I just feel like such a loser.

My mom called yesterday and was very upset and frustrated with me. I don't know why she is. My mother hasn't supported me financially or emotionally in about four years. I feel guilty that my mother seems angry and depressed over my situation. I guess she has a right to be upset, but I don't want to have to deal with her freaking out. She was going to come visit me in Albany this Friday and have a session with me and my psychologist, but I believe I am going to ask her to delay her visit a while. I understand that she is depressed, but the last thing I need is someone I have to worry about or take care of.

I always feel like I am taking care of my mother, especially when I am falling apart. I feel guilty when she's unhappy. I'm really glad that I can ask my mom not to visit, even though I wish I felt comfortable enough around her for her to come see me. I could really use the support. Perhaps another time.

Reading Ruth's diaries the first time, I was struck by their unflinching honesty and rigorous self-scrutiny; rereading them, I continue to find them extraordinary. She describes what it feels like to be overwhelmed by depression, loneliness, and self-doubt; and we begin to understand why someone would take a drug overdose to escape from pain. Our increased understanding leads to heightened empathy; whatever inclination we may have to be judgmental is more than offset by compassion and a desire to alleviate her anguish.

Had the overdose been fatal, Ruth's death might have been ruled a suicide, even though she states that she did not intend to end her life so much as to escape temporarily from her problems.[36] The overdose thus may be viewed, like most suicidal behavior, as a gamble with death. The feeling of depression and hopelessness that momentarily overcame her, causing her to seek respite from pain, recalls a statement she makes in the third diary: the realization that she is not all-powerful, that she has, like everyone else, physical and mental limitations. This may not seem a startling insight, but it is hard-earned, achieved through suffering. Ruth's diaries dramatize the disquieting observation that a serious setback can occur during a period of relatively steady recovery. The journey to psychological health is not a smooth, direct road but a circuitous route filled with detours and blockades. Ruth herself remarks that recovery takes a long time—longer, obviously, than a semester of diary writing.

Ruth gave me permission to read her ninth diary to the class, but I decided against it for several reasons. First, I did not know how she would react to hearing her words read aloud a few days after her brush with death. She was still too close to the situation to see it with much objectivity, and I did not want to do anything that would heighten her discomfort. Second, I was unsure how her classmates would react to the diary. Although she did not glorify or romanticize suicide, I felt that reading Ruth's diary would upset the other students in the class. Finally, I felt uneasy over the extent to which I might have been implicated in the overdose. If, as I wondered, the overdose was a response to the end of the semester, which she may have experienced as an impending abandonment, was her cry for help—if that's what it was—aimed, in part, toward me? There was no hint of aggression, reproach, or revenge in the ninth entry, yet I could not help feeling anxiety, perhaps a vestige of my guilt over Len's death.

Ruth did not bring up any of these worrisome issues in her final diary. Instead, her final entry was brief and unqualified in its endorsement of diary writing. She emphasized the relief she felt upon discovering that her classmates were confronting similar conflicts. "I did not feel like such a freak when I heard other students having the same thoughts or problems as I do." She also felt validated when her diaries were read aloud: "I felt as if what I wrote was interesting or important." Hearing her entries read aloud, she concluded, enabled her to acknowledge her conflicts and convinced her to return to therapy. More than two years after the course ended she continued to believe that the experience of diary writing was valuable.[37]

Unlike deaths from natural causes or from illnesses that cannot be medically treated, many—probably most—suicides can be prevented through intervention or counseling. This is especially true for teenagers, for whom suicide is usually a spontaneous, impulsive act rather than premeditated, as with older age groups. Moreover, for the vast majority of adolescents, suicidal crises are usually of short duration. Once adolescents successfully cope with a suicidal crisis, they find it easier coping with future crises, should they arise. The vast majority of people who attempt suicide do not attempt it again.

Apart from entering therapy, I believe that it is valuable for students at risk to study the lives of authors who have written about overcoming suicidal depression. The suicide literature is vast, but if I had to cite a single volume—and a slender one, for that matter—it would be William Styron's autobiographical *Darkness Visible* (1990). He describes his descent into mental illness, from the development of his depression in October 1985, when he turned sixty, to its near-fatal conclusion in December, when he rejected suicide, hospitalized himself, and initiated the healing process. An intensely private man, Styron acknowledges that his frank discussion of his suicidal depression has caused an outpouring of responses from readers who expressed gratitude to him for writing about a subject that still remains taboo for most people. His conclusion in *Darkness Visible* is that while depression remains nearly incomprehensible to those who have not experienced it, one can survive its horrors and live to write about it, as he himself does eloquently:

> If depression had no termination, then suicide would, indeed, be the only remedy. But one need not sound the false or inspirational note to stress the truth that depression is not the soul's annihilation; men and women who have recovered from the disease—and they are countless—bear witness to what is probably its only saving grace: it is conquerable.[38]

6 / Sexual Disclosures

In my mind, I'm probably the biggest sex maniac you ever saw. Sometimes I can think of very crumby stuff I wouldn't mind doing if the opportunity came up. I can even see how it might be quite a lot of fun, in a crumby way. . . . The thing is, though, I don't like the idea. It stinks, if you analyze it.—J. D. Salinger, *The Catcher in the Rye*

Holden Caulfield is, by his own admission, one of the most sexually conflicted characters in existence. Torn between intense libidinal urges and an accusatory conscience, he is both fascinated and horrified by sex. He is still a virgin, though not for lack of opportunity or desire. Wherever he goes, he encounters figures who simultaneously arouse his passion and mobilize his defenses. From his hotel window he voyeuristically peers into the other side of the building, where he sees, in one room, a distinguished looking man opening his suitcase and dressing himself in silk stockings, high-heeled shoes, a brassiere, and a corset; in another room he spies a man and woman squirting water out of their mouths at each other, laughing hysterically. "I'm not kidding, the hotel was lousy with perverts," Holden exclaims, adding, "I was probably the only normal bastard in the whole place—and that isn't saying much."[1]

The Catcher in the Rye abounds in sexual disclosures. Holden associates sex with death, splits women into madonnas or whores, wishes both to preserve and to violate innocence, makes homophobic statements while being drawn to gay men, and remains incestuously fixated.[2] Yet he is more than simply a case study in repression; he remains one of the most endearing adolescents in literature, and while he may lie to the other characters in the story, he strives to be honest with the reader, particularly about sexual ambiguities. "Sex is something I really don't understand too hot. You never know *where* the hell you are. I keep making up these sex rules for myself, and then I break them right away" (63).

Toward the end of the novel Holden takes refuge in the apartment of his compassionate English teacher Mr. Antolini, who quotes to his self-destructive student a line from the psychoanalyst Wilhelm Stekel: "The mark of the immature man is that he wants to die nobly for a cause, while the mark of the mature man is that he wants to live humbly for one" (188). Fatigued and depressed, Holden falls asleep only to be awakened in the middle of the night to find Antolini stroking his head in the dark. Fleeing in horror, he later wonders whether his teacher was indeed making advances toward him. He is never sure, nor are we. As *The Catcher in the Rye* closes, Holden is in a psychiatric institution, recovering from his breakdown, wondering whether he is prepared to face the world again, with its vexing sexual problems.

Writing about Sexuality

Like the seventeen-year-old Holden Caulfield, college students find sexuality bedeviling. Most are only a few years older than Salinger's protagonist and living on their own for the first time. Their past experience varies greatly; many students have been sexually active for years, while others remain inexperienced. Students today live in a world far more complicated than the early 1950s, when Holden burst onto the literary scene. Present students are confronted with more life-threatening dangers, particularly AIDS, which by their own admission they have not fully faced. Some students write about the joy of sex, but for others sex remains problematic, evoking confusion, guilt, and uncertainty.

Diary writing enables students to explore feelings about sexuality in a safe and anonymous setting, compare experiences with their classmates', and create a weekly dialogue in which they teach and learn from each other. It is not an exaggeration to say that diary writing becomes, for many students, part of their sexual education, allowing them to draw meaningful parallels between literature and life. Reading novels like *The Catcher in the Rye* encourages students to engage in self-analysis and self-disclosure, and while most of them were born after 1951, when the novel was published, they have little difficulty in identifying with Holden's sexual conflicts. Students write on a wide variety of topics, exploring how sexuality relates to love, intimacy, marriage, and self-esteem. Many discuss their feelings about heterosexuality,

homosexuality, and bisexuality, confronting deeply rooted fears and prejudices. They also write about sexual dreams and fantasies, sexual symbolism,
obsessions, fetishes, Oedipal relationships, Freudian slips—in short, a broad
range of subjects.

About 30 percent of the students in every class disclose sexual experiences
or feelings which they judge to be problematic, such as sexual abuse, promiscuity, and homophobia. Unlike men, who seldom write about sexual victimization, women often do; their writing is haunted by the specter of male
aggression. Some women simply make passing reference in their diaries to
having been sexually abused, a trauma which remains enshrouded in mystery and guilt long after the event takes place. Other women, generally two
or three in each class, write extended diaries on the subject. Some of these
women have never previously revealed this secret to anyone, neither family
nor friends. The effects of this self-disclosure are almost always positive.
Writing proves to be an important outlet for abused students, enabling them
to understand frightening experiences and begin the self-healing process.
They discover that their classmates can empathize with them, validate their
stories, and, in some cases, share similar experiences. Sexually abused students come to feel a strong connection to their classmates, a bond of trust.
Hearing these diaries read aloud also proves valuable for unabused students.
A diary does not have the dry abstraction of a statistic and is therefore more
powerful in conveying the terror of sexual assault.

Freud's Seduction Theory

Diaries about child sexual abuse confront us immediately with one of Freud's
most serious errors: the belief that his patients were not telling the truth
when they spoke about being seduced as children by older male relatives.
Many of these patients were young women who entered analysis because of
hysterical symptoms such as temporary blindness, paralysis, and loss of
speech—symptoms which had no organic basis but which were nevertheless
real. Freud initially believed his patients' stories, boldly tracing their anxiety
to the sexual abuse they suffered in childhood. "At the bottom of every case
of hysteria," he writes in "The Aetiology of Hysteria" (1896), there are *one or
more occurrences of premature sexual experience*, occurrences which belong to
the earliest years of childhood but which can be reproduced through the
work of psycho-analysis in spite of the intervening decades."[3]

And yet Freud soon repudiated the seduction theory because he could not accept the startling possibility that so many fathers were sexually abusing their daughters. He argued instead that his patients were confusing reality with fantasy, engaging in wish fulfillment. "I no longer believe in my *neurotica*," he confided to his friend Wilhelm Fliess in September 1897, concluding that "it was hardly credible that perverted acts against children were so general."[4] One month later he announced to Fliess that he had discovered within himself the existence of the Oedipus complex. "Only one idea of general value has occurred to me. I have found love of the mother and jealousy of the father in my own case too, and now believe it to be a general phenomenon of early childhood, even if it does not always occur so early as in children who have been made hysterics."[5] In later years Freud returned to this decisive turning point in psychoanalysis, justifying the subordination of historical to psychic reality. "Analysis had led back to these infantile sexual traumas by the right path, and yet they were not true. The firm ground of reality was gone."[6]

Why did Freud lose the firm ground of reality here? There was no logical reason for psychoanalysis to imply that historical reality and psychic reality are mutually exclusive. While the rejection of the seduction theory allowed him to pursue his groundbreaking theories of the Oedipus complex, infantile sexuality, and dream interpretation, he could have investigated these subjects without concluding that his patients were fabricating their stories. Not only did Freud fail to investigate, for example, the psychological consequences of Dora's sexual abuse as a child, but he had literally nothing to say about rape. Insofar as psychoanalysis is essentially a historical inquiry, seeking to discover how the past influences the present, the abandonment of reality could have only disastrous consequences.[7]

Several explanations have been offered for Freud's rejection of the seduction theory. Jeffrey Masson claims that Freud suppressed the truth because of the fear that he would incur the disapproval of his colleagues and the medical establishment. "With the greatest reluctance," Masson writes in the Introduction to *The Assault on Truth*, "I gradually came to see Freud's abandonment of the seduction hypothesis as a failure of courage."[8] Masson's theory strikes me as implausible, given Freud's intellectual Prometheanism, his willingness to be, quoting the philosopher Hebbel, one of those who "disturbed the sleep of the world."[9] During his lifetime Freud propounded several unpopular theories, and while we may criticize him on many accounts, he was not guilty of currying favor with his colleagues.

Freud may have rejected the seduction theory because he felt there was a lack of clinical evidence for it. Few of his contemporaries realized the pervasiveness of sexual abuse; most of the research on the subject has been published only in the last two or three decades. Psychological factors may also have induced Freud to reject the seduction theory, namely, his ambivalent feelings toward his parents. The discovery of erotic feelings toward his mother and aggressive feelings toward his father compelled him to exonerate parents in general. Marianne Krull argues convincingly in *Freud and His Father* that, on the basis of his self-analysis, Freud would have had to conclude that his own father was literally a seducer, a thesis he was not prepared to accept. "The replacement of the seduction with the Oedipus theory thus enabled Freud to examine his own childhood without having to blame his parents for his neurosis."[10]

Child Sexual Abuse

Because people seldom talk about incest, rape, and other forms of sexual abuse, generally refusing to report these crimes when they occur, it is difficult to know how many children are victimized. Different researchers report sharply different findings. No one takes seriously any more the claim made by the author of a prominent 1975 psychiatry textbook that the incidence of incest is only one per million.[11] According to one study, between 15 percent and 45 percent of all women experience at least one incident of sexual abuse before the age of eighteen.[12] Another study estimates that between 5 percent and 15 percent of the population is involved in incest.[13] Most experts agree that while perhaps three times as many girls are sexually victimized as boys, the latter are much less likely to report these crimes than the former—probably because boys may be "particularly reluctant to disclose maltreatment for fear of appearing unmanly, vulnerable, or weak."[14]

Typically, the sexually abused child knows the abuser, and there is a progression of sexual contacts. Few victims show physical signs of abuse, thus making corroboration difficult. The abuse usually occurs before the onset of puberty and may last for several years—until the child tells another person, becomes pregnant, or runs away from home. Acts of child sexual abuse are generally nonviolent, though there is always subtle coercion and often the threat of physical violence. The abused child feels isolated, stigmatized, helpless, and guilty. Additionally, the child may wish to protect the abuser from public disclosure. The mother, who is usually the nonabusive parent, often supports the husband rather than the child, thus invalidating the latter's feelings.

Most abused children never talk about their harrowing experience and, if they do, are seldom believed. Children tend to deny that they have been sexually abused, particularly when the abuser is a family member. Incest, researchers agree, reflects a dysfunctional family;[15] abused children are often under intense pressure not to disclose the crime for fear of breaking up the family. Without strong support, a child will generally retract the disclosure of abuse. Very few children lie about sexual abuse; according to one study, perhaps no more than 2 or 3 children per 1,000 have been found to exaggerate or to invent claims of sexual abuse.[16] The result of this abuse—and the years of shame, secrecy, and silence surrounding it—are low self-esteem, guilt, anger, depression, and mistrust.

The most common behavioral problem associated with child sexual abuse is post-traumatic stress disorder, in which victims later suffer dissociation, flashbacks, nightmares, and sleep disorders.[17] Many cases of multiple personality disorder also originate from child sexual abuse, as stories like *Sybil* dramatize.[18] Whereas Freud asserted that it did not finally matter whether his patients' stories of seduction were based upon reality or fantasy, research on post-traumatic stress disorder and multiple personality disorder suggests that it is vital for patients to reconstruct as accurately as possible the actual traumatic experience so that they can understand what happened, have the reality of the experience validated, learn to master their fears, and eventually integrate the experience into their ongoing development.

Nearly all my students who write about child sexual abuse are women, and they usually write about events that occurred several years ago, when they were eleven or twelve or in their early teens. Students who write about acquaintance rape tend to have been older when the experience occurs, often in high school or college. The sexual abuser of children is generally an older man such as a relative, neighbor, or friend of the family. The experience evokes terror, confusion, and shame within the child, feelings which prevent her from talking about the event with anyone.

Diaries about Child Sexual Abuse

Ambiguity abounds in diaries about child sexual abuse. The experience happened too long ago to be remembered clearly, and the emotions surrounding the event are too painful to be understood. A few students are not entirely sure whether they are remembering an actual experience or reliving a recurrent nightmare. Such diaries tend to be unusually fragmentary and vague, devoid of specifics. They are never erotic or titillating. The sexual experience is so traumatic that the writer can only summarize rather than dramatize it. These diaries are not primarily about sex but about guilt and humiliation; even as the entries enact images of violation, they remain chaste. The women report that the experience continues to burden them, causing them to fear their bodies and mistrust men. Unlike other wrenching subjects on which students write multiple diaries, child sexual abuse tends to be a single-diary issue, with the entry submitted later rather than earlier in the semester. Some diaries suggest that students had no idea they were going to write about the experience before they actually began the entry.

A chapter entitled "Sexual Disclosures" may seem to promise guilty pleasures, but there is nothing prurient or sensationalistic about the revelations contained within sexual abuse diaries.[19] They are confessional in tone but unlike the "True Confessions" featured in tabloids. The revelations contained in these diaries are neither self-conscious nor self-indulgent. Although there is always the temptation in survivor stories to bend the truth ("In the heat of the moment, in the confessional rush of relating graphic details to a supportive crowd, the truth may be stretched, battered, or utterly abandoned"),[20] I have never received a sexual abuse diary that seemed inauthentic. The diaries bear little resemblance to the vast body of literature in which the "compulsion to confess" predominates. As John Rogge observes, autobiographical confessions have been presented in countless diaries and memoirs, and these confessions, even when sincerely offered, may become extravagant or excessive.[21] Oscar Wilde's cautionary remark in De Profundis is relevant here: "A man's very highest moment is, I have no doubt at all, when he kneels in the dust, and beats his breast, and tells all the sins of his life."[22] As you will see, there is no kneeling in the dust or beating of the breast or telling of all in these diaries. On the contrary, students' disclosures of child sexual abuse are remarkably discrete and restrained, befitting the seriousness of the subject.

Sexual abuse diaries require teachers to be as empathic and nonjudgmental as possible and to maintain professional boundaries. Since many female students have been victimized by an older man, they may be mistrustful of a male teacher. It requires courage for students to write about child sexual abuse, and the teacher, like the therapist, must offer acceptance and support.

Without trust in both their teacher and classmates, students will not make these disclosures.

LEE
"And Then I Wanted to Cry Because I Thought of My Grandfather"

I want to begin with Lee because a classroom discussion of "Babylon Revisited" brought to the surface a painful memory which she had been repressing for years. Acknowledged as one of F. Scott Fitzgerald's finest short stories, "Babylon Revisited" (1931) is about a reformed alcoholic named Charlie Wales whose glamorous but dissolute life during the Roaring Twenties comes to an abrupt halt with the great crash of 1929. He is still haunted by the memory of his wife, in whose death he is implicated. After a long absence Charlie returns to Paris, the city of his former revelry, to be reunited with his nine-year-old daughter Honoria. Like *Tender Is the Night* (1934), "Babylon Revisited" explores the theme of incestuous love, with Honoria playing the role of "Daddy's Girl":

> "Daddy, I want to come and live with you," she said suddenly.
>
>   His heart leaped; he had wanted it to come like this.
>
>   "Aren't you perfectly happy?"
>
>   "Yes, but I love you better than anybody. And you love me better than anybody, don't you, now that mummy's dead?"[23]

Fitzgerald's awareness of the danger of parental overcloseness may be seen when Charlie warns himself "not to love too much, for he knew the injury that a father can do to a daughter or a mother to a son by attaching them too closely."[24] The dialogue between father and daughter often sounds like two people courting each other, with Honoria remaining detached from both her deceased mother and her Aunt Marion, who functions as the evil stepmother in the story. Although it is Marion who apparently frustrates the protagonist's efforts to regain custody of Honoria at the end of "Babylon Revisited," Charlie unconsciously sabotages himself, not only because he is unwilling to accept the responsibilities of fatherhood, but also because he fears excessive closeness to her. He loves his daughter, yet she is part of what is for him, and Fitzgerald, the dangerous world of women, who are perceived as sapping men's vitality and creativity.

Psychoanalytic interpretations of stories like "Babylon Revisited" and

D. H. Lawrence's "Rocking Horse Winner," which describes a young boy's desire to win his mother's love and approval, inevitably raise Oedipal issues: a child's sexual feelings toward the opposite-sex parent and corresponding rivalry toward the same-sex parent. Whether we view Oedipal desire as innate biological drive, as Freud did, or as the result of the child's prolonged and almost exclusive dependency on the parents, as contemporary psycho-analysts theorize, Oedipal themes abound in literature and mythology.[25] Yet few psychoanalytic topics arouse as much incredulity as the Oedipus complex, and despite my efforts to stress that it is a normal developmental stage through which most children successfully pass, students remain dubious.

Lee was clearly troubled by my suggestion of a sexual component to the father-daughter relationship in "Babylon Revisited," and even when I interpreted this desire broadly as a wish for closeness and mutual protection, she remained unconvinced. One week after our discussion she turned in the following entry, accusing me of ruining the story for her:

> I agreed strongly with the girl who said that why can't we read a story for no other purpose than just to read it. She couldn't understand why we had to look at "Babylon Revisited" as though it were dirty. I agreed with her. When I first read the story, I saw no sexual connotations between the father and daughter. All I saw was that the girl really loved her father and wanted to be with him. I understand now that there may be something there, but I can't help being angry at the idea that it is normal for a man to feel that way about his daughter and for her to feel the same way about him. It makes a father-daughter relationship seem ugly.
>
> I adore my father. I have stated in an earlier diary that when I was younger, I idolized him. I don't exactly feel the same way anymore, but I still do love him very much. I have never called him anything but "Daddy," and when I see him, I always hug and kiss him. I don't believe that I am any more demonstrative than any other daughter. In fact, I act the same way to most people in my family because that is the kind of person I am. I am not afraid to show a person that I care about them.
>
> The discussion last week left me with a very uncomfortable feeling. I have never had any sexual feelings toward my dad, and I don't think that he has ever had any toward me. In class I felt angry because I don't want to feel uncomfortable with my dad. And then you said that you believe that there will be girls in the class who will say that they have

had an incestuous relationship with a male in their family. At first I became angry, as though the insinuation was that we had all had one of some kind. And then I wanted to cry because I thought of my grandfather. I wanted to run from the class because I didn't want to hear any more. I didn't want to think about what that statement meant to me. Afterward I thought about it for a long time. Now I feel that I must say something that I have never ever said before.

When I was about twelve or younger (I don't remember too well because I have tried not to), my grandfather used to touch me in ways that at that time I didn't know were wrong. He said that it was his way of loving me. It seemed wrong to me, and I would try hard not to have to be alone with him. I never told anyone at the time because I didn't really understand it. Now I do, but I still don't plan on ever telling anyone (except of course you) because I don't believe that it would serve any purpose. I still don't like to think about it, and as soon as I'm done with this, then I will again try to force it out of my mind. I think I needed to say it now.

This class has made me think about a lot of things that I really haven't thought about before. Right now my hands are shaking, so I feel that I must end this. But first I do want to say that the incident with my grandfather has never changed the way I feel about my dad (his son). I still love my dad, and I don't think that I will ever have to fear him the way I did in respect to his father.

I can't recall specifically my comments in class that precipitated Lee's diary, but in offering an Oedipal interpretation of "Babylon Revisited," I certainly did not mean to imply that there was anything "dirty" about the father-daughter relationship. On the contrary, I probably suggested that desire is not in itself unhealthy, only when it is inappropriately acted upon. Nor did I wish to insinuate that there were women in the class who have had incestuous relationships with men—though I might have said that incest is a far more widespread problem than most people realize.

Lee's diary demonstrates how a classroom discussion of literature can bring to the surface frightening, long-repressed memories. Like most of the other women who write about child sexual abuse, she finds it distressing to remember precisely what happened with her grandfather. She does not allow herself to use the words "sexual abuse." Even when she says that she now understands what happened, she is loath to describe it. It is unclear whether she knew at the time that her grandfather's action was improper—she makes conflicting statements about this. Significantly, she seems more protective of her father's well-being than of her own.

LESLIE
"I Can't Allow Him to Come Back and Haunt Me"

Lee's response to her experience was to repress it, but other women cannot erase similar experiences from their minds. This is true for Leslie, who fears that one day soon she may come into contact with the man who made unwanted sexual advances when she was a girl.

> I'm still haunted by what he did to me so many years ago. My terrible secret is shared only with the closest of friends and no one else. Never have I dared to mention it to my parents or to any type of a counselor. I'm too embarrassed. I know I shouldn't be because it wasn't my fault. But I can't help it.
>
> I was molested. I have trouble even typing the words.
>
> It must have been about eleven or twelve years ago when it happened. He was my next-door neighbor. Don't the reports always say the offender is usually someone well known and trusted?
>
> I think he was watching my brother and me while my mother was out. He must have been a senior in high school at the time. We were sitting on the bed in my brother's room. I don't know where my brother was. He touched me and had me touch him.
>
> I don't think it bothered me at the time. I didn't know it was wrong. I didn't realize he wasn't allowed to do that.
>
> I'm not sure if it happened more than once. To tell the truth, I'm not even sure at this point if it actually did happen. I have a definite mental picture of the event, but I'm not sure if maybe it was only a bad dream or something. Could I have just blocked it out so well that I'm now doubting that it actually happened?
>
> At this point I truly am unsure whether it really happened or whether I am haunted by a vivid nightmare. Therapists would actually say I'm still blocking this out and refusing to deal with it by denying it. I can accept this as possible. I just don't know, though. I'm not sure if I'll ever know.

An old boyfriend once acted in a way that reminded me of this horrible next-door neighbor, and I started to cry. He kept asking me what he had done wrong, what had made me cry. When I calmed down a little, I explained what had happened. He was supportive and held me, which is exactly what I needed at the time.

Maybe I can tell people like him and not my mother because I'm afraid she'll do something about what happened. But what if it didn't actually happen? Then everyone would just think there's something wrong with me and that I'm out to ruin someone's life. I also don't want to have to see him again. I can't allow him to come back and haunt me.

There is the same secrecy and shame in Leslie's diary that we saw in Lee's, the same difficulty in describing what actually happened. What is most striking about the entry is the ambiguity of the event. Was it real or imaginary? Leslie cannot be sure.

There is no doubt, though, about Leslie's anxiety. She can hardly type the word "molested" without feeling dread. Like the other students who write about child sexual abuse, she feels guilty for what happened, even though she knows rationally that she was not at fault. Worst of all is the fear that one day she may again be confronted by her neighbor and find herself in another compromising situation.

JENNIFER
"I Didn't Know What He Was Doing to Me;
I Thought It Was a Natural Thing"

Leslie's diary is representative of child abuse diaries. Students believe that the experience has profoundly changed their lives and shattered their trust in others. Unless they have been in therapy, they are reluctant to dredge up the painful memories associated with molestation. Once they write about this experience, however, they feel relief. This is what two other young women, Jennifer and Karen, concluded:

Last class I don't think I was doing that much listening. The diary written by the girl who realized that she had sex when she really didn't want to made me think a lot. Actually I wanted to cry. Parts of what she said could have been me. When I was young, I was molested by a friend of the family. I didn't know what he was doing to me; I thought it was a natural thing. He told me my parents wanted him to check me out and make sure I was OK. At the time I was sure there was nothing wrong with me, but if my parents thought this was the right thing, then sure, why not?

My boyfriend in freshman year, who was a good friend in high school, was the only person I've ever told this to. He told me he would make things OK for me and said he would help me overcome the anger I had inside of me. He was also the first guy I had sex with, and after a few months of an active sexual relationship, I told him I wasn't comfortable having sex. I know he didn't talk me into starting up our sexual activities again—I did. I told myself this was a normal thing between two people, and that it was a part of life. I know now that I expected myself to have sex with him more than he did. I made that wonderful relationship into something ugly. I guess it took that one girl's diary to make me really look at myself. Thank you whoever you are.

KAREN
"I Feel Like Those Incidents Were My Fault"

Because I trust you, Professor Berman, I am going to discuss something that has been on my mind recently. No one knows about these situations except for me, the two guys involved, and you.

Sometimes I wonder about myself. Am I as normal as everyone thinks I am? Or do these incidents I hold internally have some effect on my actions without me even knowing it?

When I was younger, probably around nine years old, I can slightly remember my cousin spending the night. He was around ten. He was to sleep in the same room as my sister and me. We decided to sleep on the floor. It was like a slumber party. As the night progressed, I felt my cousin close to me. He was touching me in places most nine-year-old girls don't get touched. I didn't know what to do. I consented. He was my cousin. Why would he be doing anything to hurt me?

A second incident occurred when I was twelve. My cousin (different from the one mentioned above) was about fifteen years old. I can remember him taking me up to my room. He had me touch him until he achieved the satisfaction he was looking for.

Intercourse did not take place in either situation. Has this had some effect on me? Sure it has. I guess. I feel like those incidents were my fault. I didn't know enough to think that this wasn't right.

I tried to tell my aunt about how uncomfortable her son made me feel when he was around me. She must not have understood me. She didn't listen to what I said.

To this day, I find myself uneasy in relationships. All I am looking for is a secure, trusting, honest guy to love me. I find myself believing that all a guy wants from me is sex. When I was around sixteen or seventeen, I thought that love and sex were related. The only way I believed a guy would love me is if I gave in to his demands.

I have made a lot of mistakes in my past. I am growing up now and realizing this to be wrong. But eight years have gone by since this last occurrence, and I have been thinking about it, wondering if this could be classified as some sort of sexual abuse. I wish I knew what to do.

Professor Berman—thank you for being there, and for allowing me to have someone to discuss my situation with. It is important to express ourselves, no matter what we are dealing with.

FRED

"It Was a Perverse Act Which Was Shocking
Enough to Remember, and Mild Enough to Forget"

Only one male student has written about an experience of child sexual abuse, an incident that occurred when he was too young to understand its consequences.

The thing that I would like to talk about today may be considered horrible to some, amusing to others. I personally have chosen to look back on the event with humor—maybe because that was the easiest way to deal with it. Whatever it was, however, the event was far from funny.

When I was about six years old, I was molested. Why? Who? These are questions I could not and probably still can't answer. Now, there was nothing ultrarepulsive involved. I mean, there was no personal violation of my young body. But it was a perverse act which was shocking enough to remember, and mild enough to forget. What has brought it back into my memory is the sexual nature of this class and the self-analytic mode that it puts you in.

OK, enough suspense. This is what happened. My friend Joe and I were standing at the bus-stop corner waiting for the school bus to take us and ship us off to school. While we were waiting there, talking about whatever six-year-olds talk about, a kind-looking old man approached us. He was wearing glasses and a brown hat. Matching this hat was a long overcoat which covered the entire length of his body. OK, it was a flasher coat. Like the one you used to see on *Laugh-In* or something.

This man comes over to us, very casually, and asks my friend Joe if he could help him with something. Thinking back, it went something like: "Hey, son, I got a problem here. I seem to have something stuck in my pocket. Do you think you can help me get it out?" Now, I was not yet approached, but this man had raised my curiosity too. I mean, this guy had a problem, and he was asking two naive children to help him. A child molester who knew how to press the right buttons.

My friend Joe seemed to be trying hard to remove whatever it was in the old man's pocket. Feeling left out, I came closer to see what was going on. The man asked me to help him too. Being a child, and ignoring my mother's warning never to talk to strangers, I also tried to help this miserable guy get whatever it was out of his pocket. I'll spare you the details of what I felt there, but I'll tell you this—it wasn't a lollipop.

After several futile attempts to remove the immovable object, my friend and I agreed that it would not come out. We apologized and said "Bye," and the man said, "Well, thanks for helping." He then went on his merry way, down the block, never to be seen again.

The bus came, and we both got on. We went through the day with no recollection of what went on. It was as normal a day as any. When I got home and my mother asked me what I did at school today, I told her the usual. Then I told her about the weird man who asked me and Joe to help him with something in his pocket. My mother stared at me blankly and then said three words: "Wash your hands."

Then she called Joe's mother. The police were already there, and Joe was giving them a description of the man. They would soon be coming over to my house. I was excited that the police were coming over. My mother told me not to worry. I don't know if she understood that I still did not know what was going on. It was only after the police came that I made the connection.

They came in quietly, immediately asking to be alone with me. Now I wasn't excited anymore. I wanted my mother to be with me. "I'm sorry," they said to her, "We have to see him alone." Finally, after the policeman let me wear his badge, I gave in. They showed me several pictures of different men. One was a man with a strange mustache. One was a man with funny tattoos, going this way and that. Finally, the police came to a man who closely resembled the man I had met this morning. However, in this picture he looked ten years younger. After I identified him, they thanked me and said they had to talk to my mother. I obliged and went into the living room to let them talk to my mother alone.

After they talked, my mother looked dazed. She looked at me with grateful eyes. The police thanked me again and left quietly. "We'll be in touch, ma'am," they said. After they left, my mother took me in her arms and hugged me. I asked her what happened. All she said was, "They'll find him." When I looked at her, I realized that there were tears coming out of her eyes. I was realizing that something bad had happened to me, but I was not hurt or anything. When I pressed her for a reason to her tears, she just said quietly, "I'm just so happy that you're all right."

It wasn't until a few years later when I found out that the man who approached me and Joe was the same man who was suspected of raping and killing two children in our neighborhood.

Acquaintance Rape

Probably every high school or college female knows a person who is a victim of acquaintance (or date) rape. Defined as nonconsensual sex between two people who know each other,[26] acquaintance rape often remains unreported because women are reluctant to get their male assaulters in trouble and also because they mistrust the criminal justice system. "Less than one rape in ten is reported to police. Only 1 percent of rapes are ultimately resolved by arrest and conviction of the offender."[27] In some cases, acquaintance rape involves different perceptions of the meaning of "no," as Holden Caulfield observes:

The thing is, most of the time when you're coming pretty close to doing it with a girl—a girl that isn't a prostitute or anything, I mean—she keeps telling you to stop. The trouble with me is, I stop. Most guys don't. I can't help it. You never know whether they really *want* you to stop, or whether they're just scared as hell, or whether they're just telling you to stop so that if you *do* go through with it, the blame'll be on *you*, not them. Anyway, I keep stopping.[28]

I hope Holden exaggerates when he says that most men do not stop when a woman resists; nevertheless, according to psychologist Mary P. Koss, one in four college women has an experience that meets the legal definition of rape or attempted rape. In 84 percent of these rapes, the woman knew her attacker; 57 percent of the rapes happened on dates.[29] Acquaintance rape is often more traumatic than stranger rape because while women who have been raped by strangers develop fears of the unknown, victims of acquaintance rape may learn to mistrust even their friends, who are now perceived as potential rapists.

GINA
"No One Is as Innocent as They Look"

Women who write about acquaintance rape generally submit more than one diary about the experience, sometimes reaching an insight in a later entry which illuminates a remark in an earlier entry. The process of self-discovery can be seen in Gina's two entries:

> Quite often I sit in class and wonder at the openness of my classmates' diaries. I've never felt the urge or the need to express my secrets in writing. However, this makes me feel guilty. I feel that if I am going to be allowed to sit and listen to such important diaries, my classmates deserve the same privilege of hearing my own story.
>
> There are times when I sit in class and feel very uncomfortable. I'm unsure as to whether my discomfort arises out of the fact that people are being open about their problems, or whether it is the common reference to sex that bothers me. Possibly it's a little of both. At any rate, I will for once do my best in my Freudian diary.
>
> I am a people watcher. I stand in a room and look carefully at the people around me. I'm suspicious of everyone. No one is as innocent as they look. Not even me.
>
> To know me is to believe that I am the average American college kid. I don't appear to have a problem in the world. Always smiling, I generally have a good time with anything I do. However, within the recesses of my mind there is a deep secret.

I am a victim of date rape. I won't even begin to tell how a sweet teen-age romance turned into a vicious, recurring nightmare, but I will say that it has greatly affected my outlook toward life and men, in particular.

I don't feel comfortable around men since the incident, not even my own father. It is a chore to go out on dates and co-ed parties. I dislike getting all dressed up for fear that a man will notice me. While I continue to date and be social, it is with increasing caution. I cannot discuss sex with my girlfriends, with my boyfriends, not with anybody.

Sometimes I leave this class unhappy because we have spent the majority of the night discussing Freud's psychosexual theories or the relationship between father and daughter, men and women. I don't like to touch such subjects anymore, as they tend to remind me of my own problems. As literature is an important part of my life, I like to believe that it is free from such harsh realities. Even writing this diary makes me very unhappy, as can be seen through the style of writing. I can't even write comfortably about such things.

Perhaps the thought I wish to end with is that in little ways I believe everyone in this class finds something to hit home. Sometimes it feels right, and when it does, it just sends chills up your spine.

I have always wondered why different people affect me in so many different ways. Never can I understand how I feel self-assured with one person and cowardly with another. Some people cause me to be nasty, while to others I can't be nice enough. This type of unpredictable behavior is puzzling, but I'm absolutely baffled why I react to different *men* in different ways.

As I've written before, I am generally wary of men due to a past incident with a man I trusted. Before this incident, however, I reacted perfectly normally to the men with whom I came in contact. This weekend my behavior began to make some sense for the first time in relation to this.

This past weekend one of my closest friends came here to visit me. We have been friends for years and had quite a solid and lengthy relationship before the above-mentioned incident. It occurred to me this weekend that my behavior with my friend, a male, is perfectly normal. It's much like the way I used to be around men. I am not uncomfortable or cautious when we're together. I see a big difference in how I act toward him romantically. So, maybe the idea is that I only have problems with men that I've met *since* the incident! Does that leave me only to date men I know from childhood? Maybe. All I know is that the difference between the way I treat my boyfriend and the way I treat this friend is like night and day. I wonder what Freud would say about this. . . .

Although she ends her entry with a question about why certain men make her feel uncomfortable while others do not, Gina has reached her own interpretation, largely as a result of writing about her experience. What she seeks, then, is not advice but validation—which she received when I read her diary aloud.

HEATHER
"He Said That All Girls My Age Have Had Sex"

So, too, did Heather receive validation when I read her two diaries to the class. Her experience with acquaintance rape was similar to Gina's in that the attacker was a high school boyfriend whom she thought she knew well. Many victims of acquaintance rape are virgins at the time of the attack, and often the attacker has been drinking. Heather notes that although she has largely recovered from the experience, she still has occasional flashbacks. The first of her two diaries on the subject was written during the opening week of the semester, the second diary nine weeks later.

I, like many other women, am a victim of rape. In fact, it was my first experience of sexual intercourse, when I was a sophomore in high school. I was dating a very popular student, whom I had all the reason in the world to trust. I had known him for years and had been dating him for several months. He was athletic, witty, handsome, and fun loving. However, one night I saw a side of him that I never imagined I would see. Earlier that day my boyfriend found out that his sister was just beaten up by one of his friends. He was hurt and angry at the guy, who was in his own fraternity. My boyfriend decided that night he wanted to forget about the news and spend some time with me.

The nice candlelight dinner and romantic evening we had planned ended with me being beaten, bruised, bloodied, and terrified. He had been drinking earlier that day, and that evening he had decided that he wanted to go further, sexually. I told him I was not ready, yet he persisted with brutal force. The whole time during the violent whirl, he said that all girls my age have had sex and that he had been waiting for so long to share more of himself with me. He said that he loved me and did not want to hurt me. However, when I tried to move away, he used force and told me that I owed it to him and, if I really loved him, I would try to make him feel good. Meanwhile, he pursued an act which has haunted me since.

I told no one of the incident besides my close friend, who helped me clean up before I went home. I did not want my family to get angry at him. I just avoided him altogether as a means of forgetting. It took me a long time to be able to trust a guy again. I eventually did (for the most part), but it took me a long time to feel comfortable and have sexual intercourse. I have overcome my fear of sex (mostly) and now enjoy it very much. However, I am very skeptical of men and sometimes of relationships as well.

I find myself very bitter and judgmental when I come across anyone who remotely resembles my old boyfriend, whether it be in looks or personality. I find myself still attracted to his characteristics (athletic, funny, etc.), which I interpret as still being attracted to my first love, yet hating him at the same time. I do not wish to hold on to any good memories because they tend to make me ambivalent—more often than not I tend to see the bad. Even though the rape occurred four years ago, I still look at the bad more often after the relationship has ended. I am very friendly to people, but if I run into anyone who looks and acts like my boyfriend, I tend to ignore him and just stay away from him.

I am sometimes reminded of the incident long ago if I am put into a certain hold. That is when the flashbacks occur. I feel I am more wise now though, and I am better prepared to handle any situation if it happens again. Although I have tried to move on, I will never forget or, as it seems, be allowed to forget. No matter how close I am to my present boyfriend now, or to anyone, I will always have some doubt of men and whether or not I can trust them. Whatever trust I do have, deep down I allow myself to expect that he may give me reason to lose any trust whatsoever.

Something has really been bothering me lately. It is something that I have been doing, which is instantaneous, without thought. It is wrong, but I cannot seem to control myself lately. My problem is that I hit my present boyfriend. I have been hitting him a lot lately, and I have been trying to figure out why. I am sure that this is not too often heard of. Isn't it always the man who beats a woman? If my boyfriend were to hit me, it would be against the law. I am not talking about full-fledged beating—it is something different.

When I was raped in high school, the man who violated me hit me. I was a wreck. I at first hit back, but then I was put into a position so that I could not move. I was defenseless. I was always a tomboy—always athletic. There is nothing worse than being in a situation in which you have no control and cannot defend yourself. Ever since then, whether it be while wrestling with or just playing around with my boyfriend, or if someone jokingly cuts a blow at me, I try to prove myself by not being hurt by them, not being overpowered by them by acting stronger, playing the role of the tough guy-girl who won't take any shit. I don't want to be hurt, whether it be mental or physical. I am not always talking about punching, but rather a subtle slap.

My boyfriend knows my pain from the past. Lately I have been under a lot of stress from school, and we have been having a lot of little fights, stupid fights. If he says something uncalled for, perhaps out of jealousy, even if he is kidding around, if I think he is serious, I slap him or punch him in the arm. If I don't have a good comeback and I am severely busted on, I lightly punch the person on the shoulder.

Normally, on a daily basis I am a very caring person and intimate with friends—not sexually, but when I am in conversation, I am a touchy-feely person. I am not a boyfriend beater, but I feel that it stems from my past experiences. I feel I have to constantly defend myself in situations. I guess I just need to relax. I am trying to be aware that I act out on others physically when I feel put down. It is not that I give bloody noses or anything, but if my boyfriend says something that really hurts me, I leave bruises. He has never hit back. Obviously, I have a lot of deeply buried anger.

Writing and Relief

Lee, Leslie, Jennifer, Karen, Fred, Gina, and Heather concluded in their final entries that although revealing their experiences about sexual abuse was "scary"—a word almost all of them used—they felt better as a result of self-disclosure. As Lee observed, "The hardest thing that I have ever done was to write about my grandfather, but I am glad that I wrote about it. I think that I really needed to talk about it, and since I would never tell any of my family or friends, this was the only way I could get it out." Gina said that hearing me read aloud her diary on acquaintance rape was the most startling experience in her life; for a moment she did not even realize it was her own entry. The diary enabled her to realize that she had been sad long enough and that it was time to get on with her life.

The Reluctance to Write about Being a Sexual Abuser

Unlike Holden, who admits to thinking of "*very* crumby stuff" he wouldn't mind doing if the opportunity came up, students never disclose in their diaries the desire to be a sexual abuser. It may be that few men see themselves as sexually menacing—or that the men who take my courses are remarkably sensitive and gentle! A more likely explanation for male students' reluctance to write about sexually aggressive behavior is that they fear disapproval from the teacher or class. It is always easier to empathize with a victim than with a victimizer. Men do write, however, about their own nonsexually aggressive behavior, such as getting into barroom brawls with other men, and they also write about *other* men's sexual aggression. I don't know if many male students in my classes feel defensive when they hear me read diaries about female sexual victimization, but for whatever reason, they seldom comment on these entries.

The Wish to Dominate Women Sexually

Men's refusal to write about sexual domination becomes more striking in light of the prevalence of male aggression fantasies. In a recent survey of 114 male undergraduates, for example, a large majority agreed with the following statements: "I prefer relatively small women" (93.7 percent agreement); "I like to dominate a woman" (91.3 percent); "I enjoy the conquest part of sex" (86.1 percent); "Some women look like they're just asking to be raped" (83.5 percent); "I get excited when a woman struggles over sex" (63.5 percent); and "It would be exciting to use force to subdue a woman (61.7 percent)."[30] If these attitudes represent American male college students as a whole, they are not reflected in male students' diaries.

SCOTT

"I Wish They Would Have Never Told Me That Story"

Men do occasionally write about stories of sexual humiliation of women which they have heard from other people. The most disturbing diary I have received was about a sinister version of "rodeo" performed on campus.

A few days ago my friend told me a story about what he and his fraternity brothers did to some innocent, unsuspecting female. While one of
their friends was in a room with this girl, they all decided to hide in the
closet. After the friend was engaged in coitus with this girl, the fraternity brothers slowly revealed themselves and drew nearer to the bed.
They were all naked. When at last she saw them, she struggled to get her
clothes on, but her partner for the night held her in the rear-entry
position and stayed inside her, until she was finally able to break free
and run out of the room. This, as I discovered, was called a "rodeo." It
seems that while the girl struggles, the audience would holler out like
they were watching a cowboy ride a bull.

Honestly, at first I laughed. I really thought it was funny. I mean, my
friends aren't rapists. In fact, the word "rape" didn't come to mind until I
thought of all the implications of their actions. This girl was humiliated
in front of them, and they loved it. This "rodeo" was purely acting out
desires. Just thinking about it now makes me sick. These aren't lowlife
degenerates; these were all wealthy, middle-class boys. I guess their
drives are just the same as everyone's. But it is hard for me to understand
why people need to make someone else suffer in the process. I wish they
would have never told me that story.

I was horrified by the brutality of these fraternity brothers and wanted to
read Scott's diary aloud in order to sensitize the class to the abhorrent nature
of sexual abuse, perpetrated, in this case, by "wealthy, middle-class boys" in
the guise of a harmless prank. Yet I hesitated reading the entry, fearing it
would unleash a storm of criticism directed against the anonymous diarist.
As a rule, I do not read a diary aloud if it might make either the diarist or
another student in the class feel defensive. Scott was honest enough to admit
that his first response upon hearing his friend's story was laughter—and he
was sensitive enough to realize later that his amusement was inappropriate. I
did not want him to be feel worse than he did about the incident. I could not
stop thinking about the diary, however, and knowing how prevalent sexual

abuse is on college campuses, I decided to read it aloud. To my surprise, only one person commented upon the diary, a woman.

SALLY
"When I Heard That Diary, I Thought I'd Be Sick"

In my diary for this week, I'd like to comment on a diary read last week about a bunch of frat guys who cheered on one of their so-called brothers as he raped a girl. When I heard that diary, I thought I'd be sick. I was so repulsed that this actually happened. It's not as though I don't know that rape is a common occurrence, especially on college campuses, but since I've been in school, I haven't heard of that many.

The person who wrote that diary, if I can remember clearly, didn't use the word "rape."[31] Why? In my opinion, that girl was raped in every sense of the word, and what's worse is that a bunch of guys cheered it on! The thought makes me want to throw up! I don't care if the girl went willingly to that guy's dorm or apartment. I don't know of many girls, or guys, for that matter, who haven't gone back willingly to someone's room for whatever the reason. That's no explanation to rape someone. This sadist obviously had the whole escapade planned for the sole reason of humiliating the poor girl.

Maybe she sleeps around. Who cares? Call her a slut, then. Was this guy playing the role of God and punishing her for her actions? Who the hell is he? What were his reasons for doing this? Was it some cheap thrill? In my opinion, he is an animal. A twisted, sick individual who deserves to be shot. I can't say he is entirely to blame, though. The pack of wolves that cheered him on are as bad as he is, if not worse. They're all big boys, probably raised in good families. They were taught right from wrong. You mean to tell me that none of them felt guilty about what they were doing? Well if they don't, they all deserve to be shot as well. These aren't human beings, they're monsters.

What bothers me also is that the person who wrote the diary said he laughed about it at first. How can someone find that funny in any way, shape, or form? What I got from the diary is that he now thinks it was wrong. GREAT!!! But should there ever have been any question in his mind from the beginning that it was wrong? The girl had to get free, break away from that animal and his cheering posse! Once he heard that, he should have been 100 percent sure she was raped. No doubt about it.

All I can do is thank God this never happened to me, and I pray it never will. Honestly, I'd rather be murdered. The thought of having to live after being humiliated (for lack of a stronger word), degraded, and put through such hell and possibly have to see any of those animals again terrifies me. I want to cry for that girl and all the other women who have experienced that hell. Nobody should have to go through anything like that. Nobody!

One last comment I'd like to make is that I think the person who wrote the diary should think about making some new friends.

ROBERT
"Thinking with My Penis"

In a patriarchal society power resides in the male—and in the phallus. Since the overwhelming majority of violent crimes are committed by men, our class discussions often focus on male aggression. This subject prompted Robert to concede that he and his friends do not always think with their head.

Many people disagree with Freud's theory of repressed aggressive and sexual urges. But I, on the other hand, am somewhat in agreement with Freud. In fact, if I were to be honest, I would have to say that personally I am driven by these two forces more than I would like to acknowledge. I am constantly "thinking with my penis," as friends of mine would say. My group of friends is very unlike most friends. We have no secrets, at least sexually speaking. We tell each other what we did with girls, and what we want to do to girls. We are very explicit in our descriptions, and none of us is at all embarrassed.

When I say that someone is "thinking with his penis," I mean that he is being driven by the thoughts and desires of his sexual appetite. This person usually ends up screwing up his goals and plans because he is not thinking rationally. Many of my friends from home are consumed with the activity of thinking with their penis, and the outcome is drastic. They are so wound up with fooling around with a girl that they think of it to the exclusion of thinking in a mature, adult way.

Some of these guys have literally ruined their education because of their sexual desire. They let their sexual desires get the best of them, and now they are going to pay for it. They either have dropped out of school or are not doing very well. It is said that "birds of a feather flock together," and these birds are unfortunately bound together because of their destructive appetite, which has caused them to fall by the wayside.

I sure am glad to have had the opportunity to go away to college because it has allowed me to mature and to see that the life we were living was no good. I am not saying that my friends are bad people, but it is just that they have not been able to look at themselves from another perspective. It may seem that I am condemning these guys for wanting to indulge in their sexual fantasies, but I am not. What I am trying to get across is that there is a limit to how much a person can submit to these urges and still be able to function as a normal person in society.

It is normal to have sexual urges—heck, I have them all the time, but the problem begins to occur when these urges start to take control of your every thought. You must be able to suppress these desires if you are to live a socially acceptable life. And here is where all the problems begin. If you do not hold back these desires, then you become a slave to them, like some of my dear friends, but on the other hand, if you do manage to suppress these cravings, they must be expressed in other forms. They usually come out in sports such as football and other physical activities. But if they are not let off in this manner, they might come out in other ways, such as hostility and bitterness. Either way, they are going to come out, and it is each person's job to deal with these repressed feelings and try to handle them in a healthy way, so as not to disturb your life. Good luck!

NICOLE
"When Was the Last Time You Got Laid?"

Women also write about unfulfilled sexual desire, but their diaries tend to be more self-deprecating than men's and devoid of the threat of violent aggression that accompanies phallocentric thinking. Witness Nicole's entry:

"What did you say?" I demanded of my handsome coworker. I did not believe that I heard him right, but he shot back the same words: "When was the last time you got laid? If you got laid, then maybe you would not be so uptight, you would be more relaxed, more sure of yourself, so you could do a better job." I just could not believe he said that! My disbelief turned into rage as my ears turned red and my jaws grated together. I was at a loss for a witty response, so I turned the question back on him. "When was the last time *you* got laid?" His reply was, "On last Tuesday." That was easy for him to answer!

Then I silently questioned why he wanted to know that intimate detail about me. Was it to see if he could get me to blush, to confess that I was a lesbian, had a boyfriend, or perhaps was still a rare virgin? Maybe he just wanted to talk about sex, but darn it if he did not hit the nail on the head. That bothered me the most, that he could read me so easily. It is odd how perceptive my coworker was when he said that if I got "it," then it would help me to relax and calm down so I could get on with my life with a greater sense of confidence. Did I really *need* to make love to come to grips with my life? To me, it was not that I needed it, but rather that I desired it.

It has been ten months now since I broke off ties with my boyfriend, and right now the search for pleasure seems never ending. Just tonight when I went to dinner with my sister and her boyfriend, I was actually feeling indignant when they kissed or showed affection toward each other. It symbolized the affection, attention, and sexual feeling that I so badly lusted for and could not obtain. (Am not able to *find* yet, is what I meant!)

At the restaurant, who should be sitting directly behind us, and in perfect view of me, but a certain person who had made passes at me the year before. I had given him the shove after his intentions of a casual sexual relationship became quickly apparent. Then, I had been happy with my decision to tell him to get out of my life. Now, I am thinking, "God! If I could only turn back the clock a year; how I would give up my lunch hour for a month just to be with him for one night." Now if that is not desperate, I do not know what is! This lusting for a sexual encounter is long overdue, since the opportunity to really enjoy the act of making love has never been a reality. I have finally decided that I want to have a fling and to experience that which up to now I have only regarded as hearsay.

I just read a sentence from Freud's *Introductory Lectures on Psycho-*

Analysis (lecture 20, "The Sexual Life of Human Beings") that says: "When reality prevents you from satisfying sexual wishes, it is possible to fall ill of a neurosis as a result of a frustration."[32] Perhaps this explains my continual obsession with the men in the world (any would do), my fingernail biting, chewing ice, peeling off the labels of beer bottles, and chewing on my pen tops. What I definitely know is that I am obsessed with this lack of sexual satisfaction, and it causes me great frustration and anxiety. Poor, poor pitiful me.

Freudian Slips and Other Unusual Experiences

Women also write more frequently than men about Freudian slips, a subject that always evokes amused—and bemused—commentary. In contrast to the tense sexual abuse diaries, these entries are playful and exuberant, written, it appears, both to entertain and instruct. Freud's *Psychopathology of Everyday Life* contains a fascinating array of slips of the tongue, misreadings, and bungled actions that appear fraught with psychological significance. Students take delight in supplying personal examples of Freudian slips, particularly when they illuminate sexual themes, as the following entries, written by four different women, demonstrate.

> In my freshman year of college I had to make a long presentation to my morning class. My subject was a rather flamboyant local politician. In attempting to describe this politician's "erratic" behavior toward the media, I inadvertently used the word "erotic" instead. I corrected myself and went on with the presentation. Needless to say, I had caught my audience's attention! Since I had stayed up until 2:00 A.M. preparing the talk, I dismissed the slip to being tired. Later, when thinking over the incident, I could find no other reason.
>
> More recently, I've made another association and come up with another reason. While this politician was in office, his political antics were colorful enough to result in a feature article in *Penthouse* magazine. The article presented him as an independent rebel. Everyone wanted to read it. My family is Catholic and traditionally conservative in outlook. I can remember obtaining *Penthouse* and wondering if I shouldn't obscure the article's source. I didn't. I deliberately repressed my personal objections to the publication in an effort, I think, to demonstrate how modern and

liberal minded I was. I think I also, subconsciously, wanted to shock my mother. I think that these repressed feelings surfaced during my class presentation, and "erratic" became "erotic." It took me a long time to reach this association.

I used to work in a seafood store. I remember once, when cleaning some squid for a lady, asking her, "Do you want the testicles cut off?" (ouch!), and then retorting that my mind was probably not on work that day. My only explanation was that my boyfriend was working in the same store. Was I angry at him? Speaking of my ex-boyfriend, there was also the time I called him by his boss's name when we were in bed—the boss whom I had dated in the past. My own personal explanation? I really don't have one, other than wishful thinking.

There was another time when my parents visited me, not too long ago, and when my mother and I were out shopping, I yelled to her, "Come here, please, Grandma." This one is easy: we had just been talking about her. However, my mother was far from pleased, though it seems funny to her now. How about one with no rationalization? Like the time when I was looking for some lamination and walked into my friend's room, which was full of people, and asked if anyone had any "clear, sticky stuff"? A bad move on my part. Or when I was sixteen and was visiting my sister in college. We were going to a beach party, and I walked into a room full of guys and asked, "Can anyone give me a lei?"

My aunt was telling me about getting cable TV last week for the first time. She was most enthusiastic about all the movies that were now available. "Last night," she said, "we even saw *Carnal Abuse.*"

"Oh? *Carnal Abuse*? I'm not sure I've heard that one," I said.

"You know! *Carnal Abuse*, the one with Art Garfunkle and Jack Nicholson," she insisted.

"I think you mean *Carnal Knowledge*," I replied.

We all laughed uproariously at this, but you *know* what I was wondering: Did she hate the movie, or does she have some ambivalent feelings about sex?

This weekend I experienced the classic Freudian slip. I work in a science store where we sell everything imaginable dealing with all the major fields of science. A man came in with his son, and the father said to me, "Did you get the cloning klits in yet—I mean kits?" This didn't phase me in the least. I wrote it off as an error in speech. I helped him. Then another man came in and said, "Do you carry molecular klits— kits?" I helped this customer too. A few minutes later I had a revelation. I was hysterical for ten minutes after I realized the slips these two consecutive customers just made. Could it be that they both made the same speech error because they both said words with "l's" in them and the second word was affected by the first? Or were they both Freudian slips? By the way, this really happened, however odd it may seem. I wonder if they would have done the same thing if a male salesperson had helped them.

ELLEN
*"I Beheld the Most Repulsive Thing a Child Could
Ever See—Parents Having Sex"*

Sometimes students write extended diaries about embarrassing sexual experiences. Ellen's entry, for example, combines elements of the Freudian primal scene with French farce.

I want to talk about a very traumatic event which happened a short while ago. Though it may sound as if it is a dream I had, unfortunately it is quite real. It was a disgusting, upsetting, extremely disturbing, and nauseating experience for me, one that will remain permanently etched in my memory.

I returned home early one morning after having an argument with my boyfriend. Obviously, my arrival was, to say the least, unexpected. I opened the front door, slammed it shut, stomped up the stairs, and headed toward my bedroom. On the way, I passed by my parents' bedroom, where I beheld the most repulsive thing a child could ever see— parents having sex. I was utterly horrified and angry and shocked and nervous and confused and, well, so many emotions erupted all at once. Why didn't they hear the car door slam, or the front door, or my footsteps, or my keys jingling, or, I don't know, WHY DIDN'T THEY HEAR ME IN TIME?

I couldn't believe my eyes and ears. Never had I caught them in the room next door with the paper-thin walls. I couldn't decide what to do. I couldn't let them know I was home. I didn't want them to know I knew, saw, and heard everything. I wanted to crawl under a rock and hide and forget the whole incident. The more I thought about what to do, the more the vivid images of Mom and Dad naked, having sex, popped into my mind.

I finally decided to grab the phone, call my boyfriend, and hide in the closet. I had to tell someone about what I had seen; I couldn't keep it to myself. I stepped into the closet, shut the door, and frantically called him. I whispered as best I could, and in a shaky voice, I told him the terrible thing I had seen. Meanwhile, my parents were still going at it in their room. My boyfriend seemed to think the whole thing was hysterical. I thought it was vile. He wouldn't have laughed so hard if it were his parents he caught in the act. He probably would have puked. I wonder why he didn't.

Suddenly, in the middle of our conversation, everything got very quiet. I heard my dad get out of bed and walk toward the window. He must have somehow heard my voice or another voice. I heard the metal blinds part, and then I knew that he knew I was home because my car was parked in the driveway. "Think she's home?" I heard my mom ask. My father said, "How the hell do I know?" "Think she heard?" I heard my mother ask. "How the hell do I know. I didn't hear her come in!"

I was about to piss in my pants, fearing they were going to discover that I was hiding in the closet. Next thing I knew, my father opened my bedroom door and noticed the phone cord was pulled into the closet. "Ellen, are you home?" I opened the door slightly, and my dad jumped and quickly stepped back into his bedroom. "Ruth, she knows," he said.

Shit, they know I'm home! Why did my boyfriend and I have to argue this morning of all mornings? Why didn't I stay in my apartment? Why didn't my parents hear me come in? Why did they have to have sex with their door wide open? At least they could have gone under the covers! How am I going to handle this? So many "why's" entered my thoughts.

Later on, after my father escaped to buy bagels and whitefish salad as he did every Sunday, I finally left my room. My mom was sitting in the kitchen, smoking a cigarette and sipping coffee, as if nothing had happened. She asked me, "So, did ya hear anything?" As if the whole incident was a joke. I replied, "Not only did I fucking hear, I fucking saw!" I was really fuming. "What's wrong with you guys? Didn't you hear the front door slam? Why don't you close your fucking door?" She just puffed away while steam was flying out of my ears and my eyeballs were popping out of my head. She came out with a very sarcastic reply: "Well, hey, once in twenty-one years isn't too bad, is it?"

I really believe she was amused by this event. She expressed no shame, no guilt, no sympathy for the way I felt. My father came home, however, and had a very difficult time facing me. I had a difficult time facing him, too. He wouldn't or couldn't acknowledge what had happened and the fact that his daughter had caught him—coitus interruptus. He didn't mention a word about anything. He didn't look me in the eye. He just asked me if I wanted a poppyseed bagel with whitefish spread on it. How did he expect me to eat after what I had seen? He also told me there were a couple of black and white cookies in the bag. Black and white cookies were my favorite, but he hadn't brought them home since I was a kid. Were these cookies a sign that he was sorry or ashamed or embarrassed? Maybe this was the only way he could express that he was sorry I had walked in on all of that. I'm not sure. Unfortunately, I wasn't able to touch the cookies or the bagels. I was just too sick to my stomach.

Since that awful incident, my thoughts and daydreams are constantly being interrupted by the image of my parents having sex. It is something I want so badly to forget, but I can't. I can't repress it or erase it from my memory. I still feel bitter toward my mother for her lack of sympathy and understanding, and turning the whole incident into a joke. In some way, my sexual relationship with my boyfriend has been affected. My father has yet to discuss what went on that day, and in some way I bet he still feels awkward that I saw them.

It's strange how kids squirm at the thought of their parents having sex. Sex can be a beautiful thing, yet it turns into something repulsive and vile when you relate sex to parents. Kids dread catching their parents in the act, as I did. I mean, I suppose I knew my parents had sex. After all, I wouldn't be here if they didn't. But it still does not prevent me from feeling disgust and nausea after seeing them "doing it." That experience was probably one of the grossest, most traumatic experiences I've ever had. Why should it be? Why is parental sex so horrible for children to think about?

Ellen's diary placed me in a quandary. I knew that if I read the entry aloud, her classmates would burst into laughter—as I had done upon first reading it. The diary was irresistibly funny, and no matter how degrading the idea of parental sex appeared to her, Ellen masterfully exploited the humor of the situation in her retelling. And yet because she was still angry at her mother for "turning the whole incident into a joke," I wondered whether she would similarly become angry at her classmates. I did not want to be in the situation Scott described in his rodeo diary, deriving pleasure over a woman's sexual humiliation. After debating with myself, I decided to take a chance and read it aloud—and could see out of the corner of my eye Ellen joining her classmates in mirthful laughter.

ADAM
"My Perfectly Shaped Love Slaves Had Turned Into Bloodthirsty Vampires"

Adam's diary, no less highly crafted than Ellen's, combines Freudian dream analysis and gothic horror with an eerie *Twilight Zone* ending:

> More and more recently I have become aware of how outside elements shape one's dreams. Having been skeptical in the past, I will show how I've come to the realization that dreams are directed by events we experience in waking life.
>
> This past weekend I was at a bar partaking of the two-for-one beer special with my girlfriend and a couple of other friends we usually meet there. After several pints of beer, my friend Lew was ready to play Elvira, the pinball machine. It's probably one of the best pinball games ever made, and one which seems to attract mostly males. I think this statistic can be attributed to the colorful artistic, rather risqué caricature of Elvira. It shows her in all her glory, the black mistress of the night dress, her long black hair, and her most famous trademark, those ghostly white plump and perky breasts, which are located dead center in the scoreboard.
>
> We were playing and drinking and talking, and our conversation somehow revolved around having sex with two women at once. Lew mentioned how he once had the chance back in high school but for some reason decided against it. I told him I never had the opportunity

and didn't know what my decision would be if I ever had the chance. We always seem to talk about women and sex after we watch *Cheers* and down many brews—I'm not exactly sure why, but we do.

After we played our last game of Elvira and spent the last of our money on one beer for the road, we said good night and went home. My girlfriend stayed over, and as usually happens when we've drunk too much, we talked about going home and making love, but by the time we were in bed neither of us had the strength, energy, or ambition to move. We both just fell into dead silence and somber sleep. My mind, on the other hand, was just getting started. With all the talk about making love, combined with my conversation with Lew, the stage was set for a night of mental passion.

The specifics of the dream are a bit fuzzy, but I can recall the general outline. I found myself in a castlelike atmosphere in a bedroom with a large bed, which I was lying on. I was immediately joined by two phenomenal looking women, dressed in black leather lingerie. I didn't know these women, but I was sure I was going to. The dream went along at a very intimate pace—there was no whipping and quick movements. I was enthralled with their lovemaking, and I had the endurance of a marathon runner added with the ability to attain multiple orgasms, two of the most truly envied and sought-after qualities any man could hope to be blessed with. The dream continued for what seemed like forever, always maintaining the same rhythmic pace.

Suddenly the mood switched, as the women began to ignore me but continued having sex with each other. So I watched. Again the tempo changed, and so did their mood; they became aggressive and loud. I got nervous but stayed in bed—maybe they could teach me something new. But when one got close, I noticed an obvious change in their appearance. They were no longer gorgeous, long-haired sex-crazed dolls; they had fangs and razor-sharp fingernails. It was unbelievable, like the whole dream itself: my perfectly shaped love slaves had turned into bloodthirsty vampires. No longer were they interested in me being in them in the sexual sense, but instead they desired me in a thirst-quenching way. Somehow my dream ended with me watching them as though I was floating above them as they, unaware of my presence, lay in bed looking as fantastic as when the dream started.

I then awoke, my arms around my girlfriend, and I gave her a huge hug. She rolled over, said good morning, and asked how I slept. I replied I slept great, and she said she also slept well. As I lay next to her, running my fingers through her hair, I noticed two very small red dots located below her right ear on her neck. They slightly resembled a vampire, and immediately I recalled my dream. We always talk about our dreams, but I wasn't sure if I wanted to share this one with her. I was afraid she might ask me to analyze it—ever since I began taking this course, she has asked me to try and give a Freudian interpretation to dreams and other things. I didn't want to even try with this one, and though I'm confident in our relationship, I'm not sure if I really care to know what Freud would say about such a dream.

Homoerotic Desire

Unlike men, who rarely write about homoerotic desire, women not infrequently narrate dreams or fantasies of lovemaking with other females. These women define themselves as heterosexual yet find themselves thinking about homoerotic desire. Gender theorists such as Nancy Chodorow argue that, since daughters are more symbiotically attached to their mothers than sons are, thus experiencing a greater degree of connectedness, they may find it easier to imagine loving a member of the same sex.[33] In the following three diaries, the first two students are visibly troubled by the thought of bisexuality, while the third finds the idea intriguing.

KATE
"I Would Never Tell My Housemate About This Dream"

Wow, I had the strangest dream last night, and it worried me a lot. I've never questioned my sexuality before, and I don't plan on doing it now. I don't mean to offend anyone, but the thought makes me sick. I guess I'm writing this in my diary to help myself understand the whole thing. In the dream we had the urge to make love to each other all the time and in the strangest places. There was even one time when we were in a walk-through closet that I remember from the fifth grade. The funny part was that I was the aggressive partner teaching her how to enjoy sex, but on the other hand I seemed to have all the pleasure.

There are a few different ways I've explained this dream to myself, but I'm not quite sure that I've convinced myself any are valid. My strongest thoughts about the dream involve my housemate's bashfulness in discussing sex openly, even to her boyfriend. I think that in the dream I allow her to be open about sex. I know that this does not deal with *my* sexuality, but who said it had to?

Another view of the dream is that I'm too dependent on her, and this is just a way to express it. In the dream I make her my sex partner, whom I would depend on for sexual fulfillment. My last thought was that I am just expressing the love I have for a good friend. I'm not really sure what the dream means, but I'm not going to think about it. All I know is that I would never tell my housemate about this dream.

DARLENE
"Lovemaking with One's Own Sex"

The other night I had a dream which startled me the next day when I remembered it. In the dream, I was sexually intimate with my housemate. We are both female and heterosexual, and I don't think that I am subconsciously attracted to her specifically. But the dream bothered me (and still does), and I'd like to know the significance of it.

I have, for a while, been fascinated by homosexuality as well as confused by it. Some feel that it is a psychological disorder with which individuals are unfortunate to be struck. Others have expressed the notion that homosexuality is a quality within all of us but is repressed so much that we are unaware of these "shameful" desires.

Perhaps it was these subconscious desires that were revealed in my dream. These dreams have occurred before the other night and were followed by feelings of shock and embarrassment.

Apart from this theory that we have unconscious desires, which I feel is debatable, I feel that everyone holds a strong curiosity toward homosexuality. I will never know how it feels to have a penis, and I wish I could try it sometime, but that is impossible. I will also never know what it feels like for a man to have sex with a woman, and though someone could describe it to me in explicit detail, I still will never feel the sensation.

I think we all have this desire to experience the impossible. But I also think that we desire the possible: to know the sensation of lovemaking with one's own sex.

GRACE
"If She'd Ever Be with Another Woman, It Would Only Be with Me"

I'm writing this in reply to a diary read last week. The person who wrote it seemed pretty much disturbed by the fact that she had a sexual dream about a girlfriend. Personally, I think it's pretty normal. I don't consider myself a lesbian or even bisexual, yet I've had sexual dreams (not really sexually explicit, but still sexual) and thoughts about one particular girlfriend of mine. And I was pretty surprised when one day she told me that if she'd ever be with another woman, it would only be with me. I told her I felt exactly the same way, and we talked about it and came to the conclusion that our feelings came not from a real sexual attraction to each other but from the very deep sense of love we have for each other.

Before we talked I was a little disturbed by my thoughts—every guy I seemed to be meeting was one disappointment after another, and so I thought maybe I'm not heterosexual. But then I thought longer and came to the conclusion that being in Albany, it's not surprising to have repeated disappointments. So, as I said, I think it's perfectly normal for anyone to have these dreams, thoughts, or feelings—even for me. Now my friend and I joke and say that if either of us had a penis, we'd be perfect for each other.

ADRIENNE
"A Secret Sharer"

I have received similar diaries from women describing intense friendships, charged with erotic overtones, with other women. Shortly after a discussion of "The Secret Sharer," Joseph Conrad's short story about a young captain's encounter with his mysterious double, Adrienne submitted the following diary in which the boundaries between self and other have almost disappeared. To use Tracey's metaphor from the "Sins of the Fathers," Adrienne possesses a mysterious "alarm system" alerting her to her friend's fears and pains.

I have a secret sharer. I guess you could call her that anyway, and I know that she is a real person, unlike the story we read. She is my very best friend because she knows all about me, every dark thought, and she loves me anyway. We even look alike; my mom said she never saw anyone with the same shape and color eyes as mine until she met Maureen. We come from similar backgrounds, and we have had almost identical experiences in our lives, dating back to before we knew each other existed. We don't need words to speak, as I often know exactly what she is thinking before she ever says a word.

One night a few weeks ago I was very depressed, and I softly cried myself to sleep, so no one would hear me. I had seen Maureen the day before, so there really was no reason for her to call. At about three in the morning the phone rang, and I answered it on the first ring, even though I had been in a deep sleep for hours, because I knew it was her. "What's wrong?" she said to my hello. "Nothing," I said as I began to cry once more. "I knew it was him; I knew you were upset over him again," she said. I did not question how Maureen knew. She always knows, just as I can feel her sadness even when we are miles apart.

Last weekend she came to visit. People said that she acted just like me and used the same expressions. I guess that can easily be explained by the fact that we spend so much time together. But how do you explain that we both have the same recurring dream of our teeth falling out, and that she wakes up in the middle of the night because she knows that I am upset?

Maureen bites the skin on her hands when she is nervous. I instinctively hold her hands when we are in a tense situation so that she does not make her hands bleed and hurt herself. She is the only female in the world that I can hug and kiss besides my mom. We went on many trips together with our high school basketball team, and we always slept in the same bed. Being close to her comforts me.

Homosexual? I don't think so. More like in comforting Maureen, she comforts me. It makes me feel good to know that I can make her feel as secure as she makes me feel. How many people can say that they have a friend who always understands even when they don't agree? Who can say that there is a person out there with whom they need not measure their words or hide their feelings? The girls I live with now always laugh when I say to Maureen, "I love you too" and then hang up. But I do love her, and I have nothing to be ashamed of.

KEVIN

"I Look Back at Myself of a Few Years Ago, and I Cringe"

Many of the stories we read contain homophobic characters, and these works never fail to produce timely class discussions of sexism. In *The Bell Jar*, for example, Esther Greenwood is repelled by homosexuality and asks her female psychiatrist: "What does a woman see in a woman that she can't see in a man?" She receives an eloquent answer: "Tenderness."[34] Students use their diaries to define their feelings toward homosexuality, sometimes confronting disturbing prejudices which they vow to overcome.

There have been many things that have changed about myself since my arrival at college. I liked to think of myself as mature and, in comparison, ahead of many of my peers, yet I have learned things about myself which have brought me to some harsh realizations. I have taken several courses and participated in a training program that has heightened my level of sensitivity. I look back at myself of a few years ago, and I cringe. In many instances, I could have been unknowingly causing pain to people and alienating them by my insensitive words or actions.

During this year, I attended a lecture in which a speaker was discussing homosexuality. She was very blunt, to the point, and she really hit home. She had us perform an improvisation dealing with a straight person and a homosexual. She asked for volunteers before she told us the content of the role play, and I was chosen. When she announced that I was to play a homosexual, many people in the class laughed and said that at least I had dressed the part (I was wearing pink) and made other joking comments.

It was then when she angrily stopped the role play and began telling us a story that no one in the room will ever forget, including me. She told us of a male college freshman who wrote his parents a letter asking if he could have a male friend stay with them over the summer. His parents wrote back saying that any friend of his was most certainly welcome in their house, for as long as he liked.

The son then wrote a second letter asking if it was still OK and whether his parents didn't mind the fact that his friend was homosexual. He received a letter very soon after from his parents apologizing for their forgetfulness and explaining that they were having a few friends over themselves, and that there would thus be no room. Also, what would the neighbors think?

Knowing that their son would be home in a few days, his parents didn't expect another letter, so they proceeded to await his arrival at the airport on the proper day and at the proper time. They began to wonder where their son was when his plane unloaded all of its passengers and he was not among them. They asked a flight attendant where he could be, and he, a bit uncomfortably, told them that he would be waiting at the loading dock. They quickly went there, since they had missed their son a great deal and wanted to clear up this friend problem.

But when they came upon the loading dock, they realized that any hope of fixing this problem was over. There was their son, lying dead in a coffin. There was a short note attached to the coffin, reading: "Mom and Dad, I love you both, but I know that you could never love me now, so I can't go on living any longer. I'm the one who is gay, and if you had really loved me, you would have accepted my friend unconditionally."

I know I will never forget this story, and I have told everyone of my friends and my family about it. I wondered how much it really affected me until the other day when I was in acting class. Two students were doing an improvisation, and they began to portray the stereotyped homosexual—they were laughing and joking, and one of them said that he had AIDS. They joked about that? They joked about that! I was horrified, not just because of their blatant insensitivity, but also because I know that a very short time ago that could have easily been me. How would homosexual students have felt if they were in that class? One out of every twelve people has homosexual preferences. How would they have felt indeed?

CRAIG
"I Must Admit That I Never Did Feel Abnormal"

I was initially reluctant to read Kevin's diary to the class because the story about the gay man's suicide struck me as too melodramatic to be true. Rarely do I question a diary's truthfulness, but in this case I did. Nevertheless, I felt that even if this part of the story was fabricated (strictly speaking, the diarist was simply relating a story told to him by a teacher), Kevin's responses seemed genuine. I decided to read the diary to the class and received a week later the first of two entries from Craig about being gay.

On several occasions there have been diaries that have focused on the issue of homosexuality. I'm not sure why, but until now I've chosen not to write on the subject. I guess it's because I'm not too clear on Freud's position on the subject, but what I do know is how I feel about my lifestyle. For many years I was obsessed with trying to figure out what was wrong with me. Did my parents drop me on my head, did they fail when they raised me, or am I just a deviant pervert? I think I knew I was gay by the age of ten—I'm not sure how or why, I just did.

Society told me it was wrong; they said gays were perverts and that all they needed was a good shrink. So that was how I grew up, with an overwhelming sense of guilt and an acute sense of isolation. There was no one to talk to and nowhere to turn. I felt all alone in life, trying to understand who and what I was, and needing to know that I was OK. This has turned into what seems to be a long and turbulent journey.

What I've come to understand about myself is that there is nothing wrong with me, neither physically nor psychologically. I came to realize that I had let society dictate to me what was right and wrong as they saw fit, as ignorant as it was. Today I am glad that I allow myself to express my sexuality. I no longer date women in an attempt to change or hide my true feelings, nor do I live a secret life. I live openly with my lover of two years and have never felt more normal in all my life. I must admit that I never did feel abnormal—I always felt that it was society that was wrong.

Since other students have expressed their views on the Oedipus complex, I thought that maybe I should do the same. My experience with the subject is similar in many ways and yet so different in other ways. The relationship that I share with my mother has always been ambivalent. If I ever had a desire to sleep with my mother, it's news to me. Quite honestly, I don't think the thought ever crossed my head. I think that in my case, due to my homosexuality, the roles of my parents were completely reversed.

What I can recall about growing up is that I very much did fantasize about sleeping with my dad. I don't think I ever really thought much about it, nor do I think that I ever expected it to happen. I do remember thinking how odd it was, however, because I did know of Freud's theories. I wasn't too sure what Freud was trying to advocate, but I did know that I was dreaming of the wrong parent.

For some reason, my mother and I always seemed to clash with each other. I grew up constantly thinking that I had to prove myself to her and to some extent compete with her. I never felt that I was competing for the attention of my father, however. I can remember needing to be like my mother, to have her control, authority, and sense of self-confidence. The hate and the anger that I felt for my mother stemmed mostly from my inability to get her approval. To this day it is still difficult to live up to my mother's standards. It never seems to be good enough or even enough.

What I have come to realize is that, because I will never make my mother happy, I no longer try. I simply live my life and no longer look for her approval. As a result, my relationship with my mother is much closer today, and to be honest, it really seems as though she is much more accepting of me and the decisions I make.

As for my father, my relationship has remained very constant over the years. It is a very loving and trusting relationship that does not know the meaning of conditional love.

Understandings Gained

As a result of writing and listening to diaries on sexual disclosures, many students reached Craig's conclusion that they were not "abnormal." Although it is unrealistic to expect diarists to resolve a serious conflict by semester's end, their sexual disclosures initiated a valuable (self-)dialogue that continues, I hope, to this day. The women discovered they were not alone in being sexually victimized. By writing about their experiences and hearing them read in class, they felt empowered and connected to the classroom community. Equally important, the men discovered the extent to which an ideology of male dominance pervades American culture. Insofar as poor communication is often cited as a culprit in many sexual crimes, particularly acquaintance rape, hearing diaries on female victimization is likely to leave a strong impression on the men in the class. Those students who were sexually abused began to confront years of guilt, shame, and anger; those who had never given much thought to sexual humiliation became more aware of its repellent nature; and those whose sexual orientation ran counter to society's expectations were able to express their point of view with the assurance they would be heard.

I too have learned from my students' sexual disclosures—learned about problems of which I was unaware. The diaries have expanded my knowledge of sexual victimization and compelled me to revise some of my earlier literary interpretations. Two years ago, for example, I was teaching a summer course on Fitzgerald and lent a graduate student, Beth Gordon, a copy of *The Talking Cure* so that she could read my chapter on *Tender Is the Night*. A few days later Beth came into my office and said, "I agreed with your interpretation except for one part." When I asked her to elaborate, she referred to my discussion of the incest theme between Nicole Warren and her father, in which I suggested that the various changes Fitzgerald had made in the incest material, from his initial conception of the novel to the final manuscript, had the effect of softening the act. In his working notes for *Tender Is the Night* Fitzgerald wrote: "At fifteen she was raped by her own father under peculiar circumstances—work out."[35] The few details we learn about the incest in the published novel come mainly from Nicole's guilt-ridden father, who implies that it was an act of love in which his daughter had participated willingly:

We used to say, "Now let's not pay any attention to anybody else this afternoon—let's just have each other—for this morning you're mine." A broken sarcasm came into his voice. "People used to say what a wonderful father and daughter we were—they used to wipe their eyes. We were just like lovers—and then all at once we were lovers—and ten minutes after it happened I could have shot myself—except I guess I'm such a Goddamned degenerate I didn't have the nerve to do it."[36]

On the basis of this passage, I argued in *The Talking Cure* that Fitzgerald could not decide whether the incest was a rape or seduction. "In the novel . . . Nicole consents to sexual intercourse. The change is obviously significant in that now she must assume partial responsibility for the act, along with the consequent blurring of innocence."[37]

In rereading my interpretation, written more than a decade ago, before I studied closely my students' diaries on sexual victimization, I can now understand why Beth disagreed strongly with it. I can also appreciate why Lee was so upset by my Oedipal reading of "Babylon Revisited," an interpretation that must have struck her as making every male relative into a potential sexual abuser. Surely the responsibility for the incest in *Tender Is the Night* must lie entirely with the father, not jointly with the daughter. Even if it is true that she did not resist her father's advances—and we cannot know this for sure, since Nicole does not talk about it—the terror of incest and other sexual crimes is such that we cannot see any "blurring of innocence" regarding her actions. Had Nicole been a student of mine and written a diary about the experience of being "Daddy's Girl," she would have heightened my understanding of *Tender Is the Night*—as my students' diaries have heightened my understanding of their lives.

7 / Conclusion: Teaching Empathically

The damned little brat must be protected against her own idiocy, one says to one's self at such times. Others must be protected against her. It is social necessity. And all these things are true. But a blind fury, a feeling of adult shame, bred of a longing for muscular release are the operatives. One goes on to the end. —William Carlos Williams, "The Use of Force"

William Carlos Williams's short story "The Use of Force" (1961) is a cautionary tale for physicians and teachers alike. A masterpiece in its brevity and dramatic tension, the tale opens with a physician summoned by a family named Olson to examine their young daughter, Mathilda, suspected of having diphtheria. (Her exact age is not specified.) The parents are poor and uneducated, desperate enough to spend three dollars for the home visit yet suspicious of the physician's authority. Sensing their mistrust, the physician assumes they are concealing a secret which he is determined to uncover. His initial response to Mathilda betrays a curious mixture of professional detachment and nervous attraction. "The child was fairly eating me up with her cold, steady eyes, and no expression to her face whatever. She did not move and seemed, inwardly, quiet; an unusually attractive little thing, and as strong as a heifer in appearance."[1]

Narrated in first person, "The Use of Force" immediately calls into question the reliability of the physician's perceptions. Was Mathilda really eating him up with her cold, steady eyes, or does her expression simply reflect a child's understandable fear of a physical examination? Smiling in his "best professional manner," he asks the girl, who is sitting on her father's lap, to open her mouth. She refuses. He then tries to coax her, again with no success. As he approaches her, she suddenly springs at him and, clawing at his eyes, sends his glasses flying. With the symbolic loss of his vision, the physician's manner hardens. "Look here, I said to the child, we're going to look at your throat. You're old enough to understand what I'm saying. Will you open it now by yourself or shall we have to open it for you?" (133). Exasperated by her noncompliance, he informs the parents that he will not insist upon a throat culture if they accept responsibility for the consequences. The parents, terrified of the possibility that their child may be dying, admonish her, to no avail.

The physician's struggle to examine his patient takes on increasingly sexual and aggressive overtones suggestive of rape. "I had already fallen in love with the savage brat," he admits, noting that, in the ensuing battle, her parents grew contemptible, while she "rose to magnificent heights of insane fury of effort bred of her terror of me" (133). He commands the father to hold his daughter's wrists so she cannot move; when she screams, "You're killing me!" the mother expresses alarm, only to be ordered peremptorily out of the room by her husband.

The physician then tries to insert a wooden tongue depressor between the girl's teeth. Before he can enter her mouth cavity to take a throat culture, she violently clenches her teeth, reducing the blade to splinters, whereupon he resolves to complete the examination at all cost. Although reason dictates he should desist and try again later, he is out of control, intent only upon exerting his will over her. "I could have torn the child apart in my own fury and enjoyed it. It was a pleasure to attack her" (134). In one final, brutal assault, he overpowers her, forcing a heavy silver spoon past her teeth until she gags. At last he discovers the secret she has attempted to conceal, the diphtheritic membrane covering her tonsils. The story ends with the maddened girl, blinded by tears of defeat, again trying to fly at the physician.

Interpretations of "The Use of Force"

Williams's story illustrates how a person's best intentions—in this case, the desire to restore an ill person to health—may be defeated by lurking unconscious forces. The physician's desire for sexual mastery, his need to break down his patient's resistance and dominate her, is striking. The more she resists, the more he is determined to conquer. He never tells us why he allows his erotic attraction and pent-up sadistic fury to overcome his better clinical judgment. No psychotherapist, he lacks even a rudimentary awareness of the negative countertransference he brings to his patient.

An Oedipal interpretation of "The Use of Force" suggests that the physician, a father-surrogate, seeks to "know" the girl biblically. The secret she struggles unsuccessfully to preserve, in the form of a hidden membrane, evokes an image of virginity. The father, by physically restraining his daughter, appears to be an accomplice to her violation. A pre-Oedipal interpretation sheds light on another possible motive behind the physician's assault: the desire for domination may be a defense against the fear of being "eaten up" or engulfed by a female whose bovine strength symbolizes a primitive male fantasy of a devouring woman. Mathilda's violent splintering of the phallic tongue depressor with her teeth (an image of vagina dentata?) seems to awaken the physician's castration anxiety, thereby inciting his fury.[2]

A feminist reading of Williams's story yields still another meaning. "The Use of Force" is about the abuse of patriarchal power, male oppression of women. The physician dominates and depersonalizes the girl, reducing her to an object of penetration. His commitment to a "masculine" model of science reflects objective, detached, impersonal values; by contrast, he ignores a traditional "feminine" model reflecting subjective, involved, personal values. The physician imagines himself in a contest with the patient in which he seeks power over her rather than her empowerment. The story thus dramatizes a master-slave relationship. While his actions may prevent her from succumbing to a deadly organic disease, he traumatizes her in the process, producing a psychic injury from which she may never recover. Although patriarchal society may approve of the physician's use of force, the story explores the darker motives of the medical establishment's treatment of women.[3]

It may seem odd to begin a chapter on empathic teaching with a discussion of "The Use of Force," but I do so because of the possibility that teachers who encourage their students to engage in introspective diary writing may find themselves unwittingly in the position of Williams's physician. Teachers unconsciously may use force either by rewarding self-disclosing students or by punishing self-concealing ones. They may become subtly coercive by failing to understand their motives in helping students. Or they may succumb to the temptation to penetrate or probe their students' secrets in the mistaken belief that they are physicians, therapists, or saviors.

Conspicuously absent from the physician's relationship to his patient in "The Use of Force" is empathy and respect for otherness. There is no dialogue between physician and patient, no mutuality or attunement, no recognition of the affective dynamics of the relationship. The physician's phallic paradigm of knowledge depends upon conquest rather than empathic connectedness.

Only Connect

The model of teaching I propose for the use of introspective classroom diary writing is relational, affirming empathy, mutuality, and empowerment. The model values both the affective and the cognitive elements of learning. In this intersubjective paradigm, teacher-student exchanges form an indispensable part of the learning process. Unfortunately, intersubjectivity has not received sufficient attention from educators. Few literary critics, apart from feminists, reader-response critics, and composition theorists, have recognized the affective components of knowledge.[4] Paul de Man voices the prevailing masculine model of education when he asserts that teaching and scholarship should not be concerned with the personal dynamics of the teacher-student relationship:

> Overfacile opinion notwithstanding, teaching is not primarily an intersubjective relationship between people but a cognitive process in which self and other are only tangentially and contiguously involved. The only teaching worthy of the name is scholarly, not personal; analogies between teaching and various aspects of show business or guidance counseling are more often than not excuses for having abdicated the task. Scholarship has, in principle, to be eminently teachable.[5]

Unlike de Man, I believe that education *is* an intersubjective process in which teacher and student are directly and centrally involved with each other. All learning involves both affective and cognitive elements, and there is no contradiction, as de Man implies, between scholarly and personal teaching. Effective teaching is, in my view, affective teaching, and we need to devise methods to address the personal dynamics of the teacher-student relationship. Classroom discussions of literature awaken intense emotions within teachers and students alike—love, hate, passion, jealousy, fear—and these emotions cannot be relegated to "guidance counseling." Construing danger to arise from the teacher-student relationship, de Man propounds a paradigm of knowledge that excludes the affective issues which promote connected learning.

A recent book, *Women's Growth in Connection*,[6] published by Judith Jordan and her associates at the Stone Center for Research at Wellesley College, proposes the intersubjective model of learning I have in mind. In this model, teachers and students maintain an ongoing awareness of each other. Teachers and students strive to maintain interconnectedness, seeking to communicate and share their knowledge. This mutual attunement, which has its origins in the early mother-child relationship, expresses the need to be recognized and validated by others.

Empathy

At the heart of the relational model lies empathy, the ability to project oneself into another person's point of view without losing necessary distance between self and other. Empathy is, developmentally speaking, a precursor to sympathy but a more active and intense form of involvement. Heinz Kohut, the founder of self psychology, pioneered the "empathic-introspective" stance in therapy.[7] Kohut argues that empathy serves three major functions. First, it is an invaluable tool of observation, the method by which one person understands another's feelings; second, empathy creates a powerful bond between people, counteracting human destructiveness; finally, empathy is a psychological nutriment that sustains human life. The development of empathy is not only a major therapeutic goal but also, in my judgment, a major educational goal, in which teachers strive to heighten their students' empathic awareness of the world around them.

Self-Esteem

In a relational model of learning, the heightening of students' self-esteem becomes another valuable educational aim. Students who develop self-esteem are much more likely to succeed in their education than those who do not. In this model, the teacher is not only an imparter of knowledge but also a nurturer and empowerer. Just as many of the benefits from therapy derive from the quality of the patient-therapist relationship, so do many of the gains from education derive from the student-teacher relationship.

BARBARA
"I Do Not Accept Praise"

It is not uncommon for students to tell me that many of the issues they discuss in their diaries coincide with those discussed with their therapists.

Barbara, for example, revealed in the following entry how her difficulty in accepting praise from me reflected the problem of low self-esteem she was trying to work through with her therapist.

Because of this course, my psychotherapy has moved out of a lengthy impasse, and I find that I am able to be more open rather than drawing blanks or intellectualizing everything. Consequently, I have learned a great deal about myself—some of it I like, some of it I do not—much has been illuminated. I now have a deeper understanding and can make more connections between internalized feelings and attitudes and outward actions, some of which may be self-defeating. Some of these feelings are related to self-esteem.

Though my self-esteem has increased dramatically over the past two years (since entering therapy), it is still low.

In last week's class we talked about people with low self-esteem and how they invite others to treat them poorly and tolerate mistreatment. Though I don't believe I have invited mistreatment, I do not accept praise and feel that anyone complimenting me is mistaken—if they knew me better, they would surely change their mind. I didn't realize until recently that I sometimes do things to prove them wrong.

The first week I walked into your office you made a comment about my having a first-rate mind and that I had written an excellent paper. On a reflex I started to turn around to see who you were speaking to. (I believe I stopped myself before I actually turned around.) The next week I stopped by your office, you again complimented me. I apparently had an unconscious need to prove you wrong. I became inattentive to you as evidenced by my responses to the things you were saying. It would be easy to blame the heat of the day or my fatigue, but that would be a very flimsy excuse and not accurate. Later in class I found myself not responding at all or responding incorrectly to your questions to which I knew the answers. I now interpret this as a form of aggression toward you, a way of showing you that you are wrong in your assessment of my abilities. I apologize to you. This discovery is most unsettling, since, on an intellectual level, I consider myself to be a knowledgeable and intelligent woman. However painful this discovery has been, I am grateful for it.

Teachers can care about their students without feeling obliged to be their caretakers, a role which implies an unequal, dependent relationship. Although the patient-therapist and student-teacher relationships are fundamentally unequal in the degree to which one discloses to or learns from the other, they are both dialogic interactions associated with mutuality, respect, and openness to change.

A fundamental shift toward intersubjectivity may be seen in psychoanalysis as well as education. In *Relational Concepts in Psychoanalysis*, Stephen Mitchell argues that psychoanalysis has been moving away from both the classical drive-conflict model, which emphasizes instinctual sexual and aggressive drives, and the developmental-arrest model, which stresses the infant's relationship to the mother, to the relational-conflict model, which foregrounds the patient-analyst relationship. "An interpretation is a *complex relational event*," Mitchell writes, "not primarily because it alters something inside the analysand, not because it releases a stalled developmental process, but because it says something very important about where the analyst stands vis-à-vis the analysand, about what sort of relatedness is possible between the two of them."[8]

From a relational perspective, Williams's narrator makes no effort to analyze the doctor-patient relationship as an interactive encounter between two persons. In gazing provocatively at the girl, he sees her only as a mirror of himself—sensual, willful, savage. In the desire to examine the girl, he refuses to examine the perspective from which he sees her, thus narrowing rather than broadening his vision of her. His angry dismissal of the parents deprives him of another point of view that might have enabled him to understand the patient. He acknowledges his clinical mistakes but does not analyze the reasons for them. We are left finally with the image of a physician who violates the Hippocratic oath he has sworn to uphold.

Introspective diary writing heightens the intersubjective nature of education. The connection students feel toward their teachers and classmates offsets much of the loneliness, alienation, and depersonalization associated with the college years. Writing and listening promote students' attachment between self and other, increasing their empathic understanding and enabling them to realize the commonality of their lives. The development of community is one of the most valuable by-products of diary writing.

This connection sometimes manifests itself in startling ways. Some students have told me that when I began reading a particular diary to the class, it seemed at first to be their own—until they realized that the entry was written by another classmate. They identified so intensely with the contents of the diary that they actually thought I was reading their own writing. It was an uncanny feeling, they said, as if they had recognized the existence of a doppelgänger in the class. Other students have told me about having the opposite experience, not realizing for several seconds that I was reading their own entry aloud. For these students, the initial feeling of detachment from their diary suddenly gave way to a recognition of involvement. In both cases, the students experienced an epiphanic repositioning of self and other.

Diaries as Transitional Objects

Diaries encourage connected teaching because they represent a bridge between self and other. Diaries thus may be viewed as *transitional objects*, a term introduced by the British psychoanalyst D. W. Winnicott to describe how a sheet, blanket, teddy bear, doll, or soft toy serves as the child's first "not-me" possession. In Winnicott's view, the transitional object is the space between inner psychic reality and outer external reality, subjectivity and objectivity, the self and the world. Symbolizing the child's relationship to the breast or the primary caretaker, the transitional object becomes a defense against anxiety, depression, and loss—a security blanket, so to speak, allowing the child to remain symbolically connected to the mother during her literal absence.

The child, according to Winnicott, invests the transitional object with special qualities. The child assumes rights over the object, maintains sole possession of it, protects it sometimes and mutilates it at other times, derives warmth and comfort from it (the transitional object is invariably a soft object capable of taking on the child's unique body smells), and gradually distances himself or herself from it without forgetting it or mourning its loss. The infant's relationship to the transitional object may continue well into childhood. An adolescent, for example, may find it necessary to hold or cuddle a teddy bear or sheet while falling asleep or during moments of anxiety or loneliness.

Students are fascinated by Winnicott's theory of transitional objects, largely because many of them can still recall vividly their own security blankets. Both men and women write about past or present transitional objects, and when I read these diaries aloud, they prompt other students to write about similar objects. Some students write about a continuing literal attachment to their security blankets, clinging to them in the privacy of their dormitory rooms or fantasizing about them in class; other students suddenly remember an old transitional object which they have not thought about in years. The following two diaries are representative in describing strong attachments to transitional objects.

JASON
"I Don't Know Why I'm So Attached to This Damn Thing"

I guess it started back in '69. My dad left for Vietnam when my mother was six months pregnant with me. There was no dad for me for my first nine months. When he finally came home, he brought me my first one. Of course I don't remember it, but I'm sure I loved it. Upon return, Dad started something that still continues today.

I guess you could say I am Linus personified. Yes, I have a security blanket. Always have, for as long as I can remember. It hasn't always been the same one, but the present blanket has been with me for over ten years, probably more like twelve or thirteen years. My blanket has a runner along the edge, as do most blankets like it. It's sorta like a blanket you might wrap up a baby in. This runner has a cool touch to it, something like a silk tie might feel. What I love the most about my blanket is to run this border fabric in between my fingers. And only one piece of border, a corner piece about three inches long. For me it's the greatest feeling. It's impossible to describe.

I've been doing this "between the fingers thing" for as long as I can remember. I'm addicted. Many times in class I think about doing it. Or when I'm driving. Chances are, if I'm on the way into my house, I'm thinking about doing this. When I do schoolwork, it's next to me. When I watch TV, it's usually next to me.

A lot of people have seen my blanket. I've always had it with me in the dorms. No one has the slightest idea what I actually do with it. No one has ever asked me what it's for. I wouldn't dare tell. When we used to hang out in the dorms, it was right behind me on the bed, between the fingers, unknown to anyone.

This is something very personal—only my girlfriend knows about it. She calls it my "Wooby" and thinks it's cute. That really annoys me.

I just sat with "Wooby" in my fingers, deciding whether to hand this in. If anyone reads this, I'd be really upset. I don't know why I'm so attached to this damn thing. I really love it. I know Freud would have a field day with this one. I guess I do depend on it in a way. I do know I'd be unhappy if something were to happen to it. I hate when other people sit on it like it's nothing, especially if it's on the "corner." I get agitated, like someone just fooled with an addict's stash.

Next time you have on a tie, try this: run the tie gently through two fingers, paying attention to the feeling on both sides of each finger. That's the attraction to me. It won't be the real thing, but try it.

Maybe you'll understand.

MEREDITH
"Everyone Knew That We Were an Inseparable Pair"

When we talked about duckie and sheeties last week, I remembered my old "security object" from so many years ago. It started off as a small brown teddy bear. Its name changed as my mood did. One day I called it simply "Teddy," and on another day it was called "Spaghetti."

I took it with me everywhere until it began falling apart. It was sewed many times, and eventually all that was left of it was one of its legs. From that day on it was known as "Leg." Everyone knew that we were an inseparable pair. Not only did I keep him in bed with me at night, but I also took him with me each time I went out.

He smelled wonderful to me. I used to suck my thumb and hold him in my hand so that I could smell him at the same time. My mother knew better than to wash him.

He got lost once when I went shopping with my mother. I got hysterical, and she went back to look for him, knowing that if Leg couldn't be found, I would be devastated. She searched the entire store. A security officer wondered what she was doing looking all over the floors and on floor displays. She explained the situation, and he helped her find my best friend.

I must have dropped him at some point. Someone picked him up and, since there was only a leg left, threw him away, probably wondering what the strange fuzzy thing was. He was found in the bottom part of a department store ashtray. My mom brushed off the sand and brought him home to me. Needless to say, she still wasn't permitted to wash him.

I still remember one incident where Leg acted as my savior. I was traveling in the car with my family, and we lost the rear axle on our car. We started to spin and swerve across the road. My parents said some words of reassurance so that my brother and I wouldn't worry too much. I said, "I'm OK. I have Leg to protect me," and I meant it. I don't recall being the least bit scared. I was simply happy that I had my companion there to keep me safe.

My grandmother hated the fact that I kept Leg with me constantly. Early child psychologists discouraged this, and so she thought it wasn't good for me. I'm glad my parents didn't listen to her.

I also kept Leg with me when I was in the hospital for a few weeks before my second birthday. All the nurses knew who he was and that, despite the fact that he looked like a grungy old ratted up stuffed part, he was omnipotent to me. They even gave Leg a hospital I.D. bracelet just like mine. It was too big, though, and kept sliding off.

I gradually grew up and grew away from my "Leg," probably with a little help from Mom and Dad. It wasn't until now that I even realized she still had Leg tucked away in some closet or lost in the attic. I think when I go home for Thanksgiving I'll search for my long-lost friend. I wonder how he'll smell to me now. Maybe I'll even bring him back to school with me.

It may seem far fetched to suggest that diaries are transitional objects, a metaphoric security blanket connecting self and other, yet I believe there are intriguing parallels. Diaries may not have the wonderful smell or soft sensuousness of a "Wooby" or "Leg," but they evoke the same magical intimacy, uniqueness, and safety that both Jason and Meredith describe. Just as children talk to their transitional objects, expressing their deepest feelings and thoughts to it, secure in the knowledge that a duckie or teddy will never contradict or criticize them, so do students confide in their diaries with the expectation that they will be understood and will never be betrayed. Recall Tracey's apostrophe to the reader of her diaries in chapter 3: "You accepted my inner thoughts and did not criticize them. You are like my diary, my secret friend who has breathed my thoughts and will treasure them forever."

Many students tell me that they become inseparably attached to their diaries and return to them during times of crisis, deriving comfort and security from their presence. Past students also tell me that they save their diaries as a record of how they felt at a particular time in their lives, discovering the truth of E. M. Forster's observation: "How do I know what I think till I see what I say?" It is not uncommon for some students to turn in four or five typed pages of entries every week. For these students, writing becomes almost an addiction, albeit a healthy one, not unlike the "addict's stash" Jason mentions.

Like other transitional phenomena, diary writing not only reduces anxiety and loneliness but also maintains identity and connection between self and other. Diary writing forges a powerful bond between writer and reader, establishing a dialectical tension between "I" and "you" suggestive of Buber's "I-Thou" relationship. A diary is a creation of the writer, yet part of the world. Once it is read aloud, a diary becomes internalized by other students who then make its contents part of their own lives. Diary writing enables students to engage in play, artistic creativity, and reality testing, proceeding, in Winnicott's terms, from the pleasure principle, based on the infant's illusion of omnipotence, to the reality principle, the mature recognition of one's limits in shaping reality and receiving gratification.

The Good Enough Teacher

For Winnicott, the *good enough mother* facilitates the child's successful adaptation. "The good enough 'mother' (not necessarily the infant's own mother) is one who makes active adaptation to the infant's needs, an active adaptation that gradually lessens, according to the infant's growing ability to account for failure of adaptation and to tolerate the results of frustration."[9] The good enough mother begins by being closely attuned to the child's needs but slowly adapts less and less completely, allowing the child to tolerate frustration and imperfection.

Teachers, like parents, can be either good enough or not good enough, depending on whether they are attentive or inattentive to their students' needs. Good enough teachers are able to acknowledge their students' criticisms without becoming angry or vindictive, and they make adjustments in their teaching when necessary. Although it is not always easy for a teacher to accept a student's legitimate criticism, when the criticism is accepted and publicly acknowledged, the student feels validated and empowered. Students seldom have the opportunity to criticize or evaluate their teachers; more often than not, the only opportunity occurs at the end of the semester when they fill out anonymous course evaluations. Even when these evaluations are taken seriously, it is too late to acknowledge them to the class. When students write weekly diaries, however, the opportunity to praise or criticize the teacher is always present.

I have found that in those courses in which students write weekly diaries for me, I am more empathically attuned to their feelings and thoughts than in other courses in which students do not write diaries. I feel more connected to my diary students, more in touch with them, more sensitive to their weekly progress. I also have a greater awareness of my successes and failures in the classroom because students do not hesitate to tell me when my teaching is not good enough.

Not long ago, for example, I was teaching John Steinbeck's "Chrysanthemums," a story about a middle-aged woman named Elisa who feels entrapped in a lifeless marriage and a barren setting. A pot mender comes along seeking to sell his services to her. Pretending to take interest in her life, he cynically manipulates her into giving him some of her precious flowers to bring to another woman down the road. The encounter with the man momentarily awakens Elisa's passion and revitalizes her interest in life. When she later journeys down the road with her husband, however, she spies the once-beautiful flowers strewn along the ground, discarded by the stranger, who never had any use for them. At the end of the story, Elisa feels betrayed and defeated, "crying weakly—like an old woman."[10]

During our class discussion, Heidi suggested that the dead flowers symbolized Elisa's unborn children, an interpretation I was loath to accept, perhaps because, I am embarrassed to admit, I had not thought of it first. I can think of no other reason for my arbitrary dismissal of it. Heidi was visibly dismayed and experienced my rejection of her reading as a rejection of herself. My reluctance to accept the interpretation was especially puzzling to her because of the less plausible interpretations she felt I had advanced throughout the semester. A few weeks earlier, for instance, I had discussed at considerable length the reasons for the captain's failure to retrieve a rope ladder hanging over the ship in Joseph Conrad's "Secret Sharer." I could not convince my skeptical students that, by inexplicably taking over the night watch and then forgetting to haul in the ladder, the captain was mysteriously summoning Leggatt, his second self, on board. The rope ladder, in my view, symbolized the bridge between the conscious and unconscious self. Believing that her reading of "The Chrysanthemums" was at least as persuasive as my reading of "The Secret Sharer," Heidi submitted the following diary expressing anger at my inconsistency:

HEIDI
*"If We Say Something That Doesn't Exactly Match
Your Theory, It's Wrong"*

I have quite the bone to pick with you this week. I'm still having a problem with the class discussion of "The Chrysanthemums" last Tuesday. It seems to me that even though you profess that there are many ways to psychoanalytically interpret a story, you are only willing to accept your own theory. I understand that you are much more of an expert on the subject than anyone in the class, and that you've spent much more time analyzing the stories. I (and I'm *sure* I'm not alone) often have a difficult time buying your interpretation. Then, when someone else offers an interpretation, which is often valid, you give the traditional teacher "Yes, very good. BUT . . ." reply and continue with your theory. You tell us to analyze the story and to write our essays on our own, before your discussion of it, but if we say something that doesn't exactly match your theory, it's wrong.

You said that the theory of the chrysanthemums being children was stretching things a bit too far. So was saying that the ladder was left out by the captain in "The Secret Sharer" on purpose to let this guy up. You see the children theory to be far fetched and say, "Go for the obvious." To me THAT WAS OBVIOUS! On the other hand, this ladder thing was so obscure that I couldn't believe how long we dwelt on it. I think you've got to decide just how much thinking you want us to do, and how much imitating you expect from us. You say one thing and do another, and often you don't let people complete their thoughts before you jump in with why it's wrong and replace it with your own ideas. You really are trying to be a father figure, aren't you?

Heidi was exactly right, of course, as I wrote to her in my comments. Without realizing it, I was giving off contradictory signals to her, paying lip service to her interpretation of the story but then aggressively pursuing my own. She perceived me as an overbearing male authority figure, not unlike the physician in "The Use of Force." From Heidi's perspective, I was cramming my interpretation down her throat, and she felt angry, resentful, subjugated. By praising her insight and courage and then reading her diary aloud, I implicitly acknowledged the error of my ways—to the satisfied smiles of the other students in the class. If Heidi had not written the diary, I doubt I would have realized my inconsistency as a teacher. She helped me to become a better teacher, for which I acknowledged my gratitude.

Phallic Readers

In my examinations of fictional characters, I suspect that, like Williams's physician, I desire to penetrate and probe their essence, uncovering their secrets and mysteries, conquering and subduing them in my quest for knowledge—or should I say *power*? This is an occupational hazard for many literary critics, particularly "depth critics," who, grandiosely modeling themselves upon Freud, believe they have discovered a text's "deepest meaning." I have often enacted this role in the classroom, seeking to match my psychoanalytic readings against students' nonpsychoanalytic ones. In both my teaching and writing I have been a "phallic reader," conditioned by culture, gender, and professional training to interpret literature as a series of Oedipal or pre-Oedipal contestations. But thanks in large part to the thousands of diaries I have received over the years, especially from female students, I am learning to read more empathically and relationally.

ASHLEY
"All My Defenses Come to the Fore"

I recall another example of inadvertently silencing a student, this time, ironically, during a rushed discussion of "The Use of Force." Ashley raised her hand and suggested, in a tentative voice, that Williams's story bears the telltale signs of child abuse. If Mathilda had indeed been sexually abused by an older man, Ashley speculated, that might explain her terror of the physician, who abuses her further. I told Ashley that, while I found her interpretation interesting, I did not see any textual evidence to support it and then steered the discussion in another direction, anxious to complete the story before class ended. Ordinarily, I would not have given Ashley's comment further thought—except that, two days later, she submitted the following diary to me:

I continue to feel very strongly that the little girl in "The Use of Force" has been sexually abused. Furthermore, I believe that the doctor often confronts signs of it in his work, but that his own pedophilia precludes his full acknowledgment of it. The parents are too nervous. In the era of the three-dollar visit, it is strange that the father is the one to offer the child's symptoms to the doctor. And the mother! A veritable pimp! "Such a nice man. . . . Look how kind he is to you. Come on, do what he tells you to. He won't hurt you." The child *knows* the doctor will hurt her because "nice" men *have* hurt her. The doctor objects to the mother's use of the word "hurt" because he is aware that it will have that effect. The child's *immediate* terror is suspicious. With a child's mute understanding, she knows he is one of them. Additionally, if she had been forced to perform fellatio, she may feel that some sign of it is in her mouth and throat, and she would be terrified to have it discovered.

It is strange that the mother keeps referring to the doctor as "the nice man" rather than as a doctor. The parents are obviously poor and un-educated, and the father-abuser may be as fearful as the girl of discovery, which is why he releases her at the "critical moment." The narrator-doctor describes the parents as "contemptible" but offers no reason. "Stop it! Stop it! You're killing me!" the girl screams as she has no doubt screamed before inside her head—now released in the new horror of *two* males who seek her open mouth. The exaggeration, the idea of being "killed," is not unrelated to the perception of an abused child. "She had fought valiantly to keep me from knowing her secret." Why would she consider her sore throat a "secret" unless she thought it had another meaning.

Berman says this idea of sexual abuse is an intriguing but purely speculative one. I think it is no more speculative than the rape. I think it (the idea of the girl reacting thus to the doctor because she has been abused) is the underlying message Williams wished to deliver. The anger of the doctor toward the little girl is instigated not only by her resistance and his lust but by the very fact that pretty little temptations like her exist at all, must be dealt with, cause problems. No rage as profound as hers could have been portrayed to deliver any other message.

All my defenses come to the fore as I fight for some acknowledgment of this interpretation of "The Use of Force." Why? Because it has been my experience that when you speak up in an area where you have already admitted a negative personal experience, your viewpoint may be discounted as "neurotic" at worst and "biased" at best.

Ashley's diary raises several intersubjective issues. It would be an understatement to say she was dissatisfied with my response to her interpretation; she felt dismissed, silenced, erased by my remark. As the last paragraph of the diary intimates, Ashley's affective response to "The Use of Force" was inseparably related to her cognitive response. The story touched a nerve, enabling her to empathize with the abused girl and protest her violation at the hands of the parents and physician. Moreover, the diary enacts some of the master-slave implications of "The Use of Force." Ashley, like Mathilda, mobilized her defenses as she fought valiantly to have her *own* point of view acknowledged and confirmed. I may not have been as menacing as Williams's physician, but she clearly found my classroom response—"intriguing but purely speculative"—woefully inadequate, a repetition, in fact, of other dismissals she had experienced by male authority figures.[11]

Diary writing enabled Ashley to develop and articulate her reading of "The Use of Force." The result is an interpretation that deserves further discussion, particularly in light of the clinical knowledge of child abuse she brings to bear upon the story. Although it is easier to suggest that Mathilda is the victim of metaphoric rape than of literal child sexual abuse, I am no longer willing to dismiss the possibility. By writing the diary, Ashley not only protested the use of force by physicians and professors alike but reversed the teacher-student relationship, enlightening her instructor on the dynamics of child abuse and insisting that he read literature more carefully and listen to his students more attentively. Without the opportunity to express herself in her diary, Ashley would have remained silenced—and both the class and I would have been deprived of her powerful voice. Her diary *forced* me, in the best sense, to listen to her point of view, and when I read the diary to the class, *she* had the last word.

Women as a Muted Group

Significantly, most students who use their diaries to protest the experience of being silenced or erased are women. Rarely do male students turn in diaries like Heidi's or Ashley's. And when female students do express anger toward me for dismissing their point of view, it is not unusual for them to call attention, as Heidi does, to my role as a father figure. In a patriarchal culture, the father is the dominant authority figure inside and outside the classroom, and consciously or not, he can easily infantilize his students or children. Female students tend to be, even when they are in the majority, a "muted group"—a term that describes unequal power relationships. Mary Crawford and Roger Chaffin have observed that "women seek to express themselves by writing in other than the dominant (public) modes of expression."[12] Diary writing is especially valuable for empowering women and other muted groups. It enables them to express their resistance against the patriarchal forces that would either silence or force them to counteridentify with themselves and "read like a man."[13]

Bankers and Midwives

In *Women's Ways of Knowing*, Mary Field Belenky and her associates quote Paulo Freire's description of traditional models of education based on male authoritarianism as "banking," in which the teacher's role is "to 'fill' the students by making deposits of information which the teacher considers to constitute true knowledge." Opposed to the banker-teacher model of education is the midwife-teacher. "While the bankers deposit knowledge in the learner's head, the midwives draw it out. They assist the students in giving birth to their own ideas, in making their own tacit knowledge explicit and elaborating it."[14]

As the reader of my students' diaries, I perform the role of a midwife, assisting them whenever possible in giving birth to their own offspring and admiring their creative products without presuming to judge or criticize them. I feel privileged that my students have entrusted to me their most intimate writings and allowed me to observe their lives. In writing this book, I certainly feel more like a midwife or editor—a compiler of my students' diaries—than a single author. In rereading their diaries and typing them into my word processor, I can visualize each student and recall his or her "birth" experiences. Each of my students has made an important contribution to this book, whether or not I used their diaries. In writing about their lives, they have made me part of their families and have become part of my own. Their writing has facilitated my writing. This book never would have come into existence had not so many students served as midwives to me.

As the preceding sentence reveals, I have a strong desire to be a mother, not only in giving birth to articles and books, sublimated offspring, but in fostering the lives of students and maintaining a close, albeit limited, connection with them. I am not unlike my own Jewish mother, feeding my students with weekly handouts (which, like food, is a symbol of love), exhorting them to do well in their studies, writing letters of recommendation on their behalf for graduate schools and employers, sending and receiving holiday greetings, attending their weddings, and, intergenerationally, teaching their children.

At the same time, I am a father and do not see a conflict between my maternal and paternal roles. It was a male, after all—Socrates—who first compared the teacher to a midwife. "No one can imagine that they have learned anything of me, but they have acquired and discovered many noble things of themselves."[15] As the father of two daughters, whose growth and development are my greatest joy, I view father figures as nurturers. Although most of the books on the teacher-as-nurturer have been written by feminists,[16] I believe that male teachers can be as caring of their students as female teachers. Indeed, in light of the distressing number of students who write about the "sins of the fathers," it is crucially important for male teachers to become a nurturing force in the classroom.

Do No Harm

In closing, I anticipate criticisms I will receive from educators. Some readers may feel that, by not requiring students to connect their personal self-analyses with those of the fictional characters studied in class, I deflect attention from the primary object in a literature course: a study of literary texts. Other readers may feel that, despite my statements to the contrary, I am somehow "practicing psychotherapy" on my students or engaging in practices that are inappropriate for an English professor. In showing portions of this manuscript to friends and colleagues, for instance, I have sometimes received responses like "Aren't you worried about lawsuits from your students' parents?" or "Hasn't your dean ever called you on the carpet?"

While there may be no precedent for the kind of introspective classroom diary writing that I advocate, no student, parent, or administrator has ever issued a complaint, nor have serious problems arisen. I do not believe that teachers must have unusual empathy or clinical training in order to be effective readers of self-analytical diaries: only the desire to encourage students to engage in self-discovery, an understanding of the necessary safeguards that must be put into place, and a respect for students' otherness. Nor must introspective diary writing be restricted to literature-and-psychoanalysis courses. The diaristic model of teaching I propose can be used effectively in many humanistic courses in which the self is studied from a variety of perspectives. Virtually any discussion-oriented college course emphasizing the interpretation of human experience—literature, psychology, sociology, history, religion, women's studies—would be an appropriate site for introspective diary writing. And the brief amount of classroom time spent in reading a few diaries aloud each week will be well worth it.

In *Love, Medicine & Miracles* Bernie Siegel, a holistic cancer surgeon, provides compelling evidence that unconditional love is a powerful stimulant to the immune system. Siegel cites the following anecdote. "An oncologist once asked me, 'Since you're not trained in psychotherapy, how do you know you won't do these patients harm?' I replied, 'I love them. I may not help, but I'm sure I won't hurt them.' "[17] My feelings precisely. By encouraging our students to write self-reflectively and share their experiences with classmates, by making sure that we indicate how literature speaks to every person in the classroom, by teaching empathically, and of course by avoiding the use of force, we can truly make a difference in our students' lives.

/ Afterword by Maryanne Hannan

Homo sum; humani nil a me alienum puto. (I am human; I count nothing human foreign to me.)—Terence

You suddenly realize you are not all alone.—Student diarist

I am a diarist, and I believe in the therapeutic value of writing. There have been times in my life when only by writing could I find the rhythms that would contain the pain, sustain the necessary movement forward. There were other times when only by rereading my diaries could I believe that my shifting reality would continue to shift and that present pain would yield as mysteriously as past pain had.

I am a mother, and I believe students should not be called upon to delve into their personal lives to satisfy writing assignments. Years before, my daughter had been a victim of inappropriate pedagogy, and I was still angry.

I was a student in Jeff's class, a returning graduate student, his contemporary, and I needed to reconcile what I observed in the classroom with these beliefs. This Afterword is my attempt to do so.

When I began Jeff's class, the memory of my daughter's experience was vivid. She, I believed, had been forced to disclose more personal information than she comfortably could in order to fulfill an assignment for her high school freshman English class. The possibility of writing down the pain had already been suggested to her, and she had refused. When her father had died, I told her how helpful writing was to me, but she was not interested. It was understandable; she was a young child, and she had no faith in writing as catharsis, nor any inclination to try. Yet now she had acceded to the demands of an assigned exercise in self-disclosure, answering a series of probing questions in painfully hesitant prose.

Reading what she had written, I was touched but horrified by her honesty, her lack of guile. She confessed that the thing she most liked about herself was her "naturally blond hair" and that she wished for a "more exotic name like Brandwin or Cassandra." Her ingenuousness went unremarked. The questions sallied forth, demanding that she explore the boundaries of her experience. Her most valued possession was a birthday gift her father had sent her from the hospital: "He had bought me a book and had wrote in it." The teacher had circled "wrote" in red. Her worst memory was looking at the tarp-covered ground into which her father's casket would be placed after we left the cemetery on the day of his funeral. There was no comment on this entry.

I was outraged at the teacher's insensitivity to what he had set in motion. In asking her to dredge up this material, he had gone well beyond the wisdom in the venerable dictum of writing about what you know best. After all, she wasn't writing about not going to the Freshman Prom. And it was not just my daughter I was concerned about. In our current social climate, she is not the only student at risk. I felt protective of all our children and angry at an educational system that ignored the plight of so many.

Her teacher had restricted himself to commenting only on issues of grammar and orthographic orthodoxy. While this is obviously preferable to inept responses to the content of the diaries, I was still angry that she and students like her were forced to engage in a process of self-disclosure for which there were no adequate safeguards in place. Mandatory writing assignments of this nature, I felt, blurred the distinction between public and private, placed students' welfare in jeopardy, distorted the goals of education, and made highly unlikely that the students would ever discover for themselves the marvelous catharsis that writing was for me.

And here I was, some five years later, in Jeff's class, writing my own diaries. For myself, I had no fears. I wrote my diaries easily and had reached the point of not feeling particularly proprietary toward their content. I was happy to engage Jeff—indeed anyone—in my own questions, and I knew I had all the tools of obfuscation at hand if the going got rough. However, I was not at all convinced that this was a good teaching method. I may be able to handle it, but what about the other students? He may be able to pull this off, but what about other teachers? Could they? Was it a good idea to tap into all this vulnerability in an educational setting? What did it have to do with literature? What was the appropriate response to manifestations of clinical depression, threats of suicide?

I expressed these kinds of objections to Jeff freely all semester, and have done so since that time. He has taken my concerns seriously, while continuing to insist on the diaries' therapeutic value. It has been an ongoing dialogue, one which culminated in my offer to write this Afterword. Jeff matched my offer with one of his own. He suggested I read the diaries anonymously and critique his written interaction with the diarists. He presented the entirety, warts and all, for my scrutiny.

I took Jeff up on the offer and have read literally thousands of student diaries, paying close attention to what he says in his comments to the diarists and what selections he chooses to read in class. I have carefully tracked developing and disintegrating relationships within the diaries. I attended classes other than my own in which the diaries were required. I heard them read and watched them heard. I have continued to talk to Jeff, and he has answered at length all my questions. Yet even now as I write, he requires no commitment from me. He says only, "I trust your honesty."

Fairly early, I saw that the diaries worked much as Jeff has described them here. I have no problem admitting that the marvelous stories he tells within this book are all true. He has chosen to tell these stories because they are representative of the main themes and preoccupations of the diarists, not because they are the most riveting or provocative. There were many more stories he could have told.

Nevertheless, I continued to suspect that there was a group, however much a minority, for whom the diaries would prove invasive, indeed threatening, unproductive—worse, counterproductive. I remembered my daughter. It was my goal to give credit where it was obviously due but simultaneously to voice the concerns of the minority she represented. I expected my own story to sound as a caution: "Beware, all ye who enter here." I thought my ambivalence, carefully honed over the years, would temper the enthusiasm of the devotees and correct the skepticism of the disenchanted.

The more I examined the process, the less sure I became. I found bits and pieces of what I expected to, but in the final summation, these bits and pieces did not tell a story. There were students who at various points in the process would find the diaries unpalatable. They might write something to the effect that their refusal to write a diary was their diary, because they didn't want to share anything or play along as if they were. Invariably, Jeff responded, "Fair enough."

Such entries were rare, but I still might have been inclined to make a story of them except that these same few diarists generally concluded the semester by saying that writing and hearing the diaries had been a positive experience for them. I knew students all had the option, as I did, to grant or withhold permission for their diaries to be used in this project. According to Jeff, about 95 percent of the students over the years have given their permission, so the number who exercised the option to retain their diaries is minimal, and their reasons for doing so unknown. In the diaries I read, only one student concluded the diaries had not been valuable to him.

What clearly emerged was a series of astounding endorsements for the process by the student diarists. Student after student praised the course in unequivocal terms: "Looking back over all my college classes, this has been my favorite. It has given me a whole new way to look at literature, as well as at my own life." They usually frame compliments with claims of personal integrity. One writes, "I will admit without reservation that you are my favorite professor (no, I am not going for brownie points; I am just being truthful.)" They meant what they wrote.

Even more compelling were the stories of those who, while initially opposed or neutral to the idea of diary writing, became converts to the process. It was thrilling to see students move from positions of self-protection to open admiration. One in particular concluded the semester with: "My personal experience in this course has been one of great learning. Not the typical learning, but a solemn education of the soul." To scour the diaries for negatives and to discuss them at any length, I decided, would be misleading. Surely I could find some, but they are trivial, tangential. The real story lies elsewhere.

I found myself slowly redefining my task. I certainly did not want to write an apology, but I could not ignore what I found. Yet what exactly were the students so heartily endorsing? It was not easily reducible. I found much variation among individual diarists and even among the different classes. There was no set way. They work the best, or at least they work along the lines described here, in the undergraduate classes. One returning student gave voice to this: "It seems that the younger people are talking to themselves for the first time and are just learning that they are not the only person in the world with problems." It is an ideal forum, according to one such younger person: "This time of our lives is very confusing, and to have an outlet in which to complain or ask questions is very important."

But a significant number of students do not fit this profile. Older students, seasoned diarists, and students in therapy often have highly developed defensive styles and are reluctant to give themselves up to the process. They resent the short-term intrusion of another, be it Jeff, their classmates, any personal audience. However, even for this group (and I count myself among them), the diaries proved largely beneficial, if serendipitously so.

I revisited my own diaries. As I suspected, I had been somewhat less ingenuous than most diarists, somewhat more controlling, more demanding of Jeff. He responded at length to my questions, asking only that I keep an open mind and continue to engage myself in the process. In one diary, I had angrily recounted my daughter's story. He had responded with a full page of comments. He began by acknowledging my concern and agreeing that a prerequisite for using diaries in the classroom was a sensitive, empathic teacher. He then went on to suggest that "on the other hand, you don't really show that your daughter was harmed by the experience."

What a jerk. Two in a row. I was annoyed that he had missed the obvious (how could she not have been harmed?), but I wrote his response off to a vested interest in or, alternately speaking, a fond, foolish faith in diary writing. Since nobody else in the class is privy to Jeff's comments, I was shocked in subsequent weeks when a fellow classmate wrote: "Only the mother's pain is obvious, not the daughter's." I felt both responses were insensitive, but the fact that two people had made them, independent of each other, stuck with me. It is only recently that I have begun to see their point.

In retrospect, I see much else of value to me in both Jeff's responses and in his insistence that difficult passages be read aloud. Unlike many students, I had felt more engaged by his prods than by his affirmation. I felt that I was being taken seriously. Since then, many of the issues he urged me to explore have taken center stage. In the aftermath, his comments have proven prescient, predictive of struggles to come. Rereading my own diaries, I have come to the conclusion that they were sui generis, that what happened to me was special. I have a sneaking suspicion that most diarists would say the same thing. And how that comes about is the story that needs to be told.

Individuals have written diaries for centuries. There being no public advantage to doing so, we must conclude that the benefits are purely personal. Diarists write because they derive pleasure or satisfaction from the mere act of recording the events of their lives or the feelings elicited by these events. Over the years, there have been fashions in what is appropriate diary content, but no mandate. Some diarists are chroniclers; others reflectors.

Whatever their predilection, diarists experience a greater sense of control over their lives by reducing its details to words. What is written becomes real and therefore more manageable. To what extent the mere writing of personal diaries is therapeutic, in the sense of contributing to self-healing, remains an open question. Who is to say that inappropriate responses are not reinforced by scribal repetition? Self-congratulation is but a pen push away. One's point of view may grow increasingly reasonable, even seductive. However, the reduction of personal angst to the page does lock in an objective point of reference which is easier to move beyond than inchoate churnings, cataclysmic surges. I can say that for years when I wrote diaries, I *felt* better. I cannot attest positively to the fact that I *became* better, although I believe it.

The potential benefits inherent in diary writing have been recently recognized and formalized in various growth therapies. Probably the most common approach is the use of prescribed techniques of self-exploration within diaries which themselves remain private. Therapists frequently suggest to clients specific writing exercises in which they might find expression for their anger, their fear, or any other painful emotion.

Tristine Rainer suggests many such diary writing exercises for personal use in her book *The New Diary*. Among her excellent recommendations are writing unsent letters to and developing dialogues with significant figures, writing from another's point of view, and exploring nighttime dreams. She delineates the means for do-it-yourself personal growth via diary writing and offers antidotes lest the process become mere self-stroking. Whether to share personal diaries she regards as a matter of individual preference, but she wisely cautions those who choose to do so against having unrealistic expectations of their readers. She notes the success of diaries as an adjunct to formal psychotherapy, but always, everywhere, she affirms that "the central relationship in the diary is with yourself."[1]

A different approach to directed diary writing, or what he calls journal writing, is offered by Ira Progoff. His book *At a Journal Workshop* and his widely held workshops give diarists well-defined instructions, assignments, tasks to complete as they write. He has developed a rigid structure of interrelated parts within the journal in order "to produce a mirroring and feedback effect" in the work itself.[2] The journals thereby become independent of an authority figure and serve to strengthen the autonomy of the writers themselves. Key to his system is that the diarists at the workshop read their journals aloud to other diarists engaged in the same process. The point is to make one's private, previously undisclosed thoughts audible. That the journals be heard is sufficient; the group makes no response and, in fact, is specifically directed to give no feedback. Progoff considers the aural component so vital that when the workshop is over, he recommends diarists read their journals into a tape recorder and play them back in order to derive, at least partially, this benefit. Progoff insists on the paradox that group presence allows for private work because it gives "the benefit of the psychic support and validation of others, while we ourselves are giving the support of our sincere presence to the other participants in the group" (53). The act of making private journals public liberates, fosters personal growth.

Jeff has overseen the evolution of a system of diary writing which combines elements of both these approaches and adds features of its own. Jeff's passion is for teaching literature, for engaging his students. He does both well. However, his greatest achievement may be an unwitting one—the formal creation of a safeguarded system of personal diary writing within a classroom setting. Like Rainer, Jeff encourages natural diary writing. He suggests numerous points of departure through the psychoanalytic theory and literature he teaches, but the choice is clearly the diarist's to make. Like Progoff, Jeff appropriates the social context for individual growth by reading the diaries out loud to a silent group. Unlike either of them, Jeff reads each diary himself and responds directly to the diarist. What develops is unpredictable for any given diarist, but there is always something of value. Some part of the process kicks in. The system makes this inevitable; the system, then—Jeff's system at the University at Albany—is my story.

What is this system in its finer details? The routine is established early. Diaries are a mandatory part of the course; they are weekly and unstructured. Students write them privately. Jeff reads them privately, writes comments on them to the individual diarists. As class begins, he reads five diaries selected from the thirty to forty available. He reads them out loud to the class, solemnly. Neither he nor members of the class comment on the content of the diaries. When he is finished reading his selections, he returns all the diaries, including the ones he has just read, unobtrusively reincorporated into the pile. Students, anxiously casual, scan his comments and hastily put their diaries away. Jeff then collects a new set of diaries and, with sudden animation, initiates discussion of the literature assigned for that class. So it cycles, week after week, until semester's end.

Of what do the students write? Everything, yet it must be said that their diaries eschew the quotidian. One's hamburg and fries rarely reach print; one's overindulgence on candy bars or nachos might. The diaries are Pepysian in neither form nor content; this is not the stuff of chroniclers. Nowhere in Jeff's program is this stipulated; it just happens, or more accurately, it increasingly develops over the semester, as barriers come tumbling down.

A psychoanalytic critic himself, Jeff teaches the theory and practice of his methodology. The literature he chooses to teach yields nicely to this approach. The psychoanalytic theory he lays out at the beginning of the semester addresses head-on many issues that were for centuries found only in literature. And they were found there, buried, only by readers courageous enough to see them. Specters of patricide and mother love may haunt our great works of literature, but for centuries, the unpalatable was renamed or rejected, culture often availing itself collectively of individual defense mechanisms. Now, however, here is Jeff, sometimes passionately, sometimes dispassionately, examining the most potentially explosive material of human existence as he walks around a fluorescent-lit classroom. Here also is a group of people, most of whom have never confronted such issues, let alone personalized them, being let into the club. They are being challenged to accept as normal, even normative, what had previously resided in the dark recesses of human experience. In these circumstances, with the class studying great works of literature with the frankness psychoanalytic theory necessitates and watching their peers grapple with these issues in both literature and their own lives through the diaries, it is no wonder, under such conditions, that these diarists are not chroniclers of life's minutiae. These diarists mount cognitive assaults on the unruly. The interplay of material makes this nearly inevitable.

And how does Jeff respond? While I may have concluded that his impact is muted by the larger process of writing diaries in a classroom setting, I certainly did not begin with this assumption. Moreover, even muted impacts have megatonnage displacement potential. As I read the diaries, I recognized other students shared my curiosity—maybe even my suspicion—about what Jeff wrote on other people's diaries. One male student deems the process "fraught with dangers," wondering: "Would you tell every overweight student in your class to go on a diet? Or every smoker to stop? It might seem that you are intruding into their lives as if you knew better than they did about what is good for them, which you may, but do you have the right to 'tell' them what is best for them?" This assumption that Jeff was giving advice was out of the blue. Nowhere had Jeff made such recommendations to him, but how was he to know?

Diarists themselves perceived his comments very differently. Writes one angry student: "The one thing that bothered me most of all was that He [sic] never commented other than pushing more questions in my face. . . . All I wanted was for Him to give me a little pat on the head—you know, a small whack on the butt—to let me know i wasn't half bad at this writing crap." Another student says: "Thank you for telling me when I was being stupid or smart, or self-indulgent. It's kinda rare to find tolerant folks out there." Neither reaction seems warranted based on the actual comments Jeff has made on these individuals' diaries, but this just reinforces for me how treacherous these waters can be.

By and large, student response to Jeff's comments runs the gamut. He receives praise for being "honest, thought-provoking without being nosy or overly psychoanalytical." He is "unobtrusive, encouraging"; he is "harsh." One diarist calls him "laid back" one entry, "overpowering" the next. Another points out: "Incidentally, you come across as two different people—one, the class professor who confronts, challenges, and sometimes badgers and the other, a wonderful, loving accepting person who reads my diaries." Another praises him for sharing personal information about himself because "for me, trust and respect are mutually earned." Another gives perhaps the best endorsement: "Your comment on my diary made me think." And that is the objective, regardless of the style he uses to achieve it.

Jeff would define the style of the ideal therapist as embodying empathic understanding, nonjudgmental acceptance, and authentic engagement. Jeff would deny that he plays the role of therapist to his students, but to the extent possible, he tries to enact the qualities of an ideal therapist. I use the term advisedly, knowing that he would want neither term applied to him. He is teacher, not therapist. He is "good enough," not ideal. In his teaching, his writing, and his life, he frequently employs the phrase "good enough—teacher, parent, friend, whatever." This struggle to act honestly, to respond guilelessly, to forgive himself for his own humanity, and to move on is nearly palpable in his comments. His relationship to his own behavior objectifies for the diarists this principle in action.

Nevertheless, in his interaction with students, he strives to be ideally engaged, empathic, and accepting. His protocol for doing so is twofold: he limits his responses to supportive comments, and he raises additional questions for students to consider on their own. He does not criticize, nor does he interpret. He discourages nascent transference activity immediately. His awareness of appropriate boundaries is thoroughgoing and arises spontaneously from his own desire for such boundaries. He eschews the parent role, the teacher role, the savior role. He prefers to act from the greater bond of fellow human feeling. That is good enough; in fact, it is better.

I have read the diaries and his comments, and I am here to report. While he adheres to his principles in large measure, he also breaks every rule he has set down for himself. Even the easy-to-follow ones he violates. Grammar and spelling are off-limits for comment, but there he is, telling a diarist who is "irrate" over another's disregard for her keen sense of order, "Fortunately, you're not a compulsive speller." To a diarist referring to a matter "eluded to in class," he responds " 'alluded' (unless you're being ironic)." Another wishing to be more empathic writes "emphatic," and he merely underlines the *h* and rewrites the word, allowing her to determine if it is a mistake or a slip. He overlooks distorted syntax but always corrects factual errors, especially mistakes in title or author. He lets many misspellings go but crosses out a diarist's "mensh," replacing it with his own "mensch." Some mistakes are easier to overlook than others. (Again, the worm turns. Jeff calls me to tell me that "mensh" is an acceptable Yiddish spelling, "mensch" is not. He stands corrected; I stand corrected. The diarist is vindicated. Perhaps comments on comments about spelling should be considered off-limits.)

Another diarist submits a poem as a diary, and he meticulously critiques it. He tells her: "I'm responding to your poem in as detailed way as I can. Since it's really a poem, rather than a diary, I'm offering the kind of technical comments that I don't usually make on a diary. I hope that's OK." It's not. She responds that she is "upset" because he "destroyed it," and "if one of my better pieces merits such a negative response, I see no need to seriously continue writing."

Another diarist mulls over a friendship that she would like to see develop more. Jeff makes comments completely consistent with his protocol throughout the diary. At the end, however, he metamorphoses into Dear Abby: "P.S. My advice: Ask him out!" He boxes this comment in and decorates it with a big happy face. He is equally directive with a diarist agonizing over whether to make a marriage commitment: "It sounds like you're not ready for marriage. Why rush it? You'll know when it's time."

On the few occasions when diarists expressed a cry for help, he responded accordingly. To one he wrote that if her feelings continued, she should speak to someone. He thereby offers hope that feelings may abate and that even if they do not, there is help available. To another, in the throes of suicidal ideation, he offers himself as a stopgap measure, suggesting she call him if she feels out of control. Such exchanges are fortunately rare.

What, then, are characteristic exchanges? Jeff's responses spring from two deeply held beliefs: Knowledge is power, and sharing insight increases its healing potential. There are multiple expressions of these themes throughout the diaries. He does not fear the process of self-discovery on which students embark, frequently urging them onward with the precept "Knowledge is power" largely emblazoned on their entries. He models for them what he espouses: that a person's best chance to live happily and productively is to seek self-knowledge, to refuse unproductive denials of pain, and to share the fruits of one's knowledge with others. He shares his own struggles; he acknowledges his mistakes. In fact, the naturalness and the spontaneity of his comments are frequently more compelling than a die-hard program of correct responses would be. His humanity engages. He steps forward bravely, in class and in the diaries. His hallmark as a professor is this willingness to share his own quest, his ordinariness, his humanity, with his students, his fellow wayfarers. The process works, despite—sometimes because of—his mistakes.

So diarists dig deep and discover themselves. They share with each other, during the weekly readings, the results of their individual work. At his behest, they offer to people in their lives the fruits of their labor. Jeff tells them: "This is a fine diary. You might want to share it with your parents [or whomever has been written about]. They would be proud to read it." They do so. This book details but a few of the dramatic reconciliations students have initiated with their parents, siblings, grandparents, friends, roommates, and lovers when they have followed this suggestion.

Impressive as the stories in this book are, they are also intimidating. Teachers considering using diaries in their own classrooms might be overwhelmed by the possibilities. They might fear opening the Pandora's box that is their students' lives, even while acknowledging the potential therapeutic value of diary writing in the classroom setting. Perhaps before any such decision, we should follow Jeff's own dictum that knowledge is power. If his stated goals are to limit his responses to supportive comments and to stimulate further self-inquiry on the students' part, we have a task of practical criticism at hand. How exactly does he implement these goals?

Following are comments typical of those Jeff makes on the diaries. In isolation, here, they appear wooden and manipulative, but in the context of the diaries, set among other, very human comments, they are much less offensive, indeed dynamic. He consistently praises diarists for being "thoughtful, honest, sensitive." This is bedrock. So is the call to pursue nascent insights: "This is the most important diary you have written"; "You are asking the right questions." He supports diarists' self-evaluation: "You have been a good friend to . . ."; "That was a cruel thing for him/her to say"; "I'm sure your inner voice is right"; "I think you're on to something important here"; "I can imagine how unsettling this might be"; "Your conclusions seem perfectly reasonable." He encourages them always to accept themselves: "Don't be so hard on yourself"; "Take comfort. Most people feel the same anxieties that you do. They're normal anxieties."

In other ways, he prods. He rarely lets vague expressions of pain go unnoticed. He leads where Rainer suggests diarists go. "This is something you might want to explore in future diaries" is a constant refrain. So is "try to be more specific." Specifics lead to self-knowledge and acceptance; they are also a prerequisite for human interaction. He responds to undifferentiated lamentations very pointedly: "You have to explain things clearly so that people do understand you." Whining does not get reinforced. He urges: "Why is this event so stressful?" "What is this terrifying reality you write of?" "Why don't you elaborate on this anger [guilt, fear, sadness, whatever]?" He pushes diarists to examine what they write and even to accept ambiguity: "Both possibilities may be present, as well as others."

A diarist repeatedly describes himself as a "passive sort of guy." Suddenly he acknowledges that "every three months or so I get violent." Jeff writes: "Maybe you'd like to discuss this more." He does, and he learns a lot. Many of the stories in this book are the result of diarists' taking seriously Jeff's invitation to be more specific. Very often when they acknowledge present misery, they can begin to confront the past. The truth of another one of Jeff's comments—"I think there is something here that you want to share"—is borne out.

It is not enough that diarists be honest with themselves. He prods them to share their insights with the people in their lives and, most significantly, with the class. While students have the option of requesting their entries not be read aloud, it is not a choice he blesses. I was among this group. He invariably urges diarists who choose this option to reconsider: "If you change your mind, please resubmit this." He exhorts: "I think you would be surprised how many people could relate to this." He insists on the paradox that "by revealing one's vulnerability, one becomes *less* vulnerable." Like Progoff, he is unswervingly wed to this principle.

He does not aspire to power in the lives of his students; he acts out a faith in their own power of self-regulation. He respects their boundaries, their autonomy, and their own internal wisdom, and he encourages them to do likewise. A frequent motif is "You are describing an interesting dilemma. Let me know how it works out." In a similar vein, he writes: "You alone know the truth of this situation"; "These are important questions. Only you know the answers to them." He does not interpret students' dreams, asking them to examine their own associations. He validates their interpretations, sometimes more bizarre than the dreams themselves, with comments like, "A fascinating dream! I think you are right about its meaning." He refuses also the parental role. Over and over again, he acknowledges diarists' admissions of wrongdoing by merely praising their honesty. He leaves to them the decision to change. One diarist writes angrily about his solitary drinking, defensively admitting that he might have a drinking problem. Jeff responds: "I do *not* pity you or advise you. I think you can figure this situation out for yourself."

Such words grow out of a respect for otherness, a seasoned acknowledgment of boundaries. When given an opening, however, Jeff grabs it. One student queries, "Is it possible for me to change?" and his affirmative "YES!!!!" nearly leaps off the page. He allays students' expressions of fear with, "I know you won't let this happen." He responds eagerly to requests for information, academic advice. He reinforces career choices: "You will make a wonderful teacher [lawyer, candlestick maker, whatever]." Occasionally, he suggests diarists use his office hour to discuss specific problems: "Come chat with me about this." He encourages the practical approach: "In another diary, you might want to plan how to respond in the future." His comments are grounded in good sense and faith in the future. He tells another: "There is always a way out." He is believable.

His precepts are the value of surfacing repressed material and the wisdom of sharing those feelings with others. Our common humanity underlies these precepts. Jeff is human. Therefore, he errs. The question then becomes in what way does he veer from his precepts or enact other ones? What are his empathic failures? What are the countertransference issues? Is there not some point at which we all might say: "Get thee to a nunnery" or "Give it a rest, fathead?" Surely there is a point at which we all think it. Jeff usually acts in accord with his stated principles by either ignoring admissions of wrong-doing or by praising the author's honesty. One student with a serious but not life-threatening disability admits that she uses her illness to get her parents off her back about grades. Jeff makes what I would deem a conspicuous noncomment to her admission. Similarly, he ignores a diarist's admission that she enjoys being spanked by her boyfriend but tells her that she is probably right when she speculates that this may be related to her father's treatment of her. He often passes up the opportunity to comment on drug and alcohol use. One diarist says she used to be able to go out with friends and "get buzzed or even drunk, but now every time I go out—which is quite often—I get hammered." He makes no comment, but later when she says she is going to try to cut back to smoking half a pack of cigarettes a day, he brackets it with "sounds like a good idea." He ends by praising her for writing "a good, honest diary." Unless the diarist expresses some discomfiture with the behavior, Jeff generally leaves it alone.

On religious issues, he is consistently tolerant and supportive of differ-ence. With diarists who write of religious doubts, he shares his own. He likewise always affirms religious faith in diarists who profess it. He tells them, "Contrary to Freud's dismissive comments on religion, there is much that is therapeutic in religion." To another who is defensive about her Chris-tian beliefs, he offers this endorsement: "Your religion is a source of deep strength to you, and you remain tolerant of other people's beliefs—and dis-beliefs. This indicates, to me, how healthy your religious belief is."

He is himself intolerant of intolerance. He does not refrain from pointing out any evidence of prejudice. One diarist writes about her newly acquired "insight" about "Japs," and he responds: "This is a thoughtful diary. The only thing that makes me uneasy is the religious and cultural implications of the word 'Jap,' which I know you are using as a metaphor." He always jumps into any direct discussion of injustice. He explores the "distinction between rac-ism and the perception of racism" with a disgruntled basketball player and shares with another his own unexpected reaction during a visit to Germany twenty years before. He validates the anger of the recipient of a racial remark, and whenever he gets the opportunity, he writes to the effect that "racial tension does exist here, and thus it becomes important for us to act as sensitively as possible toward others."

He is also sensitive to issues of gender, although, in perhaps his own version of affirmative action, he is more likely to overlook offenses by females than by males. He fails to respond to one diarist who marks the men she conquers with "notches on her lipstick case." No male could have so bragged without receiving a gentle, or not so gentle, reprisal from him. One diarist referring to how "mothers should act" receives back an ominous "Hmmm. You seem to have a traditional view of mothers. What are fathers expected to do?" Another male verbally rejects society's emphasis on "superficial" things like looks, yet says: "Except the fact remains I find it much more exciting to go out with a girl who is good-looking" and "If a girl is ugly, I won't ask her out, no matter how sparkling her personality." He is told somewhat pointedly: "But not everyone attaches so much importance to good looks." To another, he says: "You sound like a misogynist here."

He tells a diarist angry about the treatment of Dead fans: "I agree with your main point here—that all of us should be more tolerant of other people, including alternate lifestyles." But then there is a student who struggles valiantly all semester with his upcoming graduation and his uncertain career plans. When he suddenly realizes that he wants to work in advertising, he is relieved. Jeff's final comment to him is: "Good luck in advertising. I hope you work for a socially responsible company." I chuckled when I read this; then again, if this is his worst empathic failure, easy lies the hand that holds the pen.

I found the depth and breadth of Jeff's self-disclosures amazing. Even if I had the courage to speak so freely of my conflicts, my aspirations, my life, I don't know if I would have the generosity to share so much of myself with, as they describe themselves, "virtual strangers." He poignantly gives witness to his own doubts. One diarist writes: "How do you find out who you are and remain safe at the same time?" and he responds: "Good question. I wish I knew the answer." Another laments a career failure, and Jeff generously describes his own difficult tenure battle. He concludes with, "As a person who has experienced humiliating defeats also, I believe I know how you feel. . . . I still have plenty of scars. But I was able to prevail, as you will too."

He draws funny faces all over. He makes corny jokes. He suggests to a diarist given to procrastination that he "Plan Ahe" with the "ad" following awkwardly on the next line. He asks a student exploring Oedipal ramifications: "Did I ever tell you that you remind me of my grandmother?" He tells another who shares his own desire for neatness: "I think you and I are the only healthy ones." Another satirizes the life of success to which she fears she is headed by postulating marriage to a "short, hairy, ugly, big-nosed Jewish lawyer." He circles "big-nosed Jewish" and writes, "Hey, that hurts."

He shares his own problems and solutions, including "an inferiority complex about money." He advises: "My own feeling is that it's better to err on the side of generosity." He admits to personal health concerns. He recommends jogging to someone in low spirits. He often describes how he came to jog himself. He tells another that he eats tofu. He writes about his parents, his wife, his daughters. The impact of such self-disclosure is often startling, and always positive. Diarists appreciate it: "Your willingness to talk about yourself and your family made the class more of a two-way street; the confiding we did in our diaries was being reciprocated."

Jeff is a popular teacher. Diarists compliment him profusely, all the while insisting on their dignity in so doing. There is often a proviso: "I would like to take this chance to compliment you. Please don't mistake this for ass-kissing. You have given me constant reinforcement in my diaries, now it is my turn. In the four years I have been here, I have not encountered a professor like you." Another writes that she "savored every minute of the class," and credit is due him because "I don't think that my love of the subject matter would have been enough to keep me there (awake) for three hours." The university has recognized him with two of its highest teaching awards—both the President's and Chancellor's Awards for Excellence in Teaching. However, he is not an idolized teacher. He does not walk around campus surrounded by adoring students. He is respected; his classes are highly regarded, yet it is entirely plausible that he could eat alone in the campus cafeteria.

Instances of transference obviously occur, but negative repercussions seem contained within the larger cycle of writing and hearing the diaries. Disappointed diarists speak out and are mollified in the process. Counter-transference may result in more socially responsible advertising executives. There is not the intensity of a patient-therapist relationship, or the parent-child one, because of the larger scenario in which the relationship evolves, its public dimension. There is much leeway in the process for Jeff and for diarists to defuse potentially harmful interactions, and most significantly, it is usually the student who determines the level of intimacy.

The diarist about whom I wrote earlier who experiences a "solemn education of the soul" is a case in point. He draws his boundaries early. He will comply with all requirements but will keep his distance. He uses only his last name. In the diaries, he says he will "present a short story in two-page sequels." Jeff responds: "Interesting idea" and, as usual, mirrors the tone as well as the content of the diaries. He therefore sprinkles the next few diaries with objective criticism: "If this were a short story, you would want to describe her beauty. . . . Showing is better than telling"; and "You would want to dramatize, rather than summarize, the parents' fights." Suddenly, the diarist decides to "deviate" from his plan because he identifies with Pip during the class discussion of *Great Expectations*. He writes about his past, concluding: "Most people, when they meet me, don't like me very much. They say I am cold and have no feelings. I also realize that it takes a long time for me to trust people because of what I've been through." Jeff does not say: "Don't be ridiculous; everybody loves you." Nor does he say: "How could they like you? You are obnoxious." He responds: "But your mistrust is understandable!"

Two diaries later, the student writes: "When I stop to think about some of the experiences of my classmates, it makes me feel that my experiences are not so bad and that they help me deal with my day-to-day pressures with less stress and anger. . . . I hope this diary does not affect the teacher's narcissistic attitude." By now, he is using his last name and first initial. At course end, yes, he uses his full name. And he writes, "When we met, we had big differences, and I said to myself that this is going to be a hell of a semester with this guy. And guess what? It was a hell of a semester because I have been taught things and have become friends with someone who I know now and have come to greatly respect. . . . Thanks for the belief in me and getting to know me as a person instead of just another student." If this is transference, let's have more of it.

On the whole, students are more interested in what they have to say than in what Jeff does. They painstakingly detail their own reactions to the diaries. They trace their feelings as they write them, their reactions as they hope or fear their diaries will be read in class. They are equally taken with their peers' responses. Jeff turns out to be just one part of the process, important as a facilitator, but almost more important as a participant. Transference is not the issue I expected it to be.

Writing a weekly diary is mandatory. All else is at the discretion of the student. They have freedom to choose what to write about, how to write it, what level of intimacy or self-disclosure to maintain. They can, and do, retrench at will. One diarist recognizes this: "Every time I got deep into a conflict, I pulled back and wrote about something less painful." This is their right, and it is always honored. The latitude they have liberates them. Each diarist chooses his or her individual path, stops for rest when desired, forges ahead at unexpected moments, and approaches the finish line with a sense of pride. The style, the pace, and the goals are as different as the diarists, yet they share so much.

Some students find writing the diaries the most powerful part of the process, as it is for Rainer. One student writes: "I enjoy your responses, but most of the therapeutic value I see is by my own self-analysis." Another says: "I believe our *own* diaries help us more, in that self-discovery and self-healing occur through our own writing." "Writing," attests another, "allowed me to work through some of the darker, more mysterious, and until quite recently unexamined sides of my personality." Another proclaims that writing "clears my mind, like a walk on a beautiful day." It enables one to "vent," another to "get past my shame barrier," another to "get things off my chest that were bottled up inside." One enjoys even the physical disposition of his diaries: "Handing them in dissociated me from what had been written." Perhaps the consensus is best expressed simply: "Even though many were not easy to write, they were strangely satisfying to have written."

Jeff tells reluctant diarists that writing "helps us master our fears and remain in control," but there are those who hold back because of the public dimension of the process. One writes: "Because I sign my name, I cannot open up." Another explains: "I would either have to know you very well or not know you at all to be comfortable sharing personal thoughts with you. Our relationship is much too in between for me to be comfortable." One dislikes the diaries because "I fear revealing myself," and another holds back out of "fear of disturbing feelings." Strangely enough, despite their reservations, these same students endorse the process as a whole.

However the process of writing is perceived by the authors, the results are impressive. Students write on topics near and far, in styles eerily spontaneous to ominously formal. Many are pleased with their output. At semester's end, one writes: "What an odyssey! I just read over my journals and am amazed at the amount of ground I covered over the course of the semester. I wrote creatively, personally, psychoanalytically, journalistically, and experientially, and I am sure in other ways too."

Students write diaries for two of Jeff's courses—Introduction to Freud, and Narcissism. In the Freud class, many begin by expressing reservations they or their peers have about traditional psychoanalysis, with its perceived overemphasis on sexual issues and the Oedipus complex. One diarist begins with a warning: "When I mention this Freudian course, most laugh. Everyone I know believes Freud was a sexual madman who hated all women and used his theories as a way of venting his sexual frustrations." For the purpose of the diaries, however, they generally suspend disbelief and attempt some "what if" scenarios. "What if there is any truth to this stuff" is gradually replaced by "How can I best use in my own life whatever truth I find here?"

Many diarists choose to enter the discussion by examining so-called Freudian slips, inadvertent behaviors that reveal more than was intended. They begin with their own parapraxes, with those they see and hear others commit. They frequently express amazement at the insights gleaned. They also commit some in situ. Often they will notice and leave their slips behind proudly as proof of their growing self-awareness and receptivity to matters psychoanalytic. Sometimes they miss them altogether, and Jeff points them out. New frames of reference develop; theory is appropriated for personal usage.

One woman admitting to a strong attachment to her father disapproves of his unfaithfulness to her mother. She worries about the effect this might have on her relationships with men: "I am afraid I will marry this *king* of a man because of the way my dad is." What greater proof of her ambivalence could she have? One diarist repeatedly fails to return his girlfriend's call, as promised, and realizes: "Never before had I thought that something such as forgetting a phone call could tell me such a great deal as to the direction in which my relationship is heading. Things are not going well for us, and I believe it is just a matter of time before the relationship terminates."

One diarist writes that she cannot accept counseling "*fact* to face." Now she knows why. Another writes that she "had *know* idea," thereby suggesting the opposite. Another reveals an unacknowledged uneasiness in recollecting "while you *disgusted* this topic in class." Another writes of being "emotionally *scared*" instead of "scarred." And then there is the student who talks of "*writhing* the diaries."

Other diarists in the Freud class enter by way of dreams. Some write detailed accounts of surrealistic nocturnal happenings; others report bland quotidian scenarios. Often they offer interpretations which Jeff accepts and reinforces. When they seek his help, he directs them to whatever associations they have to the dream images. Rainer similarly advises that serious dream work be done within the diaries. Jeff's encouragement is sufficient to prompt diarists to confront aggressively their nighttime images. One diarist, in therapy for agoraphobia, is "stymied" by a recurrent dream but then has a breakthrough: "Why did I see my mother as a wolf . . . I can't believe that the obvious meaning had eluded me, especially since it was so damn unsubtle!" Diarists often find hope, even in nightmares: "Lately in these dreams I do make it to assorted destinations, whereas in the past I used to wake up before I reached any place."

The Oedipal complex is the central gateway to the family issues that diarists so frequently confront within the diaries. Initially most judge it a preposterous notion; however, as they explore their relationships with both parents in the theoretical context of sexual rivalry and competition, they often surface surprising material. Many of the stories Jeff tells here evolved over weeks of entering through this portal, backing out, and once again reentering. One diarist, recalling that she used to want to kiss her father for practice, writes: "Now that I can relate to one of Freud's bizarre theories, I am petrified to think or apply any of the other ones more grotesque than the Oedipal/Electra complex to my life for fear of recognizing a situation." Jeff assures her that she is normal and has nothing to worry about. In her final course summation, she delights in all she has learned about herself and remembers when she was "so very stunned that I was able to relate a theory to my own life." Honest exploration and admission of Oedipal conflict often lead to greater self-acceptance and increased empathy for the same-sex parent, a kind of "Eureka!" perspective on one's own behavior. Some of these diaries represent dramatic breakthroughs; others just reinforce positive directions already established.

The Narcissism class provides diarists with theoretical discussion of borderline personalities. Just about everyone knows a textbook narcissist. They are as available as dreams and more available than slips. Insight develops from viewing these individuals from a clinical perspective which presumes an early narcissistic injury contributing to present behaviors. One diarist writes about a friend who has mistreated her for years. This friend always spoke in glowing terms of her own family, especially her mother, whom the diarist found inexplicably cold, bordering on cruel. She constantly rejected her own intuition in deference to her friend's opinion until class discussion about parental relations in *Wuthering Heights* and *Frankenstein*. Realizing then that her friend probably found it too threatening to admit her mother's cruelty, she has "far more pity and less contempt for [her friend] now than I used to." So many times, theory provides diarists with the opportunity to step back from their experience and to gain understanding and perspective on what is otherwise inexplicable behavior.

Students are encouraged to write about psychoanalytic theory as it applies to their own lives or as they see it unfold in literature. Students are encouraged to write about the literature, in whatever way it presents to them. They identify with some characters; they counteridentify with others. They revise identifications they have made in the past with certain characters, and they wonder what has changed in their lives to account for these new feelings. This is very much in line with Rainer's suggestion that diarists critique their own under- and overreactions to situations as a way to understand themselves better.

Diarists in Jeff's class, vicariously experiencing fictional characters' problems, make decisions about how to proceed with their own lives. One diarist writes her graded paper on *The Catcher in the Rye*'s Holden Caulfield and returns to him frequently in her diaries. Her final words in the course are: "I have made up my mind to take what I have and make the best of it. Holden judges people too harshly, and this is something that I am trying not to do anymore. Holden makes me think about my own life and the changes that I want to make to keep from ending up like him." Esther in *The Bell Jar* evokes many strong reactions. One diarist whose life has been painful describes the story as "threatening" and writes that in the beginning she "strongly identified with her character," but as the story progresses, she "felt very angry." Finally, Esther's suicide attempt "completely changes my attitude toward her. We all at times feel stifled, as if a bell jar has descended upon us. God knows I have. She was a coward." Others are more forgiving, less threatened.

The process described by one student as "changing the boundaries between life, learning, and writing" is enacted by another. She writes: "Like Esther, I feel in control if I leave before they leave me. I'm noticing that I'm attracted most intensely to someone who acts ambivalent toward me. I try to win their attention. My boyfriends that didn't show me that they cared, I stayed with. . . . Wow! Seeing this on paper is like a 'wake-up!' smash on the head. I reject those that show me that they care and give me what I need, and

I exhaust myself running after those that will hurt me." Diary ends. Jeff brings down the curtain: "I think your self-awareness is rapidly increasing."

A student reassesses past career choices in writing her paper on *The Bell Jar*: "As I wrote, I found myself feeling very angry at her mother. I noticed this especially when I wrote about how I felt Esther's mother had devalued her abilities. I wondered why and then suddenly I realized that I felt my mother had done the same thing to me." Another discovers excessive generalized anger toward men. After haranguing against "Hemingway's gem of a royal shit," she writes: "I realize in reacting to these two males with so much anger, I'm probably saying something about myself. Trying to think what that can be." It is a job tailor-made for this diary-writing process.

Frequently, students develop their paper topics first in their diaries; indeed, many of the diarists write what is in essence short papers on the literature discussed. Jeff often suggests that students engaged by a particular work continue to develop their response to it in their formal essay. Students reopen class discussion in the diaries, asking for clarification of issues raised in class. They take exception to some issues; they expand on others. They join the discussion belatedly, offering an "interpretation I had of the novel but was too insecure to raise in class." They restate positions they had inadequately or ineptly taken in class. Jeff frequently volunteers on a diary that he has enjoyed an exchange in class.

Dissatisfaction with the class or with Jeff can be explored safely within the diaries. One student criticizes Jeff's treatment of another student: "I felt this to be an abuse of power and a betrayal of trust . . . an abuse of power because you are the professor and the authority . . . a betrayal of trust because you had earlier said that you would never embarrass or humiliate us." Jeff responds at length. He is sorry she was upset in class; he describes his understanding of the interaction, allowing, "It's hard for me to know whether I was on an ego trip—though I don't doubt your perceptions." He then reads her diary to the class, giving others the chance to react. Her feelings are validated, and Jeff is sensitized to undercurrents in the group.

Another student compliments him on the way the class is going, and he responds: "Let me know if it ever becomes unsatisfactory." He is often called upon to defend his attendance policy. He acknowledges students' anger on this point but does not back down: "Yes, if I were a student, I too would resent my rigid attendance policy. My justification, however, is that much or, perhaps, *most* of the learning goes on *during* class. Therefore, if you miss more than a few classes, you can't possibly learn as much." Any dissatisfaction with the class or with grading on papers is similarly aired, and the result is usually positive.

Diarists often bring up reading they have done outside of class. His interest is always piqued. They suggest changes to the class syllabus. He answers in great detail, telling them if he has ever taught that work, why he does no longer, whether he might in the future. They suggest books and movies he might enjoy, and he tells them if he has read or seen their suggestions. He tells them if he has ever written on any issue they raise, and he offers to bring them copies of such material. There is academic congress; their appetite for literature is whetted. In choosing to emphasize in this book the personal growth his students experience by means of the diaries, Jeff has significantly underreported the enormous strides they make in interpreting literature by this same means. Over and over again, they rejoice that the work is theirs to interpret. Surely there is another book here, one which I hope Jeff will write someday.

What is not so comforting is that students repeatedly express anger at an educational system that has led them to think there is one "right" interpretation of a work which it is their job to "learn." One writes: "The diaries and interpretations of the novels somehow made me feel that my feelings and ideas were legitimate in a way I've never felt before. I always felt that I was supposed to interpret the novel in a certain, conventional way, and I was always afraid of being wrong." A graduate (!) student writes: "What I really value about this course is that before I took it, I have never invested such intense feeling into literary characters and my reading of novels. My literary studies have had little to do with my personal life." Students express amazement that the best of what has been thought and said before is there for their personal use.

Jeff is probably wise in leaving unwritten all the personal accolades he himself has received from students. In doing so, he avoids the muddied waters of transference, but more important, he isolates the focus to what students do for themselves in the diaries. In the diaries themselves, he usually thanks his benefactor for the kind words. Sometimes if the praise is embedded in criticism of the university, he gently suggests that education is a personal responsibility and that something the student is criticizing, such as size, might more usefully be converted to a source of strength or additional opportunity.

I need to report these comments and the embedded attitudes because they are such a salient feature of the collected diaries. I do so reluctantly, however. As a lecturer in another department of the same university and a graduate of the fine program of which Jeff is just one part, I can easily identify my own negative countertransference when I read: "I finally had an English class that was stimulating, that related to my own life, that allowed a lot of student participation, and that had a professor whose lectures were not the typically tedious ones I was so used to." I take a deep breath; a defensive posture is not productive.

Why do students find this an important educational method? One explains: "I will probably use diaries in my classroom of the future. I believe in empowering students. That is, I want to hear their individual voices, and I want to hear how they come to experience a particular book." What emerges is that students want to be heard; they want to be taken seriously, in an atmosphere of safety. Students point with appreciation to the fact that the diaries are ungraded and that they are "free to make mistakes" therein. Given such a safe forum, they rise to the occasion and speak eloquently. In providing an opportunity to function in the intellectual realm much the same as they do with personal issues, the diaries offer a safe place to be heard. The students write; they hear back: "I see your point; continue to explore this." They write again, appropriating for themselves what is rightfully theirs, a personal response to a work of literature. This is clearly a good.

Still the use of diaries of self-disclosure, unsupervised bouts of self-analysis, within a classroom setting gives pause. Are there not other ways to encourage learning and stimulate individual growth without appropriating all this personal minutiae—indeed glorifying it—in a college course? Could not students' insecurities about deviating from "standard" interpretations of literature be addressed by more sensitive direction of class discussion, more open-ended assignments? Would not a professor's incorporation of personal material into class discussion model for students the possibility of integrating life and literature?

These are questions that must be posed, because while I am making a case for what I observed—that is, how valuable the diary writing process is for intensifying literary interpretation—and while Jeff would undoubtedly agree, nevertheless that is not his major thesis here. In defense of his teaching, he quite rightly points to the graded papers the students write, the high standards to which he holds them, the controlled literary focus of class discussion, the number of books students read, and his detailed responses within the diaries to matters of literature. All of this is true. He holds scholarship in high regard. The diaries are not a substitute for academic work; they are an adjunct to it. But it is well to remember that the course and the book are two separate, albeit overlapping, entities, just as the diary writing and academic work are distinct from each other.

Furthermore, the organization of material around particular issues here is obviously for the purpose of narrative cohesiveness. It would be a false inference that the classes were similarly formatted, although at times certain themes predominate. Also, the background material presented here, the psychosociological discussion, while undoubtedly enriching Jeff's understanding of what the students write about and contextualizing the dimensions of the problem for readers, does not intrude in any obvious way on the way he leads the class. It is a literature class, not a talk show.

However, in this book, not to be confused with the course of similar name, he has chosen the story he wants to tell, and that is the use of diaries in the classroom setting for personal growth. Here he shares his excitement about the emotional and relational breakthroughs students experience as they get involved in the diary-writing process. While he welcomes the interplay between literature and life, his focus here is on personal growth. The question then arises, What, if any, impact does Jeff's preferential interest in personal growth, as evidenced in the vantage point he has chosen in this book, have in the classroom? I could discern that impact only in his choice of what to read in class. While he is fully responsive to anything a diarist writes about academic matters in his comments to them, he is not likely to read their entry aloud. He is limited to the number of diary selections he can read, and obviously his choice will have a large impact on the direction other diarists will take.

There seem to be two major principles at work. He invariably reads anything negative about himself or the class. He never lets dissatisfactions fester. He does not read anything positive about himself. Mixed reviews, criticism muted with praise, he generally does not read, telling the diarist, "I would have read this in class, but I didn't want to seem self-congratulatory." He reads diaries which confront past or present traumas or which contain personal breakthroughs. Probably most of the diaries in this book were read aloud in class. He does not read provocative literary analyses, nor does he read entries notable for being well written. His interest is in promoting personal growth, and he wants to do so in a classroom setting.

This was the sticking point for me. Sure, diary writing can be therapeutic. Sure, diaries shared with an empathic reader have even more potential to be therapeutic. But is a college classroom an acceptable place for this activity? Is the use of valuable classtime for reading the diaries justifiable? Would it not be sufficient merely to return the diaries with comments for the process to work, for the students to have their opinions validated, their paths, personal and academic, lighted? I decided it would be acceptable to read diaries aloud in a classroom setting *only* if it were necessary, that is, if the setting itself were a prerequisite. Given that other approaches might also work and not involve as much valuable classtime, I felt that merely working was not sufficient. Eventually, albeit reluctantly, I came to conclude that the classroom setting is not incidental to the process. It is at the very heart of it.

The time frame imposed by the college calendar is a significant element. Diaries are assignments with a well-defined termination point. Should one choose to continue a diary, as many say they intend to do, it will be a diary of a different sort. Just as a predetermined date of termination often accelerates private therapy, so too is this a factor in the classroom setting. Many processes in life are teleologically defined; we act in the present in accord with an imagined end. College students live life in semesters, and their deeply ingrained sense of what a semester means and what a course entails contributes to the success of the diaries. Diarists know there will be a point at which they won't *have* to write diaries anymore and a point at which they will not be *able* to do them. This creates a certain amount of urgency to do whatever it is they are going to do with the diaries and with themselves in a given time frame. Perhaps this endpoint taps into a competitive urge to impress the professor with their progress or their peers with their breakthroughs. Perhaps they are driven by a conscientious desire to complete all the requirements, even the unstated ones, of the course to the best of their ability. Whatever the reasons, most diarists conclude the class on a happy note. They are pleased with themselves and are happy to share the credit for their strides with Jeff, the class, and the diaries.

The predetermined end point also affects the nature of transference. While Jeff makes every effort to refuse the parental role, diarists are obviously tempted to make such projections. Nevertheless, it is a given that at the end of the semester, the relationship will radically change. The students will leave; the professor will continue on with another group. They may meet, but things will be different. There is value to the students in going through this process in tandem because leaving home without rancor and accepting a new independent identity are the familial issues so many, especially in the undergraduate courses, are dealing with. Through the diaries, students see their peers engaged in rites of passage, similar to their own. They see that it is possible—indeed highly desirable—to leave home and yet continue loving. Students tempted to break the ties of dependency at home harshly for fear of becoming further enmeshed or losing ground have some positive examples from their peers. They also have the counterexamples of pain and lingering malaise from classmates who have left home acrimoniously. In the diaries parents are objectified, tamed, demythologized, and life goes on. Guilt is assuaged. Diarists are prompted to try to teach their own parents this lesson, to take the lead in defining family interaction. They want to be their own person, and the thrust of the class and the diaries is that what they want is splendidly appropriate.

As the course draws to a close, students see how natural and appropriate it is for them to leave even a much-cherished nest. Jeff expects they will leave. After all, the semester is ending. He expects they have profited from the course; he expects they will go out into the world as their very best selves; he knows the world will be a better place because of them. He is not ambivalent.

The academic calendar is important. So too is an academic setting which allows access to and egress from big issues. Interaction with a sensitive, empathic professor skilled in this kind of writing is invaluable. I have arrived at my last reservation—the actual reading aloud of diaries to the class. I began as usual with my own experience: I never enjoyed hearing my diaries read, nor did I like hearing those of my classmates. I still don't get it. I didn't fear this part of the process because students can and do withhold permission for their diaries to be read. My goal, then, was not to scrutinize its potential to do harm but to identify its utility. What was the cost-benefit ratio? Was reading the diaries aloud a good use of classroom time?

I found my answer not in my own experience but in the accounts of others. I was astounded. According to most participants, it is the most riveting feature of the process. Almost every diarist of hundreds commented on this part of the experience. It elicited far greater attention than any of Jeff's comments. Many deemed it "the most meaningful part" of the course. One explained at length: "It felt good to get some of my feelings down on paper. It felt better to have someone read them and to make no judgments on them. And what a wonderful, safe feeling that is! I mean, to have someone read your deepest personal thoughts, and possibly read them aloud, and yet have no judgments made, no criticisms, just passive understanding and insight, is a very good feeling. . . . You listened, and so did my classmates, and there were no reprisals, just a silent understanding."

How can this be? The most effective element of the process I nearly missed altogether. A few disliked it, but most reveled in the experience: "I loved hearing my diaries read aloud. Somehow my diaries seemed more important than they did before, after you read them aloud." Another writes: "Hearing my own diary out loud was the most startling thing I ever experienced, as I was initially unaware that it was my own. It was extremely helpful to hear my words and feelings come out of the mouth of another. It was also scary."

Some students ask for their diaries to be read and are angry when they are not. One accuses Jeff of not reading his because it was not sensational enough. Jeff, of course, will bring any such grievance out into the open by reading the charge, so the student will have his or her wish. Others withhold permission altogether. Jeff never lets this pass, always urging students to resubmit particularly painful or self-disclosing entries so he can read them. His insistence on the value of doing so borders on the pushy. Sometimes he writes he would appreciate it; most often he tells diarists it would be useful to them. Other times, he emphasizes how helpful the diary could be to others in the class. When students do resubmit, he tells them: "I'm glad that you allowed me to read this to the class. It will be important not only for others to hear this but for you to hear me read this; it will help to objectify the situation for you." More than one student reenters or recommits to individual therapy upon hearing, as one put it, how really "sick" she sounded. Another wonders: "Is this really me?" after she "heard it through your voice." Hearing the diaries makes feelings tangible.

Until I read the diaries, I did not know that Jeff was so emphatic on this point. Until I read the diaries, I did not realize how powerful this part of the process is for most participants. Because it works and because I could not have anticipated it, I see myself writing that Jeff has either "shrewdly or inadvertently" devised a system, each element of which is necessary for its success. I cringe at the cavil. The point is moot; the system is in place, and it works. The issue must be a personal one; I know I could not have built a better mousetrap. Furthermore, I know I am the author of one of my favorite Freudian slips. In a diary, I obsequiously preface my objections to one of Jeff's literary interpretations with Bloomsian-like platitudes. I want "patricide"; I write "parricide." I am not seduced by dictionary definitions; I teach Latin roots, and I am "equal" to the task at hand.

Progoff's workshops provide an analogy to what happens in Jeff's class. His system similarly stipulates that the diaries be read aloud, but by the participants themselves. Each person reads his or her own journal to the group. No response is made to the shared journals. Progoff describes what happens at these readings in religious imagery, comparing the atmosphere in the room to that of a cathedral: "Each individual is offering his most personal possession, his life, but he is presenting it objectively, even transpersonally . . . a factual offering placed on an unseen altar before the group. Perhaps the atmosphere of depth and awe that enters the workshop is the cumulative effect of many human existences being set forth as offering in this sincere, unprepossessing way, each primarily engaged in clarifying itself to itself" (111).

Something similar happens here. Jeff is not gifted with a sonorous voice; he reads in a monotone, in muted tones. He does not need to project; the students listen attentively. He tells one student that he struggled to "mask his tears" in reading her diary to the class; I never detect his emotion. There is solemnity in the delivery and respect in its reception. In the presence of so much explosive material, there is an atmosphere of gentility, civility. Never, even in class discussion, is there any reference to the individual diaries or even to the broader social issues raised. It is as if there is an unwritten, thoroughly understood code—"These things aren't done." Progoff credits the "suffusion of love in the room" (61), the way in which "by our silent restraint, we express not only our love for the other person, but also our respect for the integrity of the life process at work in each of us" (56).

It is not just the presence of the other but the content of their diaries that progressively liberates. Jeff insists that sharing personal material has a boomerang effect. A diarist corroborates this: "The more personal the diaries got, the more I felt able to open up myself." Progoff writes: "As we find other persons speak out memories that are similar to ours, our restraints are relaxed. . . . As others speak, we also are reinforced in accepting the experiences that we have had as being the 'normal' contents of a human existence"

(197–98). Another diarist writes: "Hearing other students' diaries without any comments led me to feel sympathetic and encouraged me to write with more confidence about my own problems."

While diary writing per se encourages introspection, the reading of the diaries breaks down feelings of personal isolation. One student writes: "Listening to other people's diaries, I often felt this overwhelming relief that I was not the only screwed up person in the world." Another admits that "writing as well as hearing them has saved my life. . . . I felt like I was from a different planet." Another says hearing the diaries "linked me back to humanity," while another finds in them an "escape from the muteness—something I feel absolutely trapped in at times."

It also fosters identification, empathy with others—the sense, as one put it, that "we really are all the same." Another notes with surprise, "So many of them could have been written by me." Students develop greater respect for each other. One finds that "people are smarter" and "more insightful" than she thought. Many decide that appearances are deceptive and stereotypes misleading. Many acknowledge a class bond: "I felt closer to my classmates because I had heard some of their deepest sorrows and thoughts, and it makes one feel that you're all in the same boat and no one is there to pass judgment." They are grateful to each other. One applauds "all of us for having the courage to confide. Our mutual journal journey has meant more to me, and will probably have a more lasting effect, than all the novels we read for class. Thanks, my fellow journalists."

In accepting others, they come to accept themselves. One expresses gratitude that there was "no need to be ashamed for being human." In hearing the diaries read, the students learn how to proceed with themselves. They figure out how to confront their thoughts, their behaviors, to look at parts of themselves that are dysfunctional. They see their peers self-exploring, self-protecting. They reevaluate their own lives. One admits: "I was always amazed with the amount of suffering and self-hatred my classmates seemed to express in their diaries. This made me appreciate my fairly hardship-free life." Another student asks Jeff for a recommendation, over other professors from whom she has gotten higher grades. She defends her choice to her parents on the grounds that Jeff "knew me better than any other professor I had." What a compliment she pays herself in this choice.

They realize others care for them, and they reciprocate. One writes: "I have learned that nobody has an exclusive story and that there are people that care about others in the world." They write of a need to "reach out, if only to comfort." The desire to help others in the class actually motivates some diarists to be more honest than they are inclined to be. Everyone gains.

One student writes: "Prior to this course, I never put two and two together." Jeff has put two and two and two together and generated an unquantifiable. However I seek to describe it, I come up with oxymorons. The diaries—stark, elemental, private individual work—become public. They are a classroom project, one which will continue to develop, in private. The classroom is a silent revival meeting, a private group therapy session. The drama is in the suppression of emotion. The leveling of human experience is its elevation. In a student's words, "I am recommending this class to anyone who has the desire to be enlightened."

/ Appendix

I present here a typical course syllabus in a spring semester, followed by the instructions I give for preparing the weekly diaries.

English 215: Literature and Psychoanalysis
Jeffrey Berman
Tuesday, Thursday 4:15–5:35   HU 108

Required Books:

Freud	*Introductory Lectures on Psycho-Analysis* (Norton)
Berman	*The Talking Cure* (NYU Press)
Lawn (ed.)	*The Short Story: 30 Masterpieces* (St. Martin's)
Kafka	*The Basic Kafka*, ed. Heller (Pocket)
Plath	*The Bell Jar* (Bantam)
Salinger	*The Catcher in the Rye* (Bantam)

Jan 23	Introduction
Jan 28	*Introductory Lectures on Psycho-Analysis*
Jan 30	*Introductory Lectures on Psycho-Analysis*
Feb 4	*Introductory Lectures on Psycho-Analysis*; *The Talking Cure*, chapter 1
Feb 6	Hawthorne: "Young Goodman Brown"
Feb 11	Lawrence: "The Rocking-Horse Winner"
Feb 13	Fitzgerald: "Babylon Revisited"
Feb 18	Melville: "Bartleby the Scrivener"
Feb 20	"Bartleby the Scrivener"; Conrad: "The Secret Sharer"
Feb 25	"The Secret Sharer"
Feb 27	Jackson: "The Lottery"

Mar 3	Midterm Exam
Mar 5	O'Connor: "A Good Man Is Hard to Find"
Mar 10	Hemingway: "A Clean, Well-Lighted Place"
Mar 12	Mishima: "Patriotism"; Deadline for first essay
Mar 17	Kafka: *The Metamorphosis*
Mar 19	Kafka: *The Metamorphosis*
Mar 31	Kafka: "The Judgment"
Apr 2	Kafka: "A Hunger Artist"
Apr 7	Kafka: "Letter to His Father"
Apr 9	Plath: *The Bell Jar*; *The Talking Cure*, chapter 5
Apr 14	*The Bell Jar*
Apr 16	*The Bell Jar*; essay on *The Bell Jar* due
Apr 21	*The Catcher in the Rye*
Apr 23	*The Catcher in the Rye*
Apr 28	*The Catcher in the Rye*; essay on *Catcher* due
Apr 30	Conclusion
May 7	Final Exam (1:00–3:00)

Requirements: There will be a midterm exam, a final exam, and two essays (five pages, typed, double-spaced). There will also be a weekly diary (please see enclosed sheet). The essays will involve psychoanalytic interpretations of the literature we will be reading. The first essay, on one of the short stories, is due at the beginning of the class on which we will be discussing the story. For example, an essay on "The Rocking-Horse Winner" is due on Feb. 11; an essay on "Bartleby" is due on Feb. 18; on "The Secret Sharer," Feb. 25. The deadline for the first essay is March 12, if you are writing on "Patriotism." If you wish, you can write on one of the Kafka stories (*The Metamorphosis*, "The Judgment," or "A Hunger Artist"), but the paper must still be submitted no later than March 12. The second essay should be on either *The Bell Jar* (due April 16) or *The Catcher in the Rye* (due April 28). Late papers will not be accepted.

Attendance is crucial. You are allowed three absences; if you miss more than three classes, you won't receive credit for the course. Please try to attend every class.

Office:	HU 348
Office phone:	442–4084
Home phone:	355–4760 (Please don't call after 9:00 P.M.)
Office hours:	Tuesday, Thursday, 3:00–4:00, and by appointment

A Freudian Diary

An indispensable part of English 215 will be a weekly diary that I am asking you to keep. Each Tuesday you will be requested to submit a diary (one or two pages long, typed, double-spaced); you will receive the diary back, with my comments, on the following Thursday. The diary can be as personal or impersonal as you wish. The following are merely suggestions:

dreams you've had and attempts to interpret them
"Freudian slips" you've come across
comments you wanted to make in class but didn't or couldn't
impressions of the preceding class
questions about the story we are reading
connections between stories
agreements or disagreements with friends
parent-child relationships
attitudes toward sex, work, religion, love, education, the future
problems in your life—and possible solutions to them
anything you find provocative or provoking about class
what you like and dislike about the instructor

These diaries, I hope, will encourage you to make connections between what you learn in class and what you do and think outside class. Although one of the primary purposes of the diaries is to encourage you to engage in self-discovery, you alone will determine how introspective you want your diaries to be. I'm particularly interested in whether you find psychoanalytic theory relevant to your own life. The diaries thus represent the "lab" part of the course, in which you become both the analyst and the patient. My role in reading your diaries is not to interpret them but to support your efforts toward self-analysis.

Do not emphasize plot. (Plot is the least important element of our life.) Only include what you think is meaningful. Also, there is no need to make the diaries into polished essays. I am not concerned here with proper para-graphing, spelling, cohesion—though obviously I will be looking for these virtues in your formal essays and exams.

Before I hand the diaries back to you, I will read a few of them in class. I will always read the diaries anonymously, and there will be no discussion of them afterward. If you do not want me to read your diary to the class, please indicate so at the bottom of the page.

By the end of the semester you will have submitted to me about twelve or thirteen diaries. Don't lose any of them, since I will not be keeping a record of how many of them you have submitted. Keep all the diaries in a folder, and turn the folder in to me at the end of the term. I will make sure you have written the required number of diaries and then will hand them back to you. I will not grade the diaries, but they will be part of the required work for the course. I would like to keep the last diary, which should be a discussion of what the diaries have meant to you.

/ Notes

1 / Introduction

1   Throughout the present book I use the words "diary" and "journal" interchangeably. I also make no distinction between "diary" and "diary entry."

2   Readers may wish to know in greater detail the process by which I received students' permission to use their diaries for the present book. At the beginning of each semester I announced to my students that I was writing a book on introspective classroom diary writing and asked them if they were interested in contributing to my research. I told the students that, if they granted me permission to use their diaries, I would photocopy their writings at the end of the semester and keep them in a secure place. I promised the students that I would not refer to them by their real names, that I would change factual details that might reveal their identities, that I would not identify the particular class of which they were members, and that, if they gave me permission at the end of the course, they could later withdraw it if they changed their mind. The students had the entire semester to decide whether to allow me to photocopy their diaries. Those who gave me their approval were asked to fill out appropriate permission slips. I also received approval from the university's Institutional Review Board to conduct my research.

About 95 percent of the students in each class have given me permission to use their writings, and I now have over 5,000 diary entries written by more than 500 students. The diaries of 65 students, all of whom have now graduated college, appear in the present book.

To ensure that I carefully disguised their identities, I sent completed chapters of the manuscript to those students whose writings are particularly personal or self-disclosing. I asked the students two questions: "Do you feel comfortable with the way I have used your diary?" and "Have I made sufficient disguises?" No student to whom I have sent these chapters has withdrawn permission. In many cases, such as with the three students whose diaries appear at the end of "Suicide Survivors"—Ted, Terry, and Ruth—the writers provided interesting follow-up, or "postdiaries," written years after they graduated college, which are included in the notes.

3   Support for this statement appears in "The Index of Social Health," a new study released by a group of social scientists at Fordham University. As reported in the *New York Times* (October 18, 1993), the annual study "attempts to monitor the well-being of American

society by examining statistics from reports by the Census Bureau on 16 major social problems, including teenage suicide, unemployment, drug abuse, the high-school drop out rate and the lack of affordable housing." The results of the study indicated that in 1991, the most recent year for which complete data were available, the nation's social well-being was at its lowest point in two decades.

2 / English 215: Literature and Psychoanalysis, Summer 19—

1   See, for example, Joseph Maslow, ed., *Empirical Studies of Psychoanalytic Theories*, 2 vols. (Hillsdale, N.J.: Analytic Press, 1983).

2   Jeffrey Berman, *The Talking Cure: Literary Representations of Psychoanalysis* (New York: New York University Press, 1985).

3   During the fall and spring semesters, students write two five-page essays, in addition to a midterm and a final exam, and the reading list is considerably longer. The reading list also varies from semester to semester.

4   T. S. Eliot, "Gerontion," in *The Complete Poems and Plays* (New York: Harcourt, Brace & World, 1952), 22.

5   This statistic appears in Mary Field Belenky, Blythe McVicker Clinchy, Nancy Rule Gold-berger, and Jill Mattuck Tarule, *Women's Ways of Knowing* (New York: Basic Books, 1986), 59.

6   Sigmund Freud, *Analysis of a Case of Hysteria* (1905), in *Standard Edition of the Complete Psychological Works of Sigmund Freud*, 24 vols. (London: Hogarth Press, 1953–74), 7:122. Henceforth all references to Freud, unless otherwise noted, are to the *Standard Edition*.

7   It is unclear why these one or two students were not sure of the honesty of their own diaries. It may be that diary writing heightened their self-consciousness to the point where they believed they may have been exaggerating experiences.

8   See, for example, Janet Varner Gunn, *Autobiography* (Philadelphia: University of Pennsylvania Press, 1982); Jerome Hamilton Buckley, *The Turning Key* (Cambridge: Harvard University Press, 1984); and Paul John Eakin, *Fictions in Autobiography* (Princeton: Princeton University Press, 1985).

9   Friedrich Nietzsche, *Beyond Good and Evil*, in *The Philosophy of Nietzsche* (New York: Modern Library, 1954), 451.

10   David Nyberg, *The Varnished Truth* (Chicago: University of Chicago Press, 1993).

11   Sigmund Freud, *An Autobiographical Study* (1925), *Standard Edition* 20:42.

12   Robert Langs, "Boundaries & Frames: Non-Transference in Teaching," *AWP Chronicle* 22, no. 1 (September 1989): 1.

13   Sigmund Freud, "Recommendations to Physicians Practising Psycho-Analysis" (1912), *Standard Edition* 12:115.

14   Sigmund Freud, "Observations on Transference-Love" (1915), *Standard Edition* 12:170.

15   Ann Murphy, "Transference and Resistance in the Basic Writing Classroom: Problematics and Praxis," *College Composition and Communication* 40, no. 2 (May 1989): 175. For other essays on the role of transference and countertransference in the college classroom, see *College English* 49, nos. 6 and 7 (October and November 1987), guest-edited by Robert Con Davis.

16   Murphy, "Transference and Resistance," 178.

17   Susan Swartzlander, Diana Pace, and Virginia Lee Stamler, "The Ethics of Requiring Students to Write about Their Personal Lives," *Chronicle of Higher Education* 39 (February 17, 1993).

18   "New Rules about Sex on Campus," *Harper's Magazine*, September 1993, pp. 35–36.

19   George Eliot, *Middlemarch* (London: Zodiac Press, 1967), 189.

20   Anton Chekhov, "Gooseberries," in *The Portable Chekhov*, ed. Avraham Yarmolinsky (New York: Viking), 381.

21   Joseph Conrad, *Lord Jim* (New York: Norton, 1968), 129.

22   Ronald Hayman, *Kafka: A Biography* (New York: Oxford University Press, 1982), 4.

23   For a recent study of the reparative functions of literature, see John Clayton, *Gestures of Healing* (Amherst: University of Massachusetts Press, 1991).

24   Kohut, "Reflections," in *Advances in Self Psychology*, ed. Arnold Goldberg (New York: International Universities Press, 1980), 516.

25   Seymour Fisher and Roger P. Greenberg, *The Scientific Credibility of Freud's Theories and Therapy* (New York: Basic Books, 1977), 364.

26   Judd Marmor, "Discussion of Papers by Allan Compton, Donald M. Marcus, and Robert D. Stolorow," *Psychoanalytic Review* 75 (1988): 258. Donald Spence similarly argues in *Narrative Truth and Historical Truth* (New York: Norton, 1982) that interpretations work not because they necessarily make contact with the actual past but because they create a "coherent and consistent account of a particular set of events" (28).

In *How Does Analysis Cure?* (Chicago: University of Chicago Press, 1984), Kohut concludes that as long as the analyst remains empathic, good if not excellent therapeutic results can be obtained, even if the analyst's interpretation of the patient's psychopathology may be in error.

27   James W. Pennebaker, *Opening Up: The Healing Power of Confiding to Others* (New York: Morrow, 1990). For another recent study of the psychological benefits of writing, see Patricia Kelley, ed., *The Uses of Writing in Psychotherapy* (New York: Haworth Press, 1990).

Ira Progoff's Jungian *At a Journal Workshop* (New York: Dialogue House, 1975) has been instrumental in establishing the diary as a therapeutic tool. Other books on diary writing worth consulting are Tristine Rainer, *The New Diary* (Los Angeles: J. P. Archer, 1978); Lucia Capacchione, *The Creative Journal* (Athens: Ohio University Press, 1979); and Toby Fulwiler, ed., *The Journal Book* (Portsmouth, N.H.: Boynton/Cook, 1987). For an excellent account of how diary writing serves a therapeutic function in literature, see H. Porter Abbot, *Diary Fiction: Writing as Action* (Ithaca: Cornell University Press, 1984).

28   According to a Harvard University study, as reported in the *New York Times* (November 6, 1991), undergraduate students prefer courses that require substantial amounts of writing, and they thrive academically in such an environment. Conversely, large impersonal lecture classes, with no opportunity for writing, discourage genuine learning: " 'The thing for a student to avoid,' said Richard J. Light, a professor of education at Harvard who was director of the assessment project, 'is signing up for all large classes, drifting in and out anonymously, sitting in the eighth row working quietly and then going back to the library or a dorm room and applying the seat of the pants to the seat of the chair.' " I can think of

few activities that are more helpful to a student's academic and personal development than the kind of classroom diary writing that I am proposing.

29   Margaret Atwood, *Second Words* (Toronto: Anansi, 1982), 134.

30   Jerome Bruner, "Life as Narrative," *Social Research* 54 (1987): 15.

31   James Hillman observes in *Healing Fiction* (Barrytown, N.Y.: Station Hill Press, 1983) that "therapy re-stories life" (47).

32   J. D. Salinger, *The Catcher in the Rye* (New York: Bantam, 1951; rpt. 1986), 214.

3 / Sins of the Fathers

1   Judith S. Wallerstein and Joan Berlin Kelly, *Surviving the Breakup* (New York: Basic Books, 1980); Judith S. Wallerstein and Sandra Blakeslee, *Second Chances* (New York: Ticknor & Fields, 1989).

2   Wallerstein and Kelly, *Surviving the Breakup*, 35.

3   Albany *Times-Union*, December 9, 1990.

4   David A. Chiriboga, Linda S. Catron, and associates, *Divorce* (New York: New York University Press, 1991), 1.

5   "Breaking the Divorce Cycle," *Newsweek*, January 13, 1992.

6   James Pennebaker reaches a similar conclusion in *Opening Up: The Healing Power of Confiding to Others* (New York: Morrow, 1990). See also James Pennebaker, Janice K. Kiecolt-Glaser, and Ronald Glaser, "Disclosure of Traumas and Immune Function: Health Implications for Psychotherapy," *Journal of Consulting and Clinical Psychology* 56 (1988): 239–45.

7   Deborah Tannen, *You Just Don't Understand* (New York: William Morrow, 1990), 287.

8   Dorothy Dinnerstein, *The Mermaid and the Minotaur* (New York: Harper & Row, 1976), 111.

9   Nancy Chodorow and Susan Contratto, "The Fantasy of the Perfect Mother," in *Rethinking the Family*, Barrie Thorne and Marilyn Yalom (New York: Longman, 1982), 55.

10   Charlotte Perkins Gilman, *The Yellow Wallpaper* (1899; rpt. New York: Feminist Press, 1973). For a psychoanalytic interpretation of this story and its relationship to Gilman's life, see Jeffrey Berman, "The Unrestful Cure: Charlotte Perkins Gilman and 'The Yellow Wallpaper,'" in *The Talking Cure* (New York: New York University Press, 1985).

11   Wallerstein and Blakeslee, *Second Chances*, 84.

12   Lucy Rose Fischer suggests in *Linked Lives: Adult Daughters and Their Mothers* (New York: Harper & Row, 1986) that daughters who become mothers tend to view their own mothers more positively than before the experience of parenthood. For a study of daughters and mothers in contemporary American literature, see Mickey Pearlman, ed., *Mother Puzzles* (New York: Greenwood Press, 1989).

13   Nancy Chodorow, *The Reproduction of Mothering* (Berkeley: University of California Press, 1978), 169. See also Chodorow's more recent *Feminism and Psychoanalytic Theory* (New Haven: Yale University Press, 1989). For a critique of Chodorow and other gender theorists, see Jane Flax, "The Family in Contemporary Feminist Thought: A Critical Review," in *The Family in Political Thought*, ed. Jean Bethke Elshtain (Amherst: University of Massachusetts Press, 1982), 223–53.

14   Carol Gilligan, *In a Different Voice* (Cambridge: Harvard University Press, 1982), 42.

15   A vivid example of a daughter's fear of maternal smothering appears in the following entry, inspired, in part, by a glorious fall day:

It is a brisk autumn day, the sun is shining, and thoughts flow around the breathtaking scenes of nature. Leaf-peepers are everywhere with grins that are pumpkin-carved. Time flows backward into childhood, when I would bring those fire-hued leaves to my parents to appreciate, as other children have done time and time again. . . .

My father was the type who, no matter what I did, was able to love me unconditionally. Even when he was very angry at me, the heart inside him never changed. My mother was a different kind of tree. Where my father was the maple, supplying the world with sugar and me, a sapling, with enough sunlight through his boughs to let me grow, my mother was a pine. Her boughs were dense, and under them I could not breathe. To survive, I had to get out from under her and grow alongside without her protection. As she grew she crowded me out, and as I grew I felt her needles: she had conditions.

To me the maple and the pine balanced me out as a person. However, the pine was painful and still is, to some extent. Because of this experience I can see the double in myself. I have both tendencies. Unfortunately, my mother was a constant influence, where my father, due to his job, was not. Every person swears that they will not become like their parents, but it is another matter to accomplish this when their influence has been driven into us like a tree tap that goes right to the core. Instead of extracting it, it is feeding you intravenously. . . .

As the wind picks up and tosses around those wonderful leaves of learning, I wonder about the differences that were taught. I also wonder about the people who were produced—the narcissistic ones who threw away the leaf after the parent rejected it and the child. Empathy is the tap that must be slowly put into the narcissistic tree. Once one learns that one is loved, then it is possible to heal the wound that was so deeply inflicted.

As the leaves change into glorious colors, so are people capable of change—especially on a sunny autumn day.

16   "No matter what theory you read," Jessica Benjamin writes in *The Bonds of Love* (New York: Pantheon, 1988), "the father is always the way into the world. In some contemporary delivery rooms, the father is literally encouraged to cut the umbilical cord. He is the liberator, the proverbial knight in shining armor. The devaluation of the mother that inevitably accompanies the idealization of the father, however, gives the father's role as liberator a special twist for women. It means that their necessary identification with their mothers, with existing femininity, is likely to subvert their struggle for independence" (103).

17   Students who write about reconciliation with the absent parent almost always comment upon how grateful they feel for the restored relationship. Witness the following diary from a young woman:

My parents got divorced when I was in high school. I believe that my reaction was similar to the reaction of most teenagers of divorced parents. I thought that I was the only person this had ever happened to. I truly believed that nobody could understand what I was going through and shrugged off my friends' attempts to help me, even friends whose parents were divorced. The words I hated hearing most were, "I know what you're going through." My reply was always, "You have no idea what I'm going through." And to some extent this was true.

You see, my parents had a very ugly divorce, not that any divorce is not ugly, but this one was exceptionally so. It resembled a war more than a divorce. My once typically normal happy family had suddenly been divided into two sides: it was my mother and I against my father and brother. Both my parents refused to move out because doing so would mean forfeiting the rights to the house. Money had never been a problem in our family, and suddenly my parents were tearing apart their children over a material possession both could do without. Their house became more important than their children.

I did not speak to my father or brother who lived in my house for almost a year. It was only after I left for college that I was removed enough from the situation to be able to see what was really going on. I knew that I was losing my father. I swallowed my pride and was the one to attempt to salvage anything left between my father and me. This was not an easy process, nor was it a quick one. It has taken years for us to be able to reach the same point in our relationship where we had started before the divorce. We now have a very special relationship; we never speak about that year, yet the guilt I still feel is an enormous weight I always carry with me. My father and I never argue anymore; we're too afraid to. Every check he writes me I am almost ashamed to except [sic], and every hug he gives me brings tears to my eyes. I love my father very much and don't know how I could have abandoned him when he needed me the most. This is a feeling that will never escape me.

4 / Hunger Artists

1   Franz Kafka, *The Basic Kafka* (New York: Pocket Books, 1979), "A Hunger Artist," 85. Page references in the text to "A Hunger Artist," as well as to *The Metamorphosis* and "Letter to His Father," are to this edition.

2   Kim Chernin, *The Obsession* (New York: Harper & Row, 1981). See also Chernin's *Hungry Self* (New York: Harper & Row, 1986).

3   Franz Kafka, *Letters to Felice*, ed. Erich Heller and Jurgen Born, trans. James Stern and Elisabeth Duckworth (New York: Schocken Books, 1973), 57.

4   Frederick Karl, *Franz Kafka: Representative Man* (New York: Ticknor & Fields, 1991), 147.

5   Max Brod, ed., *The Diaries of Franz Kafka: 1910–1913* (New York: Schocken Books, 1948), 122.

6   Ibid., 286–87.

7   Ernst Pawel, *The Nightmare of Reason: A Life of Franz Kafka* (New York: Farrar, Straus & Giroux, 1984), 209.

8   Gustav Janouch, *Conversations with Kafka* (New York: New Directions, 1971), 95.

9   See Louise J. Kaplan, *Female Perversions* (New York: Doubleday, 1991), 455–67.

10   Hilde Bruch, *The Golden Cage* (Cambridge: Harvard University Press, 1978), viii. See also

Bruch's *Conversations with Anorexics*, ed. Danita Czyzewski and Melanie Suhr (New York: Basic Books, 1989).

11   Joan Jacobs Brumberg, *Fasting Girls* (New York: New American Library, 1989), 24.

12   Marlene Boskind-White and William C. White, *Bulimarexia* (New York: Norton, 1983), 20.

13   Margaret Atwood, *The Edible Woman* (New York: Popular Library, 1976). For a discussion of food in literature, see Evelyn J. Hinz, ed., *Diet and Discourse* (*Mosaic* 24 [1991]).

14   One of the symptoms of bulimia is extensive tooth decay and tooth loss, caused by the erosion of enamel due to regurgitated gastric juices.

15   "Nearly all the women I have seen who have any difficulty around weight control report serious, painful conflicts with their mothers, with whom they basically report loving and caring relationships" (Janet Surrey, "Eating Patterns as a Reflection of Women's Development" [Wellesley College, 1985, Work in Progress], 6). Surrey's essay is reprinted in *Women's Growth in Connection*, ed. Judith V. Jordan, Alexandra G. Kaplan, Jean Baker Miller, Irene P. Stiver, and Janet L. Surrey (New York: Guilford Press, 1991), 237–49. For a discussion of how women "turn their rage, frustration, and ambivalence about femininity on to their own bodies, carrying the culture's contradictory feelings towards the flesh and its ambivalence about the mother," see Patricia Waugh, *Feminine Fictions* (London: Routledge, 1989), 175.

16   *Diagnostic and Statistical Manual of Mental Disorders*, 3rd rev. ed. (Washington, D.C.: American Psychiatric Association, 1987), 65–69.

17   See Craig Johnson and Mary E. Connors, *The Etiology and Treatment of Bulimia Nervosa* (New York: Basic Books, 1987).

18   Surrey, "Eating Patterns," 3.

19   Kafka, *Letters to Felice*, 156.

20   D. W. Winnicott, *The Maturational Processes and the Facilitating Environment* (London: Hogarth Press, 1965), 185.

21   Sylvia Plath, "Lady Lazarus," in *Ariel* (New York: Harper & Row, 1966), 7.

22   Franz Kafka, *Letters to Friends, Family, and Editors*, trans. Richard Winston and Clara Winston (New York: Schocken, 1977), 16.

23   Kafka, *The Basic Kafka*, 292.

5 / Suicide Survivors

1   Albert Camus, *The Myth of Sisyphus* (New York: Vintage, 1955), 41.

2   See Norman Kreitman, "The Clinical Assessment and Management of the Suicidal Patient," in *Suicide*, ed. Alec Roy (Baltimore: Williams & Wilkins, 1986), 193.

3   Edwin Shneidman, "Overview: A Multidimensional Approach to Suicide," in *Suicide: Understanding and Responding*, ed. Douglas Jacobs and Herbert Brown (Madison, Conn.: International Universities Press, 1989), 7.

4   I realize that others may disagree with me and argue for a libertarian approach to suicide. According to this view, people have the right to take their own lives, and they should not be stopped. As the eighteenth-century philosopher David Hume argues in his essay "On Suicide," "A man who retires from life does no harm to society: He only ceases to do

good. . . . I am not obliged to do a small good to society at the expense of a great harm to myself" (quoted by Stephen Pepper, "Can a Philosophy Make One Philosophical?" in *Essays in Self-Destruction*, ed. Edwin S. Shneidman [New York: Science House, 1967], 126). More recently, Thomas Szasz has advocated a person's right to commit suicide ("A Moral View on Suicide," in *Suicide: Understanding and Responding*, ed. Douglas Jacobs and Herbert Brown [Madison, Conn.: International Universities Press, 1989], 437–47).

I, too, believe in individual autonomy and the right to commit suicide in special circumstances, such as in terminal illness. Sometimes it is selfish to keep a person alive who suffers unendurable pain and who has no realistic possibility of improvement. Nevertheless, I do not believe that Len's was a "rational" suicide, for he was young, resourceful, and in otherwise excellent health.

5   Stekel's comments appear in Paul Friedman, ed., *On Suicide: Discussions of the Vienna Psychoanalytic Society—1910* (New York: International Universities Press, 1967), 87. Although Freud never formulated a comprehensive theory of suicide, his remarks in "Mourning and Melancholia" (1917) on clinical depression emphasize the link between suicide and internalized aggression: "No neurotic harbours thoughts of suicide which he has not turned back upon himself from murderous impulses against others" (*Standard Edition* 14:252). In his classic study *Man Against Himself* (New York: Harcourt, Brace & World, 1938), Karl Menninger observed that no suicide is consummated unless there is the wish to kill, the wish to be killed, and the wish to die (23).

6   See Dan Buie, Jr., and John Maltsberger, "The Psychological Vulnerability to Suicide," in *Suicide: Understanding and Responding*, ed. Douglas Jacobs and Herbert Brown (Madison, Conn.: International Universities Press, 1989), 59–72.

7   It is not uncommon for a person to commit suicide on a loved one's birthday or deathday. This "anniversary reaction" is even more common if the loved one has committed suicide. See Lawrence S. Kubie, "Multiple Determinants of Suicide," in *Essays in Self-Destruction*, ed. Edwin Shneidman (New York: Science House, 1967), 455–62.

8   Edward J. Dunne and Karen Dunne-Maxim, "Preface," in *Suicide and Its Aftermath*, ed. Edward J. Dunne, John L. McIntosh, and Karen Dunne-Maxim (New York: Norton, 1987), xiii.

9   William Shakespeare, *The Tragedy of Macbeth*, ed. Sylvan Barnet (New York: Signet, 1963), 4.3.208–10.

10 Jeffrey Berman, *Joseph Conrad: Writing as Rescue* (New York: Astra Books, 1977).

11 Joseph Conrad, *Heart of Darkness*, ed. Robert Kimbrough (New York: Norton, 1963). Page references in the text are to this edition.

12 Joseph Conrad, *Lord Jim* (New York: Norton, 1968), 49.

13 Sigmund Freud, *Beyond the Pleasure Principle* (1920), *Standard Edition* 18:15.

14 D. H. Lawrence, *The Letters of D. H. Lawrence*, vol. 2, ed. George J. Zytaruk and James T. Boulton (Cambridge: Cambridge University Press, 1981), 90.

15 Ernest Hemingway, *For Whom the Bell Tolls* (New York: Scribner's, 1940), 165.

16 Sylvia Plath, *The Journals of Sylvia Plath*, ed. Francis McCullough (New York: Dial Press, 1982), 256.

17 William Styron, *Sophie's Choice* (New York: Random House, 1979), 438.

18   David Aberbach, *Surviving Trauma* (New Haven: Yale University Press, 1989), 23.

19   Quoted by Ellen Zinner, "Survivors of Suicide: Understanding and Coping with the Legacy of Self-Inflicted Death," in *Youth Suicide*, ed. Peter Cimbolic and David Jobes (Springfield, Ill.: Charles C. Thomas, 1990), 67.

20   "Attempted Suicide among High School Students—United States, 1990," *Morbidity and Mortality Weekly Report* (Centers for Disease Control) 40, no. 37 (September 20, 1991): 633–35.

21   See A. Alvarez, *The Savage God* (New York: Bantam, 1973).

22   See Jeffrey Berman, *The Talking Cure* (New York: New York University Press, 1985) and *Narcissism and the Novel* (New York: New York University Press, 1990).

23   John J. Clayton, *Gestures of Healing* (Amherst: University of Massachusetts Press, 1991), 4.

24   See Edwin Shneidman, *Definition of Suicide* (New York: Wiley, 1985).

25   Scott Poland, *Suicide Intervention in the Schools* (New York: Guilford Press, 1989), 170.

26   John Maltsberger and Dan Buie, "Countertransference Hate in the Treatment of Suicidal Patients," *Archives of General Psychiatry* 30 (1974): 627.

27   There is some slight evidence that high school suicide prevention programs may be less successful than once thought and may actually have counterproductive effects. One study, based on self-completed questionnaires, suggests that some suicide attempters apparently believe that suicide prevention courses may encourage people to commit suicide. See David Shaffer et al., "Adolescent Suicide Attempters," *JAMA* 264, no. 24 (December 26, 1990): 3151–55. Most researchers, however, continue to believe strongly in the value of suicide prevention programs.

28   Cited in Poland, *Suicide Intervention in the Schools*, 68.

29   Dunne, McIntosh, and Dunne-Maxim, *Suicide and Its Aftermath*, xvi.

30   I showed Ted a draft of this chapter a year and a half after he completed the course and asked him to comment on his feelings reading it. Here is what he wrote:

   Reading the journals and the effect your friend's suicide had on you made me feel less alone. As I stated in one of my journals, the topic of my mother's suicide has never been broached by anyone in my family. Writing the journals was the first time I had ever really tried to discuss how I felt after my mother died. Reading the chapter really made me feel less alone. I was able to see that others had conflicting feelings about suicide, and how others were affected by suicide attempts or by a loved one's suicide. I hope readers of your book will be able to understand the utter hopelessness a person can feel, and thus be able to help a friend or a loved one who is suicidal or who has been greatly affected by another's suicide.

   A couple of times when I reread my journals I shuddered, for it brought back the feelings I had when I wrote them. Yet the pain seemed less when I wrote the journals. Journal writing, particularly about my mother's suicide, has helped me deal better with my problems. Being able to put into words the hopelessness I felt makes dealing with my mother's suicide less painful. The journals give me something tangible to look at and think about. Being able to say, "Yeah, I wrote this and this is how I felt, and I know I have not totally come to terms with her death, and maybe I never will," is much less painful than keeping everything inside.

The chapter shows the writers of the journals began to reveal more and more each week. I also noticed how my journals revealed more each time, which seems to mean I was getting closer to my true feelings: the feelings of anger, hopelessness, and melancholy. I know I will always remember and be affected by my mother, but I feel a certain strength in the struggle I have been through in dealing with her death. What I found most positive about the chapter was that, even though the writers were unsure and many times scared, they continued to struggle and try. Even after the horrors these students have seen and been through, they are still living and trying to come to grips with their problems. I hope a reader who is depressed and lonely can find some comfort in the suffering that I and the other writers have been through.

31 See Ronald Maris, *Pathways to Suicide* (Baltimore: Johns Hopkins University Press, 1981).

32 Vladimir Nabokov, *Lolita* (London: Weidenfeld & Nicolson, 1959), 147.

33 "One may take it for granted that patients who threaten suicide or self-mutilation will excite a certain degree of malice in most examiners," John Maltsberger writes. "Many will feel quite uncomfortable when such impulses threaten to force through repression into conscious awareness. The consequent anxiety will make you want to get away from the patient—in a word, to respond aversively" (*Suicide Risk* [New York: New York University Press, 1986], 135). See also Herbert Hendin, "Psychodynamics of Suicide, with Particular Reference to the Young," *American Journal of Psychiatry* 148, no. 9 (September 1991): 1150–58.

34 Ken Kesey, *One Flew over the Cuckoo's Nest* (New York: Viking Press, 1962).

35 Two and a half years later, after she completed the course, Terry was still enthusiastic about the value of diary writing. I asked her if she would be willing to reread her diaries and write a "postdiary" for the present book, and here is her response:

Why does writing diaries make a difference to me? Well, writing helps me to focus, to put something down and to own it. Depression and anger are overwhelming because they're vague. Think about it. Somebody pisses you off. So you start thinking about every injustice done to you in the history of your lifetime, even the kid who tied your shoelaces together in the first grade. Then someone says, "What's wrong?" You either say, "Oh, nothing" or think of everything that has ever gone wrong in your entire life, become filled with rage, and answer by talking about whatever insignificant thing set you off in the first place.

You can't do that with writing because your computer terminal looks back at you with this look like "Yeah, right." And you have to give in because the only other alternative is to smash the monitor, but if you do that you'll have to buy another one. So you give in and start writing about what is really bothering you, whatever skeleton that is. And a weight is lifted off you, because it's there in front of you, it's not a giant unexplainable monster. It affirms you, you can look at it and say, "Yeah, I really got shit on." And you can see where the shit is coming from. Sometimes I forget where the shit is coming from. I guess we all do.

I don't mean to botch the main point here, but even more important to me than writing was hearing the diaries read in class. And even more important was hearing my own diary. Till this moment I can remember you reading the first few lines and feeling surprised that I had been picked. But most important, I remember the other students. I remember them laughing at my jokes, nodding their heads at my situation, giving looks of genuine concern—and most important, I remember looks of empathy. It was truly one of the most relief-filled days of my life. I had always been made to feel that it was my fault that I had gotten sick and that I deserved all the pain. But here was a whole class of students—a whole class, and they sympathized with me, THEY SUPPORTED ME!!!!! You can't imagine what that does for someone who has been shunned all her life for emotions that she always felt were beyond her control. I went home that night and cried—cried because I was so unburdened, so happy that someone had finally truly and honestly believed that it wasn't my fault. I would not trade that for any amount of money in the world.

I guess the big difference now is that depression and anxiety no longer control my life. I have other things now—I work a part-time job, am an officer in two service organizations, do TONS of volunteer work, and even made the dean's list last semester. But it's more important than that. I *really* want to live. I've noticed very few people can say that, but I can. And it's a wonderful feeling, especially when you've wanted to die since the third grade.

I'm still angry. I'm angry because my parents never did anything when school teachers told them I looked depressed a lot. I'm angry because I lost parts of my childhood and youth that can never be reclaimed. I'm angry because we tell kids, "Don't take drugs—see an adult if you're hurting," but we've got a sixty-day treatment for druggies, though very little for kids who are "just unhappy." But that anger has a positive side too because I can empathize with just about anyone. And I have a sense of humor because pain and humor are really two sides of the same coin (think of slapstick comedy). And I know that there's a God out there somewhere, because I would have never made it this far without Her.

I am such a different person now, even though in some ways I'm the same. I'm really starting to like parts of myself, to take risks, to help others, to have fun, and to finally tell off the people in this world who so desperately need it. I am so glad I saw it this far, and I am so glad because I know that with hard work, it's getting better all the time.

Anyway, I hope this wasn't too long or too boring or too sentimental. And I hope there's a kid out there who identifies with this if my diaries ever make it to press. Maybe one day I'll write a book about my life, and it will help someone else.

Good luck with the manuscript.

P.S. Oh yeah, one more thing. At the risk of sounding kiss-ass, there's one more thing I wanted to tell you, Prof. Berman. Thanks.

36 In a widely quoted 1979 English study into the reasons people give for taking overdoses, the desire to die ranks at the bottom of the list. More important reasons include the wish to make others feel sorry, to create guilt in others, to convey one's desperation, to influence another person, to escape from intolerable pain, to seek help, to find out whether one is loved, to show how much one loves others, and to make things easy for others (cited by René F. W. Diekstra, "Renée or the Complex Psychodynamics of Adolescent Suicide," in René F. W. Diekstra and Keith Hawton, *Suicide in Adolescence* [Dordrecht: Martinus Nijhoff, 1987], 60).

37   Ruth gave me permission to use all her diaries for my book, but I felt it was important to show her *how* I was using them and to make sure that I had sufficiently disguised her identity. I also wanted to be certain that she hadn't changed her mind about granting me permission. Because she had moved out of the Albany area after graduation, I had difficulty locating her, but when I did, I sent her the present chapter and asked for whatever responses she cared to offer:

> Dear Jeff Berman,
>
> I am sorry it took me so long to reply with a closing diary. I don't know why, but I had a lot of resistance to finishing the entry. If it is not too late, feel free to print whatever you like. I do not feel threatened in any way about anything I have written being printed in your chapter.
>
> I hope you are doing well with your classes this semester, and that you are doing well yourself. I enjoy my job and am thinking about entering graduate school next year.
>
> I read the chapter on suicide and thought it was, for the most part, interesting. I was bored while reading my journal entries. They seemed unnecessarily long and written in a tone of self-absorption and pity. I don't like thinking of times when I was depressed. I am doing fine now and feel it is not real sometimes. Depression is an intense feeling. I crave intensity. I feel alive when I have strong feelings.
>
> I think my diaries were so honest because I want to be real, to be connected with reality. I daydream so much that sometimes I almost live in a fantasy world.
>
> I don't feel I have had any dramatic breakthroughs as a result of diary writing, although I see some of my weaknesses more clearly as a result of diary writing. I don't feel or perceive myself quite as "messed up" as my diaries read. I feel embarrassed when I read my diaries. I feel uncomfortable when I read how desperate, pathetic, and unhappy I sometimes am. One concrete thing I learned is how dependent I am on other people such as my ex-boyfriend.
>
> If I am feeling depressed, diary writing doesn't usually help that much. If I am feeling depressed, it's more helpful if I do a physical activity like cleaning or exercising. But if I am feeling in a huge amount of pain or feeling very worked up or passionate about something, writing may help to alleviate some of the intensity. When my boyfriend and I broke up, I wrote a whole slew of very emotional letters which I will never mail. It made me feel better.
>
> When I was young I kept a diary for a number of years. When I felt bad or excited about something, I would write for hours, but now I have much resistance to writing in a diary. I don't naturally write unless I am so distraught that I see no other viable option. I sometimes hate how I feel, and writing it down makes it too concrete. I try to forget any bad times I went through. My feelings often scare me, and I don't want to remember them.
>
> Sometimes it made me feel less alone when I heard diaries read aloud in class, and sometimes listening to the diaries brought up feelings of isolation. Some people who wrote diaries sounded really healthy and well balanced. I compared myself with these people and felt different or weird. But when I identified with other students, I felt good because there were other people like me.

Sometimes I was bored listening to the diaries and just wanted to hear my own read. I am self-centered and do not have much patience to listen to other people's problems being read in a diary format. If someone is speaking face-to-face to me about their problems, I have a larger amount of compassion and am able to listen for a long time. Sometimes, though, I was very interested in what was being read.

I am very interested in your work and am excited for your new book to be published. You place an unusual slant on literature which I enjoy. It is a good feeling when a professor takes an interest in you, and I have enjoyed our brief correspondence. I will be in touch. Good luck with the book.

38 William Styron, *Darkness Visible: A Memoir of Madness* (New York: Random House, 1990), 84.

6 / *Sexual Disclosures*

1 J. D. Salinger, *The Catcher in the Rye* (New York: Bantam, 1951; rpt. 1968), 62. Page references in the text are to this edition.

2 For a discussion of incest patterns in the novel, see James Bryan, "The Psychological Structure of *The Catcher in the Rye, PMLA* 89, no. 5 (1974): 1065–74.

3 Sigmund Freud, "The Aetiology of Hysteria" (1896), *Standard Edition* 3:203.

4 Sigmund Freud, *The Origins of Psychoanalysis: Letters to Wilhelm Fliess*, ed. Marie Bonaparte, Anna Freud, and Ernst Kris (New York: Basic Books, 1954), 215–16.

5 Ibid., 223.

6 Sigmund Freud, "On the History of the Psycho-Analytic Movement" (1914), *Standard Edition* 14:17.

7 For a stinging indictment of Freud's abandonment of the seduction theory by one of the earliest researchers of child sexual abuse, see Florence Rush, *The Best Kept Secret* (Englewood Cliffs, N.J.: Prentice-Hall, 1980). See also Susan Brownmiller's *Against Our Will* (New York: Simon & Schuster, 1975), a history of aggressive male domination over women.

8 Jeffrey Moussaieff Masson, *The Assault on Truth: Freud's Suppression of the Seduction Theory* (New York: Penguin, 1985), xxix.

9 Sigmund Freud, "On the History of the Psycho-Analytic Movement" (1914), *Standard Edition* 14:21.

10 Marianne Krull, *Freud and His Father* (New York: Norton, 1986), 68.

11 Cited by Jean Goodwin, *Sexual Abuse* (Boston: John Wright, 1982), 160.

12 Stefanie Doyle Peters, "Child Sexual Abuse and Later Psychological Problems," in *Lasting Effects of Child Sexual Abuse*, ed. Gail Elizabeth Wyatt and Gloria Johnson Powell (Newbury Park, Calif.: Sage Publications, 1988), 101.

13 Cited by Blair Justice and Rita Justice, *The Broken Taboo* (New York: Human Sciences Press, 1979), 16.

14 Jane Levine Powers and Barbara Weiss Jaklitsch, *Understanding Survivors of Abuse* (Lexington, Mass.: Lexington Books, 1989), 10.

15 See Jean Renvoize, *Incest* (London: Routledge & Kegan Paul, 1982).

16 See Emily Driver and Audrey Droisen, eds., *Child Sexual Abuse* (New York: New York

University Press, 1989), 28. The FBI estimates that only 2 to 4 percent of all reported rapes are false.

17   John Briere and Marsha Runtz, "Post Sexual Abuse Trauma," in *Lasting Effects of Child Sexual Abuse*, ed. Gail Elizabeth Wyatt and Gloria Johnson Powell (Newbury Park, Calif.: Sage Publications, 1988), 94.

18   See Flora Rheta Schreiber, *Sybil* (New York: Warner, 1973).

19   Thomas Mallon discusses how the "very word *diary* excites us with the promise of guilty secrets to be revealed" (*A Book of One's Own* [New York: Ticknor & Fields, 1984], the chapter "Confessors," 247).

20   Katie Roiphe, *The Morning After* (New York: Little, Brown, 1993), 42.

21   John Rogge, *Why Men Confess* (New York: Thomas Nelson & Sons, 1959), 166.

22   Oscar Wilde, *De Profundis* (New York: Philosophical Library, 1960), 112.

23   F. Scott Fitzgerald, "Babylon Revisited," in *The Fitzgerald Reader*, ed. Arthur Mizener (New York: Scribner's, 1963), 310.

24   Ibid., 316.

25   See James Twitchell, *Forbidden Partners* (New York: Columbia University Press, 1987).

26   See Andrea Parrot and Laurie Bechhofer, *Acquaintance Rape* (New York: John Wiley & Sons, 1991).

27   Judith Lewis Herman, *Trauma and Recovery* (New York: Basic Books, 1992), 73.

28   Salinger, *The Catcher in the Rye*, 92.

29   Reported by Robin Warshaw, *I Never Called It Rape* (New York: Harper & Row, 1988), 11.

30   Virginia Greendlinger and Donn Byrne, "Coercive Sexual Fantasies of College Men as Predictors of Self-Reported Likelihood to Rape and Overt Sexual Aggression," *Journal of Sex Research* 23, no. 1 (February 1987): 1–9.

31   Scott did use the word "rape" in his diary, but his account of sexual humiliation must have been so upsetting that his respondent did not remember this detail.

32   Sigmund Freud, *Introductory Lectures on Psycho-Analysis* (1916–1917), *Standard Edition* 16:309. The passage is translated slightly differently in the paperback edition we use in class.

33   See Nancy Chodorow, *The Reproduction of Mothering* (Berkeley: University of California Press, 1978).

34   Sylvia Plath, *The Bell Jar* (New York: Harper & Row, 1963; rpt. 1971), 247.

35   The notes to *Tender Is the Night* may be found in "Appendix B" of Arthur Mizener's biography of Fitzgerald, *The Far Side of Paradise* (Boston: Houghton Mifflin, Sentry Edition, 1965), 345–52.

36   F. Scott Fitzgerald, *Tender Is the Night* (New York: Scribner's; rpt. 1962), 129.

37   Jeffrey Berman, *The Talking Cure: Literary Representations of Psychoanalysis* (New York: New York University Press, 1985), 82.

7 / Conclusion: Teaching Empathically

1   William Carlos Williams, "The Use of Force," in *The Farmers' Daughters* (New York: New Directions, 1961), 131. Page references in the text are to this edition. According to Robert

Gorham Davis, Williams, though no admirer of Freud, had *The Interpretation of Dreams* in mind when writing "The Use of Force." See Davis's "Note on 'The Use of Force' and Freud's 'The Dream of Irma's Injection,' " *William Carlos Williams Newsletter* 2 (1976): 9–10.

2 For an extended discussion of how women appear throughout Williams's stories as agents of castration through aggressive orality, see Terence Diggory, *William Carlos Williams and the Ethics of Painting* (Princeton: Princeton University Press, 1991).

3 At least one literary critic has rationalized the physician's actions in "The Use of Force." "The doctor's confessed feeling of 'adult shame' notwithstanding, the end justifies the means—the use of force (also exerted by the father) is necessary because Mathilda's tonsils are seriously infected" (Robert Gish, *William Carlos Williams* [Boston: Twayne, 1989], 71). By contrast, James Terry and Peter Williams argue that Williams's physician had "alternative courses of action, for example, treating the child as if she had diphtheria, thereby obviating the need for the confirmatory throat examination" ("Literature and Bioethics: The Tension in Goals and Styles," in *Literature and Medicine* 7 [1988], 7).

4 For a thoughtful study of the role of intersubjectivity in teaching literature, see Michael Steig, *Stories of Reading* (Baltimore: Johns Hopkins University Press, 1989). See also David Bleich, "Intersubjective Reading," *New Literary History* 17 (1986): 401–21.

5 Paul de Man, *The Resistance to Theory* (Minneapolis: University of Minnesota Press, 1986), 4.

6 Judith Jordan, Alexandra Kaplan, Jean Baker Miller, Irene Stiver, and Janet Surrey, *Women's Growth in Connection* (New York: Guilford Press, 1991).

7 See Heinz Kohut, "Introspection, Empathy, and Psychoanalysis," *Journal of the American Psychoanalytic Association* 7 (1959): 459–83.

8 Stephen Mitchell, *Relational Concepts in Psychoanalysis* (Cambridge: Harvard University Press, 1988), 295.

9 D. W. Winnicott, "Transitional Objects and Transitional Phenomena," *International Journal of Psycho-Analysis* 34 (1953): 94. For a discussion of how literature functions as a transitional object, see Murray Schwartz, "Where Is Literature?" *College English* 36 (1975): 756–65.

10 John Steinbeck, "The Chrysanthemums," in *The Short Story: 30 Masterpieces*, ed. Beverly Lawn (New York: St. Martin's Press, 1987), 283.

11 I have omitted the personal elements of Ashley's diary.

12 Mary Crawford and Roger Chaffin, "The Reader's Construction of Meaning: Cognitive Research on Gender and Comprehension," in *Gender and Reading*, ed. Elizabeth Flynn and Patrocinio Schweikart (Baltimore: Johns Hopkins University Press, 1986), 22. The other essays in this volume are very helpful in describing the relationship between gender and reading.

13 See Judith Fetterley, *The Resisting Reader* (Bloomington: Indiana University Press, 1978).

14 Mary Field Belenky, Blythe McVicker Clinchy, Nancy Rule Goldberger, and Jill Mattuck Tarule, *Women's Ways of Knowing* (New York: Basic Books, 1986), 214, 217. The reference to "connected teaching" that I used earlier comes from this book.

15 B. Jowett, trans., *The Dialogues of Plato* (Oxford: Clarendon Press, 1875), 4:295.

16 See Margo Culley and Catherine Portuges, *Gendered Subjects* (Boston: Routledge & Kegan Paul, 1985).

17 Bernie Siegel, *Love, Medicine & Miracles* (New York: Harper & Row, 1988), 138.

Afterword, by Maryanne Hannan

1   Tristine Rainer, *The New Diary* (Los Angeles: J. P. Archer, 1978), 287.

2   Ira Progoff, *At a Journal Workshop* (New York: Dialogue House, 1975), 32. Page references in the text are to this edition.

/ Index

/ Student Diarists